Faith, Fallibility, and the Virtue of Anxiety

FAITH, FALLIBILITY, AND THE VIRTUE OF ANXIETY

AN ESSAY IN RELIGION AND POLITICAL LIBERALISM

Derek Malone-France

palgrave macmillan

FAITH, FALLIBILITY, AND THE VIRTUE OF ANXIETY

First published in hardcover in May 2012 by PALGRAVE MACMILLAN® in the United States—a division of St. Martin's Press LLC, 175 Fifth Avenue, New York, NY 10010.

Where this book is distributed in the UK, Europe and the rest of the world, this is by Palgrave Macmillan, a division of Macmillan Publishers Limited, registered in England, company number 785998, of Houndmills, Basingstoke, Hampshire RG21 6XS.

Palgrave Macmillan is the global academic imprint of the above companies and has companies and representatives throughout the world.

ISBN: 978-1-137-32439-9

The Library of Congress has cataloged the hardcover edition as follows:

Malone-France, Derek, 1972–
Faith, fallibility, and the virtue of anxiety : an essay in religion and political liberalism / Derek Malone-France.
pages cm
Includes bibliographical references.
ISBN 978-0-230-11071-7
1. Religion and politics. I. Title.

BL65.P7M344 2012
201'.72—dc23 2011045314

A catalogue record of the book is available from the British Library.

Design by Scribe Inc.

First PALGRAVE MACMILLAN paperback edition: February 2013

10 9 8 7 6 5 4 3 2 1

In memory of my father Ronald Charles France 1945–1992

Contents

Preface ix

1 Introduction: Context, Terminology, and Structure 1

2 Anxiety: From Problem to Virtue 21

3 Anxiety, Secrecy, and Authority in the Abrahamic and Liberal Traditions 51

4 Faith, Freedom, Reason, and Responsibility 77

5 Divine Anxiety and the Metaphysics of Freedom 99

6 Process Metaphysics and Democratic Deliberation 137

Notes 157

Index 177

Preface

The seed of this project was planted more than a decade ago, when I was a beginning student in the Philosophy of Religion and Theology program at Claremont Graduate University. I had the opportunity to take a contemporary theology course with the great process theologian John Cobb, Jr., at CGU's partner institution, the Claremont School of Theology. While commenting on the pervasive impact of existentialism on late-twentieth century theology, Cobb observed that the "problem of anxiety" was widely recognized as the central issue concerning contemporary theology. Over the years since, my own reading of contemporary theology has largely confirmed that characterization. Though I feel sure, now, that if I had pushed Cobb to clarify his meaning further, he'd have qualified his statement in something like the following way: The questions raised by the ontic and epistemic dynamics analyzed under the label of 'anxiety' by existentialist philosophers and theologians have fundamentally shaped the contemporary conversations within philosophical and systematic theology, even where the conceptual framework of the existentialist analysis is merely implicit (or covert) and the specific terminology of existentialism is absent. At the time, however, my response to his observation was entirely dominated by one clarion thought: "It's not the people who feel this sort of anxiety who worry me. It's the people who don't."

That thought festered, as the subsequent years brought ever more reason for concern with the threat that is posed by the kind of dogmatic certainty that allows some people to override or suppress their own existential anxiety in ways that lead to the aggressive assertion of particularistic moral, social, and political values. Whenever I could set aside brief moments between working on other projects that I had already under way, I began to outline a kind of neo-Kierkegaardian analysis of the dynamics of anxiety and faith in which I inverted certain central claims of Kierkegaard's pseudonymous personae, such as Johannes de Silentio, Johannes Climacus, and Vigilius Haufniensis, resulting in a conceptual transvaluation of anxiety, from problem to *solution*—or, as indicated in my title, to *virtue*. At the same time, much of my other work, both in terms of my research and my teaching responsibilities, was pulling me in the direction of political philosophy and theory. And I began to have the unexpected but, again, internally compelling sense that there was an important, even foundational, connection to be made between the epistemic dynamics associated with Kierkegaardian anxiety and the moral and political norms associated with classic liberal political theory, in its Lockean-Millian mode.

Over the last several years, I have had the opportunity gradually to develop my understanding of this connection and the main arguments of the present work in dialogue with a diverse set of interlocutors, including, first, my colleagues in the Human Rights Challenges at Home and Abroad program, the Thompson Writing Program, and the Departments of Philosophy and Political Science at Duke University, with whom I had the pleasure of working as a Mellon Postdoctoral Fellow; and, now, my fellow faculty in the Department of Religion and the University Writing Program and my colleagues in the Department of Political Science at George Washington University. I have also benefited tremendously from feedback I have received during presentations of draft portions of this work at meetings of the American Academy of Religion, the American Philosophical Association, the Society for Philosophy of Religion, and the Society for the Study of Process Philosophies, as well as at a special symposium on process philosophy and political theory hosted by the Martin Marty Center for the Advanced Study of Religion at the University of Chicago, and cosponsored by the Center for Process Studies at Claremont, in October 2010. More specifically, I would like to thank the following individuals who have provided especially formative, substantive, and/or sustained feedback on the project (in no particular order): Elizabeth Kiss, Claudia Koonz, Troy Dostert, James A. Keller, Joseph Harris, Simon J. Cook, Van Hillard, Charles Larmore, John Woell, Richard Amesbury, Kevin Schillbrack, William Power, Catherine Keller, Franklin Gamwell, George Lucas, Donald Viney, William Hasker, Patrick Horn, George Shields, Ingrid Creppel, Bill Winstead, Steven Kelts, Robert Adcock, Dan Dombrowski, Brian Henning, Jude Jones, John Quiring, Ronald Hall, George Mavrodes, Terrence Tilley, Michael S. Jones, Samuel Fleischacker, and William Schweiker. And last but by no means least, in terms of interlocutors, I would like to thank my wife Katherine Malone-France, who spent many hours listening to me begin to outline my ideas while we ran the trails beside the Eno River outside of Durham and has continued to be my primary sounding board and an incisive friendly critic as I have worked them out more fully since then.

I am indebted to my editor, Burke Gerstenschlager, who saw the potential in the preliminary material I'd worked up through these presentations and conversations, signed the project with Palgrave MacMillan, and, then, gave me the time I needed to complete it, even when unexpected administrative duties slowed me down a bit along the way. I'm also grateful to his assistant, Kaylan Connally, who has done much of the work of shepherding the project.

Finally, thanks, also, to the journals *Faith and Philosophy* and *Process Studies*. Portions of Chapters One and Two of the present work first appeared in *FP* under the title: "Liberalism, Faith, and the Virtue of 'Anxiety'" (Vol. 24, No. 24 [October 2007], 385–412). Portions of Chapters Five and Six first appeared in *PS* under the titles: "Between Hartshorne and Molina: A Whiteheadian Conception of Divine Foreknowledge" (Vol. 39, No. 1 [Spring-Summer 2010], 129–48); and "Process and Deliberation" (Vol. 35, No. 1 [August 2006], 108–33).

Derek Malone-France
Washington, DC

CHAPTER 1

INTRODUCTION

CONTEXT, TERMINOLOGY, AND STRUCTURE

The liberal personality thrives not on a harmonious inner life, but on both 'internal' and 'external' value plurality, and a consequent unease or dissatisfaction.

—Stephen Macedo, "Charting Liberal Virtues"[1]

And beside this, giving all diligence, add to your faith virtue.

—2 Pt 1:5 (AV)

THE FIRST DECADE OF THE TWENTY-FIRST CENTURY brought renewed energy, and urgency, to the study of religion and politics. In particular, there is great interest at the moment, both within and beyond the academy, regarding the interaction between religious consciousness and liberal-democratic citizenship.

Is it possible for those who are fully, existentially committed to particular religious perspectives on reality, human nature, and the moral good to be *equally* committed to classic liberal political norms of tolerance; noncoercion; democratic decision making; guaranteed individual liberties of conscience, expression, and action; and equality of rights? Conversely, is it possible for liberal-democratic political societies to accommodate religious citizens in a way that does not threaten the integrity of their religious commitments and allows for at least some substantive forms of public expression of those commitments? Must one choose between living out one's religious faith in a fully authentic way and genuinely embracing the logic and consequences of contemporary liberal-democratic pluralism? Questions such as these have come further to the fore, in both scholarly and popular discourse, in light of certain political, cultural, and intellectual dynamics, the tangled confluence of which has complicated and intensified the discussion of each.

Foremost among these dynamics has been the confrontation with global terrorism in the name of certain militant forms of Islam. The promise and optimism of the new millennium was subverted almost as soon as it began by the trauma of the September 11 attacks and by the still-unfolding consequences thereof—some inevitable and some that were quite avoidable. The atrocities committed that day, and the religiously based justifications for them given by those responsible, have produced a sprawling, cacophonous conversation, ranging widely from the halls of academe to the editorial sections of newspapers, to political campaign events, and to the dining room tables of both Muslims and non-Muslims alike about whether *any* form of Islam is ultimately reconcilable with liberal-democratic society.

Some commentators rushed to label the struggle with Islamic extremism as a "clash of civilizations,"[2] drawing on the political scientist Samuel Huntington's famous thesis about the future of global conflict and implying—among other things—a categorical difference between Islam, on the one hand, and Judaism and Christianity, on the other, in terms of their compatibility with liberal democracy. Yet at the very same time, there was the perception by many secular and mainline religious observers that evangelical and fundamentalist Christian notions and attitudes were playing a problematic role in the first American presidential administration of the new century. Invocations of God and faith as motivating and legitimating the political ends of the president and his party provoked a range of denunciations—some focused on the particular manner in which these invocations were deployed, while others more broadly attacked the role of religion in American political discourse in general. And so, the ongoing scholarly conversation about the place of religion in the public sphere that had been particularly building steam since the early 1990s spilled out into that public sphere, vying for attention alongside much rougher and less nuanced forms of discourse on the matter.

Meanwhile, there has remained the countervailing perception by many American religious conservatives that the United States is veering ever further and more dangerously away from what they see as its foundational "Judeo-Christian" values. Moreover, as the contemporary cultural consensus on issues such as gay marriage has continued to shift toward an ethos of pluralism, religiously founded social conservatism has become a bridge between historically divided communities, creating new—and often fraught—political coalitions. For example, many leaders in African American churches were uniting with their conservative white Christian counterparts in opposition to gay rights, even as the politico-cultural imbroglio over comments by then-candidate Barack Obama's minister, Jeremiah Wright, was revealing continuing misunderstanding, distrust, and antipathy between these two camps and their respective flocks.

And all three of the aforementioned dynamics have fed into the absolutism, stridency, and growing prominence of the attacks on religion, per se, by certain of its critics. The most influential of these, at present, are the so-called New Atheists, who systematically conflate religion in general with religious extremism (and, ironically, pursue their own agenda with something quite like religious dogmatism and zealotry).[3] For them, all religion is a form of vicious superstition that must be uprooted from human existence to be replaced by the enlightened and omnicompetent wisdom of the scientific method. In fact, on their view, mainline religion is ultimately even more threatening than extremism, precisely because mainline religion is able to masquerade as a reasonable form of worldview that deserves respect and inclusion in the decision-making processes of contemporary liberal-democratic societies, while it actually functions as a backstop for antimodern forms of ignorance and oppression.

An underlying theme that connects the various conversations around these and many other, related dynamics is the association of religious consciousness with a particularly aggressive sort of certainty. Such certainty does not merely provide the believer with an internal sense of confidence and peace. It undermines her capacity to acknowledge and evaluate alternative perspectives, and it prompts an impulse to impose her views on others. The question, then, is whether these two effects go, inseparably, hand in hand.

In his seminal essay "Charting Liberal Virtues," quoted at the beginning of this chapter, the contemporary political theorist Stephen Macedo gestures toward a central feature of the psychology of classic liberalism: a permanent—and productive—sense of *epistemic anxiety*, especially in relation to value judgments and the knowledge claims that frame them. *Principled* liberalism requires acceptance of such a sense of anxiety as an inescapable aspect of authentic human experience. For the logic of liberalism—at least the sort of liberalism I will defend in this book—depends on an open-ended acknowledgment of the final uncertainty of all human understandings, including one's own. If one is utterly certain, beyond any measure of doubt, about the rightness of one's own perspective, morals, lifestyle, and so on, then one has no reason to be either epistemically anxious or liberal.

Of course, some measure of liberalism may be embraced simply as a necessary modus vivendi imposed by circumstance. One may not have the necessary numerical, economic, or technological advantage to be able to enforce one's will (piecemeal or wholesale), in which case one may compromise with others in order to avoid having someone else's will enforced on oneself. But such a purely pragmatic affirmation represents a merely strategic, not a principled, liberalism. Genuine liberalism is not simply a political *technique*. It is a commitment to certain fundamental moral, anthropological, and, even, metaphysical assumptions—and their normative implications. Liberalism makes use of political techniques in order to manifest its commitments, but it should not be confused with these techniques on account of that fact. *The Federalist*[4] is not merely a user's manual; it is also an argument for a liberal understanding of the human condition. The quintessentially liberal pledge to "defend to the death" the right of another to speak an opinion of which one disapproves[5] would represent a violation of the very rationale for accepting liberal norms from the point of view of the merely pragmatic democrat. And such a pledge is pure lunacy from the perspective of anyone claiming an absolutely inerrant understanding of the right or the good. To repeat, then, an authentic—and steadfast—affirmation of classic liberal values requires a certain epistemic stance, a stance that involves some measure of anxiety, the sort of anxiety that is bred of doubt.

One of my primary aims in this book is to show that the inverse of this logic also holds true. Insofar as one acknowledges, even implicitly, that one is fallible and, therefore, incapable of "utter certainty," then one must feel some anxiety about the epistemic status of one's beliefs and judgments. And insofar as one feels such anxiety, one is *normatively obligated* to affirm basic liberal-democratic principles, especially as relating to individual autonomy, the right of dissent, and the normativity of noncoercive deliberative discourse. More specifically, I will argue that the sort of anxiety just described represents an *epistemic virtue*, a cognitively basic response to the reality of human fallibility that should be understood as not only absolutely central to the liberal ethos and foundational to liberal norms but also *definitively required by authentic religious commitment*. That is to say, I will maintain that when religious faith per se is properly conceptualized, it becomes clear that it should in no way be seen as contravening commitment to political liberalism. And similarly, when political liberalism is properly conceptualized, it becomes clear that it in no way contravenes commitment to a religious faith—unless said religion *requires* that believers practice aggression and coercion toward others.

In constructing my argument, I will be weaving together threads from a number of scholarly conversations that, for the most part, have been taking place in isolation from one another over the last decade. Hence part of the potential value of this project, as I see it, is to call the attention of various groups of thinkers to one another and to the very real and constructive connections that can be made between their respective discourses on religion and politics despite the profound differences in their scholarly approaches. More specifically, throughout the remainder of this work, I will move back-and-forth between political philosophy and theory, philosophy of religion, and philosophical theology, with supporting references to issues and concepts in epistemology, metaphysics and ontology, political history, religious sociology, legal theory, and so forth. As I do so, I will attempt to articulate the insights from these various fields in ways that will be intelligible to informed nonspecialists, while preserving their full specificity and sophistication. This is not an easy task. Hence I have adopted a recursive approach, particularly in relation to the theological dimensions of my argument. Through the course of the second, third, fourth, and fifth chapters, I will circle back over the central theological concepts being employed from various angles in order to develop a fuller and clearer formulation of them and to give unfamiliar readers an opportunity to assimilate their meaning. (I will outline the specific structure of the remaining chapters in the following.)

Such recursivity is particularly necessary in relation to the theological ideas at play here because of what I take to be the significant differential between the levels of attention that the two main groups within my academic audience pay to one another. Most of the philosophers of religion and philosophical theologians that I know are well and widely read in contemporary political philosophy and theory. But very few of the political philosophers and theorists that I know have shown a similar interest in contemporary philosophy of religion and philosophical theology. This is, I think, a shame.

By drawing particularly on conceptual resources that are embedded within the Abrahamic religious tradition in order to construct an argument in favor of classic political liberalism, I will seek to clear a path for believers in this tradition to embrace such liberalism in a new way. But beyond that, I also believe that my analysis of religious faith, through the lens of Abrahamic theology, sheds fresh light on the normative logic of liberalism and, ultimately, provides a stronger foundational justification for liberal-democratic norms than one finds among the most prominent alternatives available in contemporary political philosophy. Hence while I am constructing my conception of liberalism and its warrant in relation to some very culturally, historically, and intellectually specific touchstones, the resulting conception can, I believe, be deployed in an absolutely generalized way, as a freestanding justification for classic liberal norms as providing *the proper moral ideal for the general organization and regulation of political society*.

Since my argument—and, I hope, my audience—crosses several different fields of study, and because some of the basic concepts I am employing here have multiple and complicated histories of usage, it is important to begin with some initial clarification of my own employment of a few of these terms and how they relate to one another in the context of my argument. It is also important to stress, though, that these are only initial clarifications. The full implications of my use of these terms and of their relations to one another will emerge over the course of the remainder of this work. Similarly, in beginning to explicate my use of certain terms, I will also necessarily begin to outline certain elements of my argument, and I will do so in a way that elides over some issues that will be important to specialists but that would prove initially distracting to nonspecialists. I ask the specialists on any given point to be patient, as further elaboration often will come in subsequent chapters. And I point them toward the notes, which I have used sparingly, but which sometimes contain further discussion of points that are relevant but not significant enough in the context of my overall project here to justify digressions in the main text.

MODERNITY, ANXIETY, AND LIBERALISM

The notion of 'anxiety'—*angst, anxiété*, and so on—played an important role in late modern philosophy and theology, beginning with the great Danish philosopher and theologian Søren Kierkegaard's psychophilosophical explorations of human subjectivity and belief and culminating in prominent philosophical and theological anthropologies of the early and mid-twentieth century. In both its philosophical and theological formulations the term *anxiety* generally denoted a profound awareness of human finitude and the various existential predicaments associated with it. One such predicament arises from the epistemic implications of finitude: On the one hand, we are rational beings, with the capacity to explore the nature of the world around us and to construct interpretations of its structure and significance. On the other hand, we are also finite beings, whose perspectives and, therefore, understandings are contingent and incomplete. Hence our conceptions of 'the truth,' particularly with regard to human purpose and moral judgment, are not, and never can be, absolutely reliable.[6]

In the early modern West, the *systematic* recognition of humanity's fallibility-in-finitude emerged along with the rise of deism during the seventeenth and early eighteenth centuries and found support in the critiques of ecclesiastical authority that took root in both philosophical and theological discourse during the Enlightenment.[7] Yet, during this period, absolute faith in the authority of canonical religious texts (and clerical interpretations of them) was not merely abandoned; it was, for most thinkers, replaced with an equally absolute faith in the authority and power of 'reason.' Thus it was not until the mid-nineteenth century—when the 'unity' and ultimate verifiability of the conclusions of reason began increasingly to be called into question—that the *problem* of human fallibility truly emerged in an acute form.[8]

Kierkegaard may have been the first to fully perceive both the philosophical and religious dimensions of modern anxiety, and his writings on the subject spurred the development of important philosophical and theological perspectives that took human finitude as the starting point of their analyses. In philosophy, the various problems associated with human finitude became a central focus of perhaps the most culturally prominent school of philosophical thinking of the twentieth century: existentialism. In theology, the anxiety provoked by an awareness of the implications of human finitude found prominent and perspicuous formulations in the writings of thinkers like Rudolf Bultmann, Reinhold Niebuhr, and Paul Tillich.[9]

While fallibilism has remained a significant theme in both philosophy and theology, the concept of anxiety, however, has largely disappeared from the current discourses of these fields. In epistemological terms, any systematic appeal to anxiety regarding human fallibility has been supplanted by the formulation of coherentist understandings of knowledge and cognition. In moral and political terms, the notion of 'tolerance'—representing the positively formulated, prescriptive flip side of epistemic anxiety—has come to dominate much of the discussion. Of course, methodologically speaking, such a shift from a negatively framed to more positively framed formulations of the issue was quite natural. Yet in making this shift away from theorizing the notion of anxiety itself, contemporary liberal philosophical and religious thinkers have given up a powerful methodological concept, one with the capacity to provide vital support to liberal norms.

There are challenges associated with attempting to use 'anxiety' in this way, to be sure, the foremost of which is to overcome the natural resistance to such a use of this term because of the common association of 'anxiety' with negative psychological states. This is a legitimate concern, especially given the fact that there are other terms, such as 'humility,' which, prima facie, may seem to bear the same relevant denotation but which do not carry the same negative connotations in common usage. I will defer responding to this concern fully at this point and refer the reader to the remainder of this work. In particular, the relationship of anxiety to humility—and I do believe that there is an important relationship here—will be taken up explicitly in the next chapter. However, I will at this point offer one very general historical rationale for attempting to resurrect the sort of explicitly epistemic use of anxiety that I am referencing here.

The anxiety about their own fallibility as human beings that gradually emerged among a significant portion of the literate public in the West during the modern period was one important element in the development, evolution, and survival of political liberalism. This idea is closely connected, but *not* reducible, to the commonplace historical claim that liberalism emerged out of the chastening effect that the European 'wars of religion' had on evangelical and sectarian enthusiasms. Certainly, all sections of society tired of the bloodshed that prefaced European modernity, but there was also an anxiety that sprang most directly from the erosion of the epistemic authority of religious institutions and the historical normativity of the biblical narrative. This is an anxiety that owed more to the persistence of the deists than to the excesses of the Cromwellians, and its power only increased as nineteenth-century thinkers like Charles Darwin and David Strauss further undermined the bedrock assumptions on which religious (and other) groups had predicated their competing claims to historical and normative orthodoxy. And if such epistemic anxiety was an important psychological and social precondition for the development of pluralistic liberal norms, then it seems reasonable to assume that its maintenance is a necessary condition for the preservation of such norms.

Moreover, the increasingly strident and divisive claims to moral certainty and superiority being lodged by the opposing sides—both religious and nonreligious—in many of the major public debates today suggest that we face much the same struggle against the urge toward absolutism that our Enlightenment predecessors faced in their time. Hence we would do well to promote the sorts of attitudes that helped shape their response to this challenge, which was successful enough to reconstitute the very nature of political society in the West.

One may object that, insofar as basic liberal values are related to respect for the 'dignity' or 'sacredness' of the human individual, there may be other routes to authentic liberalism than that which runs through anxiety. After all, historically speaking, 'liberalism,' even in its classic sense, is a multivalent term, encompassing various related, but substantively differentiable, conceptions. But the question is whether each of the various forms of 'liberalism' that emerged out of the Enlightenment is equally authentic, equally steadfast in its commitments to those principles that distinguish liberalism from more authoritarian modes of moral-political consciousness and practice. I cannot offer an exhaustive survey of all the particular diverse forms of liberalism that sprouted from the fertile theoretical ground of the Enlightenment. However, a brief discussion of the divergence of the two most historically important branches of classic liberalism should be sufficient to indicate, in a preliminary way, the basis for my claim that only a liberalism that refers to a sense of epistemic anxiety is, ultimately, authentic and sustainable—as well as to indicate the relevance of this view for religious faith.

Beginning with Isaiah Berlin's seminal essay "Two Concepts of Liberty,"[10] political philosophers and theorists have widely recognized a fundamental distinction between the sort of liberalism that very early took root in modern English political philosophy through the works of thinkers like John Milton, John Locke, and (later) John Stuart Mill and the quite different form of liberalism that emerged in France and Germany through the combined influence of Jean-Jacques Rousseau and Immanuel Kant. There are also important distinctions to be drawn within each of these groupings, as Berlin was well aware. But if we focus on the basic *epistemic stances* at work in each, this broad categorization has considerable merit and utility. For our purposes, Berlin's discussion of Kant is particularly useful because it takes a sort of teleohistorical view, tracing the connections between the inner, epistemic logic of Kantian liberalism and the successive illiberal developments in Continental political thought that followed from it.

Critics have often observed that Berlin simplifies matters for himself by ignoring, or at least minimizing, certain statements by Kant (and Rousseau) that do not fit neatly into his tidy analytical distinctions and historical narrative. There is certainly truth to this criticism, but it also, I think, misses the point. In "Two Concepts," Berlin is specifically interested in examining the theoretical and practical consequences that follow from two fundamentally divergent overarching perspectives on human freedom. He adopts a broadly evolutionary perspective with regard to Kantian liberalism, rather than offering a more complex and nuanced exegesis, because he is less concerned with how Kant mediated the various tensions in his formulations than with how these tensions played themselves out in the thought (and practices) of those who took themselves to be following in his footsteps as a measure of how well suited Kant's formulation really is to the task of grounding support for liberal norms. Since this is also our concern here, Berlin's analysis is apropos.

Two points should be borne in mind, though: First, I do not wish to suggest that the issue of whether liberalism can be adequately supported without explicit appeal to the implications of human fallibility maps simply onto Berlin's famous distinction between 'negative' (Locke, Mill) and 'positive' (Kant, Rousseau) conceptions of liberty—though fallibilism certainly seems to fit more naturally with negative conceptions. Second, in drawing on his critique of Kant's positive conception of liberty, I am not endorsing Berlin's particular negative conception as the only viable alternative. There have been a number of "third" concepts of liberty put forward in the decades since Berlin formulated his bipolar categorization.[11] One that has strong resonance with the approach to classic liberal norms that I will defend in this work is the 'liberal-republicanism' that has been developed over the last several decades by thinkers such as Charles Larmore.

Larmore identifies a strain of classical republicanism that defines liberty in terms of 'nondomination.' If taken strictly in terms of the epistemological issues with which we are primarily concerned here, this conception of liberty can be fit into Berlin's overarching schema as a 'negative,' rather than 'positive,' conception. However, it differs from Berlin's (Hobbesian) formulation of negative liberty in two important ways: First, unlike Berlin, republican theorists of the sort that Larmore has in mind count not only actual but also possible interference by others as an infringement on liberty. That is, one is less free not only if another acts so as to limit one's choices but also to the extent that another has the power so to act, even if that power is voluntarily unexercised (whereas Berlin claimed, for example, that negative liberty was consistent with the existence of a benevolent despot). Second, this liberal-republican conception of negative liberty does not understand all government regulation as necessarily contravening liberty in some way—that is, as a "necessary evil"—because such regulation can, in fact, produce and support types and degrees of liberty impossible in its absence. Moreover, the existence of some robust forms of governmental regulation is necessary in any political model that seeks truly to maximize liberty *for all*, because any such model must take account of the reality and history of the concrete conditions in which it finds individuals already related to one another. This is precisely the reason that I do not see fallibilism and epistemic anxiety as legitimating either anarchism or libertarianism, because both of these perspectives ignore the empirical and historical dimensions of existing human relations in articulating their aims for the present and future (not to mention the chances for their success as actual social systems in the real world). I will say more about that in Chapter 4, 5, and 6.

The realistic understanding of the conditions of actual freedom in the concrete historical world and the positive role that governments can play in relation to those conditions that one finds in Larmore's liberal-republicanism connects with my own understanding of how the virtue of epistemic anxiety ought to be enacted by citizens and governments of what I am very broadly calling liberal-democratic societies. Thus, for example, I am strongly in favor of classic republican-style constitutional checks on democratic majorities' power over minorities—since majorities are no less fallible for their number. I should also clarify, at this point, that when I refer to '*classic* liberal norms,' I am not endorsing the particular school of liberalism that sometimes goes under the label of 'classical liberalism' that is associated with such contemporary figures as Friedrich Hayek and Milton Friedman. Like libertarianism, to which it is closely related, classical liberalism, in this sense, involves certain principles and presuppositions that actually, in my view, reduce, rather than expand, the range of freedom for most members of society. Again, I will say more about this in later chapters.

So on my reading, the liberal-republican conception of liberty as nondomination is highly consonant with the conception of liberal norms that I am linking to epistemic anxiety in this work. Notably, as Larmore observes, proponents of this conception traditionally "defined liberty as not living at the mercy of another's will and did so not least with an eye to that form of domination which springs from according some single but contested vision of the human good a favored status in the political community."[12] As I say, I will return to some of the previous points in subsequent chapters. However, my aim is *not* to articulate a fully formed political theory here. My goal is to establish a very general justification for a very general framework of political norms, not a detailed formulation of my own particular preferences about how those norms should be specifically embodied in practice—many of the details of which I consider properly matters for public negotiation.

Returning then to Kant, we have a perfect example of an Enlightenment liberal who arrives at a respect for human dignity and a principle of moral autonomy through an alternative route, one that bypasses the requirement of anxiety for which I am arguing. Indeed, Kant's philosophy iconically represents the urge to rescue some element of certainty from the jaws of epistemic doubt. Rather than referencing human fallibility and an attendant sense of epistemic anxiety regarding that fallibility, Kant invokes the *majesty* of human reason, in its capacity as moral lawgiver, as the basis for his validation of individual autonomy. True freedom, according to Kant, consists in obedience to the moral law. Although the moral law is unitary, one and the same for all, obedience ideally arises voluntarily through the autonomous exercise of the individual's practical judgment, a product of the self-legislating function of rationality. The problem, however, is that people do not always agree about what rationality reveals to be the proper moral judgment in a given situation, or even what abstract 'maxims' (to employ Kant's terminology) ought to govern our conduct in general. But this can only mean that not everyone is as rational as everyone else. Given the nature of the relationship between the faculty (and capacity) of rationality and right belief and conduct on Kant's view, this imbalance presents a potential challenge to the logic of autonomy. Berlin observes,

> [For] Kant and rationalists of his type . . . the limits of liberty are determined by applying the rules of 'reason,' which is more than the mere generality of rules as such, and is a faculty that creates or reveals a purpose identical in, and for, all men. In the name of reason anything that is non-rational may be condemned, so that the various personal aims which their individual imaginations and idiosyncrasies lead men to pursue . . . may, at least in theory, be ruthlessly suppressed . . . The authority of reason and of the duties it lays upon men is identified with individual freedom, on the assumption that only rational ends can be the 'true' objects of a 'free' man's 'real' nature.[13]

Combine such a view of rationality with some claim of absolute authority—be it political or spiritual, based on some process or sign purportedly revelatory of the imprimatur of reason—or "truth," and one has opened the door to the most severe abridgments of the very freedom of conscience that Kant begins by validating.

This is certainly not to suggest that Kant's own defense of liberal norms was halfhearted or insincere. As Berlin is careful to acknowledge, Kant's *intent* was to shield the individual from illegitimate encroachments by 'authority,' whether political or religious, not to provide justification for such encroachments. Yet, as Berlin shows, despite his own best intentions, Kant's conception of rationality and its connection to the law (both moral and civil), in historical conjunction with Rousseau's naïve assumptions about the moral and practical reliability of the regulatory expressions of the 'general will,' led (more or less directly) to the state-deifying conception of the relationship between political and moral right found in the Romanticism of Johann Gottlieb Fichte and G. W. F. Hegel, the antiliberal and deterministic stance of Karl Marx's communism, and the totalitarian sensibilities (and, ultimately, practices) of their political successors in both Germany and the Soviet Union.

Noting the irony in this progression, Berlin asks, "What can have led to so strange a reversal—the transformation of Kant's severe individualism into something close to a pure totalitarian doctrine on the part of thinkers some of whom claimed to be his disciples?" The answer, it seems to me, lies precisely in Kant's failure to link his defense of moral and political autonomy to a recognition of human fallibility and its implications in relation to claims of authority. Kant is correct, in my view, to connect support for liberal norms to epistemology, but he neglects to take sufficient account of human epistemic *limitations* in his formulation of this connection. It is not that respect for the dignity of the human individual qua rational agent has no role to play in the logic of liberalism. Respect for the individual's capacity to reason for herself is a necessary, but not a sufficient, condition in the establishment of this logic. It requires a complementary relation to the sort of fallibilist delimitation of the claims of authority supported by an attitude of rationalized epistemic anxiety.

Kant's prescription that the individual should never be treated merely as a 'means' but always as an 'end' does *not* necessarily translate into a proscription against illiberal coercion *if* one believes that the individual's salvation—be it political or spiritual—depends on the acceptance of a set of beliefs and practices for the validity of which one claims absolute assurance. Under such circumstances, one may—consistently with Kant's principle, if not his intent—determine that it is crucial that the individual adopt the relevant point of view, even if coercion is required to guarantee this outcome. Similarly, one may determine that the use of force to prevent the dissemination of *alternative* beliefs and practices is required to ensure that the individual (or community) not be led astray from the "proper" path.

Though his intent may have been otherwise, Rousseau expresses the logic of such coercion in his famous proclamation that "whoever refuses to obey the general will shall be constrained to do so by the entire body, which means only that he will be forced to be free."[14] Fichte, then, provides the necessary bridge from republicanism to totalitarianism when he adds, "To compel men to adopt the right form of government, to impose Right on them by force, is not only the right, but the sacred duty of every man who has both the insight and the power to do so."[15]

Thus there is a historical case for the claim that any form of 'liberalism' that is unconditioned by the moderating influence on ideological absolutism provided by a sufficiently robust recognition of fallibility (in the form of an attitude of epistemic anxiety) cannot ultimately sustain itself without sliding over into an aggressively dictatorial illiberalism. The potential authoritarianism implicit in the logic of Kant's and Rousseau's works gradually revealed itself in the thought of their successors and, tragically, in the form of actual totalitarian regimes—with which the nations that had, contrarily, adopted the liberalism of Milton, Locke, and Mill were forced to struggle, in order to defend (among other things) the value of individual autonomy against the claims of the state. Kant and Rousseau surely would have been appalled by what their "disciples" wrought, but that does not change the (revealing) fact that it was *their* disciples—not Milton's, Locke's, and Mill's—who drifted to totalitarianism.

Religion, Fallibilism, and Commitment

The relevance of this discussion in the context of religious belief should be obvious. If we replace the abstract political individual with a hypothetical religious apostate or heretic, and the state with the church, then we immediately see the consonance between Fichte's position and those forms of religious consciousness that privilege some particular (fallible) conception of "the truth" over the right of the individual to exercise moral and intellectual autonomy. Henceforth, I will refer to this sort of epistemologically oppressive mind-set, in the context of religion, as *orthodoxism*, with the *ism* here indicating the aspect of aggression that separates the mind-set of such believers from that of their peers who have faith in some religious "orthodoxy" but who do not see that faith as a warrant for coercion.

The logic of Fichte's pronouncement about the "duty" of coercion is regarded with horror in light of the historic consequences of the adoption of this attitude as a principle of sociopolitical regulation in both Nazi Germany and the Soviet Union. Similarly, such an attitude in the context of religious belief provokes horror in those who see the historical abuses of Christian dogma—for example, in the Inquisition, the brutal suppression of "heretical" views in Geneva under John Calvin or Christian missionizing in the context of Western colonialism—as profoundly immoral (and, indeed, unchristian) and those who hear echoes of this attitude in the belligerent dogmatism of contemporary Protestant fundamentalism and ultraorthodox Catholicism. (As the example of the Soviets indicates, I do not at all mean to suggest that religion is unique in producing such problematic attitudes and behaviors. More on that later.)

Of course, contemporary Western religious orthodoxists do not generally advocate such methods of "discipline" or conversion as was applied in previous historical examples. They make use of the ballot box, the lobbying firm, and so on. But as I will discuss further in Chapter 3, there is no hard and fast line to be drawn between the attitude of the contemporary orthodoxists and their religious antecedents. Moreover, it is important to remember that the current cultural and political consensus that repudiates those older, more brutal methods of coercion developed *in spite of* the attitudes (and efforts) of past orthodoxists, *not* because of some internal check that they set on themselves out of respect for the dignity of others. Historically, the slippery slope into genuine brutality in the name of religious orthodoxy has been all too slick and the slide all too common (if not inevitable), when religious zeal is unqualified by an acute awareness of the fallibility of human understandings.

To be clear, the sort of fallibilism I have in mind here is not meant to signify, or imply, either global skepticism or unqualified relativism. Nor is the productive uncertainty that I am prescribing meant to contradict the legitimacy of deep affirmational commitment to one's own understandings (religious or otherwise). The normative thrust of the requirement I am articulating here is aimed at the level of sociopolitical intercourse. It is perfectly reconcilable with *personal confidence* in one's beliefs, so long as that confidence does not pass over into an unqualified certainty or express itself coercively in relation to others.

In other words, the 'doubt' that liberal citizens must maintain is not the doubt of the skeptic. As I will explain in much greater detail over the course of this work, when I speak of a permanent—and productive—sense of epistemic anxiety, I do not mean to suggest that one should maintain a constant state of aversion to belief or conviction. Nor do I mean to suggest the adoption of a relativistic stance that would hold that all beliefs are *equally* dubitable. Some beliefs (e.g., my own belief that I am the author of these words) approach absolute certainty in their justification, while others (e.g., the belief that the natural procreative relationship between male and female human beings implies a normative prohibition against sexual relations between members of the same gender) are necessarily much less certain—partly because they require extensive relation to a complex of other (controversial or potentially controversial) presuppositional beliefs for their justification. I will have much more to say about this in Chapters 2, 3, and 4.

One important modern line of thinking about fallibilism that deserves a mention here is the pragmatic-progressivist fallibilism that one finds in various forms in the work of thinkers such as Charles Sanders Peirce, John Dewey, and Karl Popper. Here we find fallibilism as an expression of the underlying epistemic logic of the scientific method and as a goad to critical thinking and open-ended deliberation in other arenas of human life, as well. According to these thinkers, the recognition of the fallibility of our concepts and beliefs should motivate engagement in discursive and deliberative processes that provide avenues for verification or falsification and/or the enrichment of thinking offered by alternative perspectives. Dewey and Popper, in particular, focused attention on the political implications of this sort of fallibilism, offering theories of democratic deliberation based, in part, on their respective construals of these implications.

Deliberative fallibilism of this sort is an element within the overall perspective I will formulate over the course of this work as a whole, but it is a subordinate element. My primary, overarching argument is *not* that liberal democracy is the best form of government because democratic deliberation produces the most tested and refined thinking about issues, policies, and so on. Rather, I am arguing that democratic forms of deliberation—within a framework of checks against majoritarian domination—are the most morally appropriate form of political decision making because they involve the least degree of moral-political coerciveness that is reconcilable with the full range of concrete conditions of human social existence (I include representative democracy here). That said, I will make periodic references to the form of deliberative fallibilism propounded by Dewey and Popper throughout the remainder of this work, and I will discuss its relation to theories of deliberative democratic discourse at length in Chapter 6.

One important conceptual distinction that will help to clarify the sense of fallibilism that undergirds my argument for epistemic anxiety is the distinction between *logical certainty* and *epistemological certainty*. I draw this distinction from the work of the "process" philosopher of religion and political philosopher Franklin Gamwell (I will discuss process philosophy and theology in Chapters 5 and 6), who invokes it in his defense of the appropriateness of certain kinds of a priori reasoning, despite the recognition human fallibility. Gamwell's explanation of the distinction is clear and concise enough to be quoted here at length:

> In contrast to factual or logically contingent claims, a priori claims are said to be logically necessary and, in that sense, invariable or certain. But the question is whether this logical meaning of certainty is the same certainty as that whose achievement is inconsistent with human fallibility. A defense of transcendental understanding might further distinguish between *logical* and *epistemological* certainty, such that understandings claiming to be logically certain are also epistemologically fallible, and only epistemological certainty is impossible. On this account, the distinction between logically contingent and logically necessary claims is a distinction *within* the realm of fallible thought,

> and transcendental claims no less than empirical ones are never true because someone says they are but, on the contrary, can be validated only by appeal to human experience and reason as such.[16]

In other words, it is perfectly sensical for me to claim, for example, that the principle of noncontradiction is logically certain—that is, I do not believe that its falsity is logically conceivable—while admitting that my claim is subject to the qualification that, as a fallible human being, I could be wrong about it. I do not believe that I am. And in truth, I cannot really imagine any circumstances under which I would come to believe that I am wrong about it. Nevertheless, I recognize that it is possible that I am wrong, and I behave accordingly in discussions of this principle with those who claim that it is false—which includes some quite intelligent people, as it happens. I may argue with them and attempt to persuade them that they are incorrect, but I will not censure them for disagreeing with me. Nor would I wish to coercively compel them to agree with me, even if I could do so. What I would add here is that there is a strong analogy to be made between a priori claims of the sort that Gamwell has in mind and certain sorts of religious claims, in relation to the distinction that Gamwell offers. When, for example, a religious believer claims that some doctrine has been made "certain" through the intervention of some form of miraculous revelation, the legitimacy of this claim depends on the recognition that the certainty of the doctrine in question is bounded within the limits of the believer's own fallibility. The believer may not be able to imagine any circumstances under which she would relinquish her claim regarding the relevant doctrine's status as certain, but she might nevertheless acknowledge that her certainty about it is fallible and, therefore, not a legitimate basis on which to impose that doctrine on others. If she fails to make such an acknowledgment, then, she will have implicitly denied her own fallibility, thereby arrogating to herself the epistemic standing of an omniscient divinity.

There are, of course, various ways in which religious believers (*and others*) attempt to evade the implications of human fallibility in relation to their own most cherished beliefs. Often such evasion takes a form that is patently arbitrary and hypocritical. But in the context of the related fields of philosophy of religion and philosophical theology, some arguments for the infallibility of certain sorts of beliefs have been made that deserve to be taken seriously. I will engage with these arguments at various points in Chapters 2, 3, and 4.

Finally, before turning to a specific outline of the structure of the remainder of this work, let me say a brief initial word about my use of the term 'epistemic virtue.' Just as a 'civic virtue' is generally one that has to do with the manner in which one relates to one's fellow citizens, an 'epistemic virtue' is one that has to do with *the manner in which one relates to one's own beliefs and to the processes by which one acquires or has acquired them.* Thus epistemic virtues have normative implications regarding how one decides what to believe, which beliefs to maintain, and how to act on those beliefs (and, hence, epistemic virtues can also be civic virtues). I will elaborate further on this notion and my application of it throughout each of the remaining chapters.

Structure of Remaining Chapters

Now that I have provided a sort of thematic and conceptual outline of my project, in Chapter 2, I will further explicate what I mean by 'epistemic anxiety.' I will begin with a discussion of the background philosophical and theological tradition from which I am drawing this concept. I will, then, distinguish my use of anxiety from other uses of the term and from other, related concepts, and I will contrast the epistemic stance that I am prescribing to skepticism, thereby clarifying the nature and scope of the 'doubt' that I am associating with anxiety as I am defining it here. Next, I will discuss the relationship between epistemic anxiety and other liberal virtues such as tolerance and humility, arguing for anxiety as the most foundational liberal virtue. Finally, I will rebut several potential objections to the epistemic perspective I am formulating here that are related to prominent positions within Anglo-American analytic philosophy of religion and theology.

In Chapter 3, I will circle back over the concept of anxiety and its relation to religious faith by way of the story of Abraham's "trial" at Mount Moriah, during which he is ordered by God to sacrifice his son Isaac. Here I will draw on the seminal modern analysis of this story given by Kierkegaard's pseudonymous persona Johannes de Silentio in *Fear and Trembling,*[17] in order to further clarify both the traditional Abrahamic conception of faith, as it relates to modern ethical thought and liberal political theory, and my own reconception of faith as conditioned by epistemic anxiety. This will also allow me to engage with an important line of thinking in contemporary Continental philosophy of religion and theology. Along the way, I will also connect the concepts and dynamics at work in the Abrahamic dialectic of faith to the basic issues and arguments being contested in the contemporary debate over what is the proper role, if any, of religious reasons in the liberal-democratic public sphere—a debate that importantly crosses over the Anglo-American/Continental divide.

In Chapter 4, I will further develop my own position as an alternative to the current options in the debate over religion in the public sphere. I will argue that both categorical liberal prohibitions against the deployment of religious reasons in arguments over coercive political regulations and the most prominent religious responses to such prohibitions are flawed. I will uphold a qualified prohibition, which I will apply not only to religious but also to secular particularistic metaphysical, anthropological, and moral reasons. I will, then, briefly characterize the understanding of the task of theology that is implied by my position in this debate. And finally, I will reflect on the figure of Socrates as exemplary of the mode of faithful discursivity that follows from an embrace of epistemic anxiety.

Chapter 5 represents a pivot point, at which I will turn from offering an overarching analysis of the epistemic dynamics and moral exigencies of religious faith and liberal-democratic society and a worldview-neutral justification for the latter to propounding the particular metaphysical and theological perspective that I believe best supports, in a complimentary way, this overarching justification and its normative implications. I will begin by discussing the contemporary 'open theism' movement, with its rejection of the classical theistic conception of God as completely eternal in all respects, immutable, and possessing of absolute knowledge of the actual future. Drawing on the 'organic theism' formulated by the twentieth century British-American philosopher Alfred North Whitehead and further developed by the 'process philosophy and theology' movement that identifies with his thought, I will argue for a strong form of open theism, as both more logically coherent and morally and spiritually preferable to classical theism.

Finally, in Chapter 6, I will connect the Whiteheadian metaphysics and ontology that I present in Chapter 5 to the issues and concerns at play within the contemporary 'deliberative democracy' movement. I will argue that process thought can provide needed support for central principles and presuppositions that cut across all forms of deliberative theory and that a process theory of democratic deliberation represents an ideal complimentary perspective from which to develop a particular approach to liberal-democratic discourse that is consonant with my overarching fallibilist justification for such discourse.

Chapter 2

Anxiety

From Problem to Virtue

> For my thoughts are not your thoughts, neither are your ways my ways, saith the LORD. For as the heavens are higher than the earth, so are my ways higher than your ways, and my thoughts than your thoughts.
>
> —Is 55:8–9 (AV)

Traditionally, the Abrahamic religions—Judaism, Christianity, Islam—have all treated faith in 'revealed truth' as, among other things, an epistemic compensation for the imperfection of human reason. In terms of what we now would call existential psychology, this compensation has typically been understood as offering an antidote to the 'problem of anxiety.' On this traditional view, not only the anxiety associated with our *ontic* condition (our mortality) but also the anxiety associated with our *epistemic* condition (our fallibility) is alleviated through the embrace of a faithful certainty in the core dogmas of the religion.

Notably, this understanding of the epistemic anxiety that is occasioned by our recognition of our own nonomniscience, as being a problem in need of solution, only becomes more self-conscious—it is never fully abandoned—in the analyses of modern religious existentialist thinkers from Søren Kierkegaard to Rudolf Bultmann, Reinhold Niebuhr, and Paul Tillich. As radical as these thinkers' responses to the tradition are on other points, they largely retain the presupposition that it is a negative thing for humans to feel epistemically anxious. Anxiety about one's own finitude and fallibility, we are told, is a threat to the integrity of the self—rather than being a natural (and, indeed, a *virtuous*) element in the consciousness and conscience of any psychologically mature and epistemically responsible fallible being.

KIERKEGAARD ON ANXIETY AND "THE FALL"

In traditional Christian theology, the "fallenness" of human nature is predicated on the very emergence of consciousness of the distinction between "good" and "evil." As soon as the question of alternatives arises, there is a rupture in the relationship between the human and the divine. Indeed, in terms of the narrative presented in Genesis, this rupture surely must be understood to predate Eve's and, later, Adam's actual consumption of the fruit. Their disobedience to God in the act of consuming it logically presupposes and is made possible by Eve's prior entertainment of the *possibility* of such disobedience. That is to say, the Fall occurs, for Eve at least, the moment that she even *considers* the counternarrative presented by the serpent as an alternative understanding of her situation, as opposed to that which she has received from God. In that moment of deliberation, both her consciousness and her conscience are formally decoupled from the will of God. There could be no turning back, then. Even should she have decided not to eat the fruit, the experience of having entertained an alternative to obedience would have left its indelible imprint on her in the form of an awakening to her own potentiality for self-determination that had been merely latent to that point. The fruit itself and her act of consuming it are, therefore, mere signifiers of the transformation of her self that had already occurred, even before she reached out to pluck it from the tree. (Eve is so much more interesting than Adam not least because her fallenness is self-actuated and originary, whereas his is passive and derivative. *She*, not he, is the template for real personhood.)

Kierkegaard, one of the most insightful analysts of the epistemological implications of Christian theology that the tradition has produced, examines the connection between the capacity to entertain alternatives and separation from God with characteristic profundity in his pseudonymous deliberation on *The Concept of Anxiety*—tellingly subtitled: *A Simple Psychologically Orienting Deliberation on the Dogmatic Issue of Hereditary Sin.*[1] As always, it is important to distinguish, formally at least, between Kierkegaard himself and the authorial persona he adopts in this work—namely, Vigilius Haufniensis. Here (and we will forgive, for the moment, his misappropriation of Eve's rightful place at the center of this analysis on behalf of Adam), Haufniensis observes that "[e]very attempt to explain Adam's significance for the race as *caput generis humani naturale, seminale, foederale* [head of the human race by nature, by generation, by covenant] . . . confuses everything. He is not essentially different from the race, for in that case there is no race at all; he is not the race, for in that case also there is no race. He is himself and the race. Therefore that which explains Adam also explains the race and vice versa."[2]

Thus Adam (or, more accurately, Eve) represents not the progenitor but, rather, the archetype of human sinfulness. We are not sinful because Adam (or Eve) sinned. We are sinful because we are *like* Adam (and Eve). Accordingly, Haufniensis writes, "The Genesis story presents the only dialectically consistent view. Its whole content is really concentrated in one statement: *Sin came into the world by a sin.*"[3]

Yet the 'qualitative leap' represented by each and every individual's own originary act of sin obviously presupposes the capacity for such a leap, and Haufniensis identifies the emergence of this capacity with the presence of anxiety, which "is freedom's actuality as the possibility of possibility."[4] And what is the "possibility of possibility"? It is precisely the entertainment of alternatives; for where there are no alternatives, there is only necessity issuing into actuality. Thus when Haufniensis tells us that "[t]he narrative of Genesis also gives the correct explanation of innocence. Innocence is ignorance,"[5] we are dealing with ignorance *not* as the absence of knowledge per se, but, rather, as the absence of the recognition that one can make use of one's knowledge in order *to choose*. In the state of innocence, therefore, "the whole actuality of knowledge projects itself in anxiety as the enormous nothing of ignorance."[6] But this "nothing" is not so much a *void* as it is an *opening*, a lacuna in the logic of necessity that presents itself as a space in which something *else*, something *other than what is*, might be found. That is, as possibility.

Immediately upon recognizing her own relation to possibility, the individual finds herself plunged into the realm of decision and responsibility. She cannot retreat from this recognition because even that would be a choice. And precisely because she is finite and fallible, she enters this realm without the assurance that would come from certain knowledge of the true, the right, and the good. Anxiety is, therefore, the natural and universal human response to the soul-quaking implications of autonomy.

Such anxiety, Haufniensis tells us, is unknown to angels. For angels are rich in knowledge but bereft of freedom. They do not entertain alternatives to God's will. Their existence is thoroughly bound up in necessity. Their being is undifferentiated. Their actions are nothing other than the result of their functions. Their will is not their own.

As Haufniensis puts it, "Even if Michael had made a record of all the errands he had been sent on and performed, this is nevertheless not his history," for "an angel has no history."[7] History arises from the qualification of "spirit" as differentiated and free—that is, as relating itself to possibility and manifesting itself through choice. In other words, historical being is fallenness, and fallenness is historical being.

Hence angels need no salvation, since they are never alienated from God's will. Human beings, on the other hand, require salvation precisely because we stand in an individuated relation to possibility that provokes anxiety. Our anxiety necessitates the exercise of our freedom, and our fallibility makes it inevitable that our freedom will lead us astray. Haufniensis, succinctly summarizing the drift of nearly two millennia of traditional Christian theological doctrine, writes, "Only in the moment that salvation is actually posited is this anxiety overcome . . . When Salvation is posited, anxiety, together with possibility, is left behind." In other words, salvation—which Kierkegaard fairly consistently, across his many pseudonymous personae, identifies with the achievement of "an absolute relation to the absolute"[8]—represents an exit from history. To be sure, the saved individual remains within the scene of history, but she no longer relates to it as one who is pulled to and fro by possibility. For her will—like Abraham's when he takes Isaac to Mount Moriah—has been given up to God. In this sense, the saved individual is, putatively, one who makes of her own self a sacrificial offering to God. She relinquishes her relation to possibility; she transcends freedom through an infinitely free choice to relate herself *faithfully* to the absolute.

In traditional Abrahamic understandings, such a conception of faith is, accordingly, posited as a reconciliation with the divine that is predicated on a return to the uncritical state that exists prior to the Fall, in which no question of alternatives arises, because the answers are all pregiven to the believer in the formulations of orthodox doctrine and the pronouncements of the church or tradition (or of the individual believer's own, self-authorized reading of text or sign).

Accordingly, faith is understood as effecting not merely a moral but also an epistemic reconciliation of the human and the divine. Indeed, *the former is a function of the latter.* Faith in certain revealed "truths" regarding the human condition and the proper response to it is taken to bridge the gap between our finite and fallible minds and God's perfect understanding and will—not in the sense of providing human beings themselves with perfect understanding, of course, but rather by providing a putatively inerrant representation of those aspects of God's perfect understanding that are relevant to our salvation.

Anxiety in Twentieth-Century Existentialist Theology

Rudolf Bultmann's kerygmaticism provides a telling example of how this problematic traditional conception of reconciliation was carried over into contemporary existentialist theology, even as such theology sought to divest itself of the legalistic and "mythic" content of traditional theology. Having stripped away the accretive layers of cultural and mythohistorical content from the *evangelium*, leaving only the core doctrine of the salvation in Christ, Bultmann, nevertheless, tells us that "genuine patience of disposition consists in this—in our readiness to hear, in the 'no' by which *God negates our desires and our will*, His secret 'yes.'"[9] And he decries the human propensity toward a "highhandedness that tries to bring within our own power even the submission that we know to be our authentic being."[10]

Yet is it not true that any "submission" that we claim to make to God is, in fact, an act of choice conditioned and qualified by our own freedom and fallibility? When I claim to relate myself to 'the absolute,' is it not, in truth, always *my own construction of the absolute* to which I relate? To be clear, I do not mean to suggest that our various constructions of the divine cannot embody some genuine truth about it, only that no such construction can escape the limitations of the finitude and fallibility that essentially and ineluctably characterize all human understanding. Hence "our desires and will" can *in no way be negated* through faith. Rather, any faithful relation to any construction of the divine carries with it the very forces of desire and will that condition the individual's choice to affirm *that*, rather than some other (or no) construction thereof. No relation to any understanding of 'the absolute' (if that is even how the divine should be conceptualized) can overcome our relation to possibility, precisely because any and every fallible human understanding of the absolute necessarily represents only one possible understanding among many. Thus anxiety cannot be "overcome"; it can only be suppressed. And as I discussed in relation to Kantian liberalism in Chapter 1, it is precisely such suppression of anxiety that psychologically precedes and enables political coercion.

If I believe that it is possible to be "certain beyond a doubt" about the rightness of some moral claim, then, arguably, I can feel justified in asserting that I have the right to override the autonomy of those who disagree with or live at variance from this claim, *for their own good.*

Of all the twentieth-century existentialist thinkers—including not just the theological, but also the philosophical existentialists like Martin Heidegger and Jean-Paul Sartre—Reinhold Niebuhr and Paul Tillich come closest to making the move past a *problematized* view of anxiety to one that explicitly recognizes the concept's positive normative dimensions. I will discuss Tillich's construction of the issue in Chapter 4. Here I will use Niebuhr's bivalent conception of anxiety to further clarify the logic of my own appropriation of the notion as an epistemic virtue.

Niebuhr's treatment of anxiety reflected his engagement with the ideological dynamics of the Cold War. He blames human anxiety about the limitations of finitude for the ideological impulse that leads to absolutism, not only in the context of religious systems of belief but also in secular systems like Marxism, of which he was a relentless opponent. His general description of the psychology of absolutism is worth quoting at some length:

> Man knows more than the immediate natural situation in which he stands and he constantly seeks to understand his immediate situation in terms of a total situation. Yet he is unable to define the total human situation without colouring his definition with finite perspectives drawn from his immediate situation. The realization of the relativity of his knowledge subjects him to the peril of skepticism. The abyss of meaninglessness yawns on the brink of all his mighty spiritual endeavors. Therefore man is tempted to deny the limited character of his knowledge, and the finiteness of his perspectives. He pretends to have achieved a degree of knowledge which is beyond the limit of finite life. This is the 'ideological taint' in which all human knowledge is involved and which is always something more than mere human ignorance. It is always partly an effort to hide that ignorance by pretension.[11]

Thus for Niebuhr, anxiety is not only an inescapable consequence "of the paradox of freedom and finiteness" but also "the internal precondition of sin," where 'sin' is understood as the illegitimate adoption of an absolutist stance with regard to one's own perspective, opinions, values, and so on. Yet as Niebuhr goes on to observe, "[A]nxiety is not sin. It must be distinguished from sin partly because it is its precondition and not its actuality, and partly because [anxiety] is the basis of all human creativity as well."[12] In other words, it is not the attitude of anxiousness itself but, rather, the all too human tendency to attempt to purge oneself of unwanted anxiety, by ignoring both the feeling and its implications and indulging in the self-delusion of epistemic privilege, that debases human consciousness and freedom through an abandonment of responsibility (or, as Niebuhr's philosophical counterparts would say, 'authenticity'). Niebuhr is right to say that "[a]nxiety is the internal description of temptation."[13] But temptation is only a natural, ineluctable concomitant of moral freedom. To be morally free is, by definition, to be tempted. Temptation is not, in itself, an evil. On the contrary, it is the precondition of all moral achievement—as Kierkegaard observed, one cannot laud the right choices of angels, for they are not choices at all.[14]

To be clear, I am not suggesting that we ought to cultivate temptation. Though the possibility of being tempted is a precondition not only for sin but also for moral excellence, this certainly does not imply that one should seek out temptations in order to test or prove oneself morally. My point is simply that the connection that Niebuhr draws between anxiety and temptation does not undermine the notion of anxiety—in the creative sense of "anxiety about perfection"—as functioning positively in the manner that I am advocating. Indeed, along these lines, Niebuhr speaks of 'faith' not as a means to purge the individual of anxiety but, rather, as a means to "purge anxiety of the tendency toward sinful self-assertion."[15]

Thus Niebuhr raises the possibility of an unproblematic, even empowering, form of anxiety. In doing so, he draws on Kierkegaard's suggestive references to "anxiety over nothing"—the anxiety "that is posited in innocence . . . [which one] observe[s] in children . . . as a seeking for the adventurous, the monstrous, and the enigmatic." This anxiety is found, according to Kierkegaard, "in all cultures where the childlike is preserved . . . The more profound the anxiety, the more profound the culture."[16] As Kierkegaard scholar and translator Reidar Thomte puts it, this is "'anxiety over nothing'—that pregnant anxiety that is directed toward the future and that is a pristine element in every human being."[17] Niebuhr describes this positive form of anxiety as the psychological ground of human creativity. Niebuhr calls such creative anxiety 'anxiety about perfection,' which he contrasts to the more insidious 'anxiety about insecurity.'[18] Anxiety about perfection is occasioned not by fear of uncertainty but, instead, by the desire to push one's understandings and creative accomplishments ever forward to further the bounds of one's knowledge in the face of the seemingly limitless possibilities presented by human experience and activity.[19]

Niebuhr claims, however, that "Anxiety about perfection and about insecurity are . . . inexorably bound together in human actions and the errors which are made in the search for perfection are never due merely to the ignorance of not knowing the limits of conditioned values. They always exhibit some tendency of the agent to hide his own limits, which he knows only too well."[20] And this is surely true. But the fact that no human can achieve a perfectly unadulterated embodiment of the virtuous form of anxiety does not make such anxiety any less virtuous in character, nor should it keep us from encouraging the individual to cultivate the virtue of a *more* perfected, *less* adulterated anxiety. It is common to virtues that they exhibit within themselves the potentiality for vice when they are taken to extremes or aimed in the wrong direction. Thus thrift may become greed or acquisitiveness, confidence may become pride, open-mindedness may become licentiousness, and so on. Moreover, as already discussed, it is not 'anxiety about insecurity' itself that constitutes the error of unqualified absolutism but, rather, the reaction against such anxiety in the adoption of an *orthodoxist* consciousness.

All human beings are necessarily fallible. Thus fallibility is an epistemic *condition* of humanity as such, but, like other epistemic conditions, it can be ignored (at least at a conscious level). Anxiety, on the other hand, is *both* a *condition of human existence* and a *response to such existence*. As a condition, anxiety represents a central element in what was once called 'philosophical anthropology': the elucidation of the fundamental conditions of human nature and existence, both ontic and epistemic. But its status as such a condition is derivative from its (logically prior) status as a universal response to the definitive condition of fallibility in which each human being finds herself, qua human being.[21] And it seems to me that where such anxiety about fallibility is embraced, rather than fled, where it is internalized as a check on epistemic arrogance and pretension, it is a virtuous response. For it is only in the acceptance of some level of ultimate insecurity—some fundamental preservation of anxiety within the context of committed belief—that one can overcome the temptation to deify one's understandings. Only thus can one act on one's own convictions always in such a manner as to fully respect the right of others to hold and act according to contrary convictions. Hence an appropriately moderated, but consciously sustained, sense of epistemic anxiety should be viewed as a sign of intellectual and psychological maturity. Indeed, my claim is that such anxiety represents the central epistemic virtue bequeathed (unintentionally) to contemporary democratic society and theory by our Enlightenment predecessors and that this epistemic virtue can help to support and sustain moral, religious, and political virtues, such as humility and tolerance.

An underlying and permanent sense of epistemic anxiety among a democratic citizenry is a socially and politically healthy thing, precisely because it serves to maintain citizens' acknowledgment of their own fallibility—both as individuals and as members of religious and other groups—and, thereby, discourages the sort of illegitimate absolutist and exclusivist attitudes that tend to undermine the reasonability and productivity of democratic discourses. While an overly anxious attitude regarding one's beliefs can lead to an undesirable moral and political paralysis—or an overly reactionary assertion of supposed "certainty" meant to mask the deeper sense of insecurity, an appropriately moderated and rationalized attitude of anxiety can go far in promoting other democratic virtues, such as intellectual curiosity, cooperativeness and a willingness to compromise, and genuine tolerance of others' beliefs and lifestyles.

Moreover, anxiety, in the sense just outlined, represents a powerful, and in some ways less problematic, alternative to the notion of 'tolerance' as the organizing virtue in discussions of the basis of democratic norms. The notion of tolerance has frequently been criticized as seeming to imply an attitude of mere grudging agreement to coexist. Simply to 'tolerate' another in no way obligates one to attempt more fully to understand the other's perspective or beliefs, nor does it compel one to question the supposed certainty of one's own views. Tolerance, as a mode of engagement with others, can signal just as stalemated and stagnant a conversation as does intolerance. Reasonable anxiety regarding one's own positions, on the other hand, does obligate one to attempt more fully to understand and more fairly to assess alternative positions. This is so precisely because anxiety, unlike tolerance, is an explicitly epistemic and not merely a moral-political virtue. Insofar as a reasonable sense of anxiety about one's own epistemic limitations promotes an acknowledgment of the provisionality and revisability of one's opinions, one is encouraged to take democratic discourse seriously, as a cooperative and (relatively) noncoercive mode of inquiry, will formation, and action. Democratic legal prohibitions against prejudice and forced social or moral conformism gain a normative force that is absent when one is merely constrained by law to "tolerate" those whom one is, nevertheless, "certain" are wrong. (I am not suggesting that tolerance is *necessarily* connected to an underlying assumption of the wrongness of alternative perspectives, only that it does not, in and of itself, provide any check against such an assumption.)

The sort of epistemic anxiety that I am describing here is, it seems to me, precisely the necessary bridge concept between authentic religious faith and Enlightenment liberal norms of tolerance, noncoercion, democratic decision making, equality of citizenship rights, and guaranteed individual liberties of conscience, expression, and action. Such anxiety is the product of the recognition of one's own fallibility as it applies within the context of one's personal beliefs, including one's religious faith and the acknowledgment of the necessary distinction between the content of one's faith and the absolute truth about reality (whatever that may be). As such, the conscious maintenance of such a rationalized epistemic anxiety is the central, indispensible virtue to be manifested by citizens of modern liberal-democratic societies. It is the essential psychological and social desideratum that allows us to live together in the just peace of mutual respect, despite our strong personal commitments to whatever beliefs we may affirm for ourselves with the inner confidence of faith.

My point here is not that anxiety should wholly displace tolerance from discussions of liberal norms. Rather, I am proposing that epistemic anxiety provides a necessary component of the normative warrant for liberal norms such as tolerance. The underlying logic of my argument is straightforward: fallibility is an inescapable condition of human experience and understanding. The proper response to this condition is the adoption of a stance of epistemic anxiety (as I am here defining that term), because an unqualified confidence in one's own beliefs—in spite of the recognition of fallibility—would represent a failure adequately to account for the truth of one's fallibility in the formation of one's beliefs (and one's attitude toward them). Furthermore, classic liberalism represents the proper *sociopolitical instantiation* of epistemic anxiety, because the norm of noncoercion that it propagates is the procedural manifestation of such anxiety in the context of interpersonal action. To deny the liberal principle of noncoercion in the face of human fallibility is to willfully evade the epistemic anxiety that naturally attaches itself to human subjectivity by virtue of its finitude and fallenness. And to express such an evasion is to idolatrously deify one's own understanding and to violate the sacredness of other human beings' moral and intellectual autonomy through an expression of a self-validating will-to-power masquerading as a righteous concern for the salvation of those who are coerced.

THE PHENOMENOLOGY OF EPISTEMIC ANXIETY

So far, I have characterized the particular notion of anxiety on which my argument is predicated in terms of a conscious acknowledgment of the intrinsic fallibility of human understanding (especially one's own). In order to further clarify precisely what I mean by 'anxiety,' it will be helpful to contrast my use of this term with certain other, somewhat related, usages of the same word.

First, as should be obvious at this point, the form of anxiety that I have in mind must be distinguished from the common, everyday sense of the word, referring to mental stress or tension associated with some negatively anticipated event, challenge, or trial, as well as the related clinical sense of the word, referring to some form of persistent, neurotic attitude associated with some—real or imaginary—object of dread. Both of these types of anxiety can lead to precisely the sort of hardening of sentiment and opinion—as a reaction against the feelings of uncertainty they represent—that I wish to discourage. Just as Kierkegaard and his existentialist successors are careful to distinguish anxiety from 'fear,'[22] the former must similarly be distinguished from *nervousness*. To be 'anxious' about one's epistemic limitations as a finite being is to be self-consciously aware of one's existential situation and motivated to account for it adequately in one's beliefs, claims, and behavior. To be 'nervous' about these limitations is to neurotically react to them in a way that, paradoxically, denies their inescapability, because such a reaction inevitably leads one either to seek succor in the false comfort of an absolutist mentality (that seems to erase, but in fact merely represses, the unpleasant insecurity from which one takes flight) or to embrace despair, indifference, and nihilism.

On the other hand, when it is associated with some particular issue of policy or social or ethical concern, the common, nonclinical variety of emotional anxiety can sometimes motivate people to open up to an exchange of ideas aimed at solving some problem or formulating some course of action. The political scientist George Marcus has discussed the political psychology of such deliberation-inducing anxiety in *The Sentimental Citizen: Emotion in Democratic Politics*.[23] According to

Marcus, citizens tend to think and act according to habituated patterns of behavior except when some unanticipated or novel stimulus triggers the emotional response of 'anxiety' about how to think and/or act in light of this new datum or question. He writes that "people are able to be rational because they are emotional; emotions enable rationality . . . Rationality is not an autonomous faculty of the mind, independent of emotion; rather, rationality is a special set of abilities that are recruited by emotions systems in the brain to enable us to adapt to the challenges that daily confront us."[24] Accordingly, he maintains that only visceral, stimulus-specific anxiety provokes the engagement of the subject's rational capacities, motivating the 'anxious' subject to employ her deliberative consciousness to come to some resolution of the problem or question at hand and, thereby, alleviate her anxiety. "Reason," he says, "does not come from reason's own prompting."[25]

There are some problems with Marcus's account of the role of anxiety and deliberation in the democratic sphere, however. First, he makes ordinary citizens overly dependent on political elites, such as members of government and the media, who are given almost sole responsibility for recognizing emerging problems and issues and employing emotive rhetoric in order to inspire the requisite anxiety among the people at-large.[26] This is a problem precisely because, in a democratic society, it is ultimately the underlying attitudes and inclinations of the *demos* itself that are reflected in the choices that politicians and the media make about what sorts of discussions to have and how to portray those discussions to the public. If the public does not maintain a constant sense of engagement with emerging issues, then they will not demand (nor will politicians and media outlets provide) the sort of discourse that promotes genuinely democratic and deliberative decision making.

Also, Marcus seems not only to invest too great a trust in political elites not to abuse the power of anxiety provoking rhetoric, but also too readily to assume that the mobilization of public anxiety will, more often than not, lead to reasoned discourse, as opposed to reactionism and narrowed sentiment and imagination. This problem is directly related to the previous one: a populace that is accustomed to maintaining a *reasonable* level of deliberation-inducing anxiety *at all times* will be less likely to fall prey to waves of *irrational* anxiety associated with specific socially or politically traumatic or revolutionary events or circumstances.[27]

Finally, Marcus's account of anxiety remains superficial precisely because he views anxiety only as an emotive state, without significant or coherent cognitive content—part of the "unaware and inarticulate" realm of emotional response, which he sharply divides from conscious thought.[28] Hence he is unable to appreciate the cognitive significance of anxiety as an intellectual, and not merely an emotional, state or response. Nor is he able to formulate the possibility of a systematic (or methodological) anxiety that permanently maintains the engagement of deliberative openness by permanently maintaining a sense of anxiety associated with the absence of both ultimate certitude and static sociopolitical equilibrium.

Nevertheless, as a description of the psychological connection between the emotional component of anxiety and its intellectual, moral, religious, and political implications, Marcus's account can provide a first step toward a deeper phenomenology of the more thoroughgoing epistemic anxiety I am advocating. In particular, his emphasis on anxiety's "crucial function" of "inhibiting ongoing habit," without which "reliance on habits would be so dominant that it would preclude the consideration of alternatives,"[29] is obviously consonant with the current account of the virtue of anxiety. And his empirical evidence of the positive impact of anxiety on political judgment is valuable in helping to establish the validity of this account.[30] In a sense, the sort of epistemic anxiety I am propounding represents a systematic intellectual and practical generalization of the mind-set of deliberative openness that Marcus describes as the ideal outcome of issue-specific anxiety. The transient emotive state of anxiety that he describes can represent the psychological precursor to the adoption of the deeper, permanent epistemic anxiety of the self-reflective democrat, but only insofar as this transient state of uncertainty and deliberative engagement is consciously detached from, and generalized beyond, the provoking stimulus in relation to which it arises. The *feeling* of anxiety must be intellectually internalized and transformed into an explicit awareness of one's own, and others', intrinsic fallibility.

Obviously, one who adopts a stance of epistemic anxiety will, at times, experience the psychological correlate of emotional anxiety. Yet such emotionally weighted anxiety must not take on an urgency that contravenes the impulse to remain open to dialogue. Nor should it sink into a morbidity that relinquishes deliberation for despair. Indeed, it is important to note the difference between 'anxiety' and 'despair,' where the latter indicates not merely a recognition of human fallibility but also an abandonment of the ideals of objective rationality and truth that are presupposed by deliberation as such. This is the point at which the present defense of epistemic anxiety departs most sharply from the existentialist tradition it references. The anxiety that I am advocating here does not presuppose the dissolution of the idea of objective reasons (or even values). It recognizes our character as self-defining beings who make choices about what to believe, choices that are limited by our own finitude and that are, therefore, fallible. And it acknowledges that it can be "anguishing to know that our freedom is so far-reaching as to leave our existence permanently unsettled in this way."[31] But it need not go so far as to pronounce, as the existentialists typically do, that there is no source of values that transcends finite human understandings and to which such understandings can legitimately make reference.

It is no less 'authentic' to believe, wholeheartedly, that one has apprehended some objective truth about the human condition or right conduct but, in recognition of one's own fallibility, to avoid any imposition of one's view onto others, than it is to toss aside the notion of moral objectivity entirely and simply "own" one's choices as though they made reference to nothing outside of the arbitrary (or perhaps anthropologically imposed) conditions of one's own will. One need not accept Sartre's claim that "nothing, absolutely nothing, justifies me in adopting this or that particular value,"[32] in order to be true to the insight that one's choices among possible values or actions may be flawed or incomplete, or may (at least in some cases) have equally valid alternatives. *Mauvaise foi* is expressed in claims such as that one could not possibly be mistaken in one's belief about 'x,' or that one's belief about 'x' is exempted somehow from the normal rules of reason and evidence, or that some beliefs are epistemically privileged, or that some interpretation of a text is self-evidently "inerrant." There is no bad faith or self-deception in the claim that one holds firmly to certain beliefs or accepts certain interpretations for reasons that seem to transcend the caprice of mere self-definition, uninformed by objective reference, if one simultaneously acknowledges the possibility that one is mistaken about these reasons. So long as one abstains from leveling unqualified judgments at those with whom one disagrees or trying to force them to submit to one's view irrespective of their own wishes and beliefs, and remains open to being persuaded otherwise, there is no illegitimate flight from anxiety.

Kierkegaard sees the embodiment of authentically lived anxiety in the person of Socrates,[33] who remains in a permanent state of epistemic anxiety precisely because he—unlike Kierkegaard's 'knight of faith'—refuses to make the subjective leap into 'the absurd.' Instead, Socrates relentlessly confronts the limits of his own understanding, while simultaneously bursting the epistemic bubbles of his various interlocutors. Socrates's wisdom lies in his consistent awareness of his own 'ignorance,' and his generalization of this awareness as an epistemic principle that leads him to be suspicious of all unqualified knowledge claims and to compulsively pursue deliberative debate with others. Such wisdom, or 'Socratic ignorance,'[34] as Kierkegaard calls it, does not preclude personal commitment. Indeed, Socrates is willing to die for his beliefs. But what Socrates would presumably not be willing to do is to take the life (or infringe illegitimately on the freedom) of another in order to promote his own beliefs. *Socratic anxiety*, as I will now begin to call it, requires circumspection and humility, but not indecision or paralysis.

David Hume—who consistently recognized the imperatives of belief and action, in the face of his own skeptical doubts about human understanding—beautifully characterizes the attitude and practical implications associated with Socratic anxiety in his *Dialogues Concerning Natural Religion*.[35] At one point, his skeptical character Philo responds to the charge that skepticism, like stoicism, represents a philosophy that can be entertained at an intellectual level but that is impossible to live out in a truly consistent manner. Philo replies,

> I allow of your comparison between the Stoics and the Skeptics . . . But you may observe, at the same time, that though the mind cannot, in Stoicism, support the highest flights of philosophy, yet, even when it sinks lower, it still retains somewhat of its former disposition; and the effects of the Stoic's reasoning will appear in his conduct in common life, and through the whole tenor of his actions . . . In like manner, if a man has accustomed himself to skeptical considerations on the uncertainty and narrow limits of reason, he will not entirely forget them when he turns his reflection on other subjects; but in all his philosophical principles and reasoning, I dare not say, in his common conduct, he will be found different from those who either never formed any opinions in the case or have entertained sentiments more favorable to human reason.[36]

Now it is not my intention, here, to equate Socratic anxiety with skepticism. I, for one, entertain "sentiments more favorable to human reason" than those, at times, expostulated by Hume. Yet as a committed liberal democrat, I find his description of a mode of reasoning and living that is chastened by a recognition of one's own (and everyone else's) ultimate fallibility very appealing.

I, personally, do believe that human understanding can claim some genuinely objective knowledge of the world as it is independently of our own mental-linguistic constructions—even if this knowledge can only be *expressed* through the employment of such constructions. As I mentioned in Chapter 1, I also believe that there are certain logically necessary, a priori truths, such as that expressed by the 'law of noncontradiction.' But there is no obviously correct, no 'self-evident,' set of moral regulations or judgments that can simply be deduced from such knowledge with unambiguous certitude. (Nor is there any legitimate shortcut around fallibility through the arbitrary epistemic privileging of certain 'scriptures' or other supposed repositories of infallible wisdom.) While I have strong opinions about many issues, and may even feel at times that I cannot understand how any reasonable person could disagree with certain propositions, I always know that equally reasonable people do in fact disagree over even the most fundamental moral, religious, and political issues. That is not to say that all positions in any such dispute are equally reasonable. Philo goes too far when he says, for example, that "[w]e know so little beyond common life, or even of common life, that, with regard to the economy of the universe, there is no conjecture, however wild, which may not be just."[37] But there will always be a range of reasonable alternatives in relation to any issue of metaphysical, moral, or political significance.

Given the acknowledgment that it is, in principle, always possible that I am the one who is mistaken, even regarding my most deeply held beliefs, I cannot legitimately claim the right to coerce others to believe as I do. Nor can I—in the absence of some voluntary agreement to the contrary—claim the right to force them to act in accordance with my principles rather than their own. This position need not imply pacifism, and it certainly does not imply anarchism. One of my central points is precisely that the recognition of human fallibility that is represented by this doctrine of anxiety has normative implications at a metapolitical level, implications such as that the use of force or coercive power may be employed to prevent others from violating the freedom of their fellow human beings out of some misguided sense of epistemic or moral superiority. Anxiety about fallibility would have been a good reason for the nineteenth- and twentieth-century struggles against slavery and fascism, for example, not a reason to have tolerated such practices.

Hume (through Philo) continues, in the same passage quoted earlier, to remark, "To whatever length anyone may push his speculative principles of skepticism, he must act, I own, and live, and converse like other men; and for this conduct he is not obliged to give any other reason than the absolute necessity he lies under of so doing."[38] Since the bearer of Socratic anxiety is not necessarily quite so pessimistic about human reason as the Humean skeptic, "the absolute necessity" to act, live, and, especially, converse with others may be understood by the Socratic liberal not as an arbitrary and imposed requirement of human existence but, rather, as a valuable epistemic compensation. Yes, we are thrust into a world that showers us with data while limiting the perspective from which we apprehend it. But we are not thrust into this world alone. We have the company of others, who likewise perceive the world from limited perspectives, but perspectives not our own. And our differing perspectives offer opportunities for correlation and contrast, for verification and falsification—or at least concurrence or challenge.[39] Thus we stand also under the obligation (not 'absolute' but normative) to condition our belief with humility—for humility is one fundamental moral and religious virtue that follows directly from the epistemic virtue of anxiety.

We can and should advocate our respective views. We must argue. We have every right to attempt through all legitimate means to persuade. But we cannot arrogate to ourselves the right to coerce (at least not outside of the legitimately negotiated coercive requirements of democratic decision-making procedures). For in doing so we deify our own, decidedly nondivine and finite, understandings. The phenomenology of epistemic, or Socratic, anxiety encompasses various levels (from the emotive to the intellectual), and it has both methodological and practical implications. In practical terms, though, it boils down to a genuine respect for disagreement; a principled preference for substantive dialogue as a means of decision making; an affirmation of reasonable compromise over unilateralism in moral, social, and political affairs; a strong reluctance to call on force to reshape circumstance before all other viable options have been exhausted; and a principled refusal to impose restrictions on the right of individuals to define the terms of their own lives, so long as their decisions cause no substantive harm to others.

ANXIETY AND TOLERANCE

The idea that genuinely recognizing human fallibility requires allowing the free exchange of ideas, respect for others' opinions, and remaining open to the possibility that one is mistaken is hardly revolutionary. It *was* revolutionary when John Milton put it forward in *Areopagitica*,[40] and again when John Locke reiterated the theme in his *Letter Concerning Toleration*.[41] It was less revolutionary but importantly expanded and clarified when John Stuart Mill championed it in *On Liberty*.[42] But Milton could not—because of his own religious commitments—take his argument to its logical conclusion, and he ends up with a significant residue of epistemic privilege in his stance toward the truth claims of (Protestant) Christianity, a residue that survives in Locke. Mill's theorization of fallibility (largely) achieves the consistency that Milton and Locke failed to realize. But Mill himself sets the stage for the methodological transition away from theorized fallibility by following Locke in turning immediately to the notion of 'tolerance' as the moral-political virtue ne plus ultra of political liberalism.[43]

The problem with tolerance from a nonliberal perspective is that theoretically it is presented as a sort of metavirtue that ought to transcend all various substantive points of view, but practically it presents itself as an externally imposed mandate that is inconsistent with the prescriptions of some substantive points of view. In other words, the claim that tolerance represents a perspective-neutral principle of rational discourse is challenged on the grounds that tolerance conflicts with certain religious and moral conceptions that stress the need for universal adherence to some set of epistemically privileged doctrines. Hence the issue is often treated as a conflict between the civic virtue of tolerance and the religious virtue of faith. But as the preceding discussion of epistemic anxiety suggests, this strictly polemical view of the relation between liberal tolerance and religious faith rests on fundamental misconceptions of each of these notions.

In his classic work on the relationship between faith and knowledge in religious belief, the contemporary philosopher of religion John Hick observes that "[a]ccording to the most widespread view of the matter today faith is unevidenced or inadequately evidenced belief." He then goes on to add,

> Faith thus consists in believing strongly various propositions, of a theological nature, which the believer does not and cannot *know* to be true.

> To know here is taken to mean either to observe directly or to be able to prove by strict determination. Where this is possible, there is no room for faith. It is only that which lies beyond the scope of human knowledge that must be taken, if at all, on faith or trust. When in such a case we do adopt some belief, the lack of rational compulsion to assent is compensated by an act of will, a voluntary leap of trust.[44]

The problem with this explication lies in the qualification expressed in the first line of the quote: "Of a theological nature." This implies that 'faith' is not an element in decisions about what to believe in other arenas. In other words, this formulation assumes that in all the non-theological realms of human inquiry and belief it is possible always (or at least very often) to "observe directly or . . . to prove by strict determination." Furthermore, this view assumes that it is generally the case in nontheological matters that interpretations of that which is "observe[d] directly" and outcomes of "strict" proofs are uncontroversial, because there is a "rational compulsion to assent." But is this the case?

To be sure, it sometimes *seems to me* that the evidence or arguments regarding some issue so strongly support one view of the matter that I feel rationally compelled to assent to that view. Yet almost invariably there is someone else—someone whom I would not be willing to simply dismiss as "irrational"—who disagrees. Moreover, even in the most "objective" (and I do not mean to belittle this term) fields of inquiry, it is often simply not possible to directly observe or strictly demonstrate the answer to questions of real significance. This does not mean that thought shuts down in the face of such uncertainty. Inquiry, like life, must proceed in the absence of final certainty. Hence science, very much like religion, proceeds in agreement where agreement is possible, and it is the backdrop of general agreement that allows for the pursuit of those points about which no such agreement exists, sometimes leading to discoveries or new theories that destabilize or demolish the prior consensus from which they proceeded. This is the pragmatic-evolutionary character of scientific inquiry and of life in general.

Thus some measure of 'faith,' in the sense described by Hick, is present in all areas and expressions of human inquiry and understanding.[45] To be clear, I do not deny that there is a significant difference in the *degree* of such faith that is required to affirm, say, the basic principles of the theory of natural selection, as opposed to the claim that the

Nicene Trinitarian formula expresses some fundamental truth about ultimate reality. The latter certainly seems to me to depend more heavily on subjective inclination and controversial metaphysical and epistemological assumptions than does the former. I am simply denying that there is a *categorical* difference between the two, in terms of the epistemological standing of those who affirm them respectively.[46]

I certainly do not mean to imply that there are not generally reasons to believe in one way rather than another. But such reasons rarely, if ever, "compel assent"[47] for everyone who encounters them—and those who believe that they do may be mistaken. The failure to recognize that thought and action always depend on some degree of faith that one has seen things rightly not only encourages nonreligious people to unjustifiably disdain the notion of religious faith per se but also encourages many religious people themselves to accept the notion that the objects of belief relevant to their religious lives lie "beyond the scope of human knowledge" and are, therefore, exempt from the normal rules of evidence. Strict fideism makes no sense if questions such as "Is this text demonstrably the 'Word of God'?" are in fact open to some measure of rational adjudication.

The cognitive universality of faith, in the sense that I am discussing it here, is also a reason to reject the currently pervasive tendency among liberal theorists to treat religious reasons in the public sphere, qua religious, as being inherently suspect in a way that nonreligious reasons generally are not. If we shift the previous example from the strictly limited conceptual confines of the theory of natural selection, per se, to the full-blown worldview associated with the more philosophically developed neo-Darwinian expressions of the New Atheism by thinkers like Richard Dawkins and Daniel Dennett, with all of its attendant (and controversial) atheistic, deterministic, materialistic, reductivistic, mechanistic, and sensationistic metaphysical and epistemological assumptions, on what basis can one claim that such a worldview is admissible as a basis for argument in the public sphere, whereas Nicene Christianity is not? No nonarbitrary line can be drawn between religious and nonreligious worldviews in a way that would legitimate such theoretical discrimination between the two at this level. In whatever regards the introduction of the one into the public sphere is suspect, so must it be with the other.

Therefore, the issue is not whether religious believers, in particular, have a right to assert their own convictions as the basis for political regulations impacting those who do not share those convictions.

Instead, the issue is *in what manner*, and *within what limits*, ought any individual or group—religious or otherwise—seek to assert particular, worldview-dependent normative understandings or regulations in the context of a society that is *pluralistic as a matter of first principle*. And this formulation of our proper concern also helps explain my focus on virtue here. Part of the answer to the questions implied by the previous formulation will be procedural, but another part of it will necessarily be dispositional. This is precisely why I am linking my justification for classic liberal-democratic norms to an account of anxiety as an epistemic virtue. As I will discuss further in Chapter 6, while liberal theory has generally stood counterposed to virtue theory in contemporary political philosophy, the most sophisticated visions of liberal–democratic social forms—in my view—are to be found in *hybrid* liberal-virtue theories, of the sort that one finds in current American 'deliberative' democratic theory. (I will return to the specific issue of the proper role of religious—and other worldview-dependent—reasons in the liberal public sphere in Chapter 4.)

The putative uniqueness of religious belief, as being a matter of faith, also provides support for the traditionalist (monotheistic) religious notion that faith is a mysterious, divinely bestowed third element standing between the believing subject and the object of belief, encouraging some 'believers' to view the 'unbelief' (notice, not 'alternative belief') of others as a product (and sign) of the latter's moral degeneracy or spiritual deficiency, rather than simply a matter of intellectual disagreement over an issue on which it is possible for reasonable people to disagree. This misconception further obscures the too little discussed resources for combating absolutism that exist within religious traditions, like Christianity, in which the urge to absolutism has been historically pronounced.[48] Such intolerant believers embrace what we may call *Calvin's contradiction*, after the theologian who, perhaps, most brazenly weds the notions of religious certainty and textual and interpretive 'inerrancy' with the directly contradictory notion of humanity's moral and epistemic 'fallenness.'[49] Jean Calvin's steadfast refusal to consider the implications of his view of human 'depravity' for his own claims regarding the nature and meaning of scripture has conditioned Protestant belief ever since, setting the stage for the flight from anxiety that has helped to push the self-satisfied certainty of many Christians in tragically (and sinfully) aggressive and intolerant directions.

Indeed, this all too common propensity to circumscribe the epistemic implications of finitude within the bounds of an absolutist and exclusivist religious understanding represents one important reason the traditional virtue of 'humility' cannot play the role I am ascribing here to anxiety. Humility certainly can be connected to the epistemic conditions of finitude, and, yet, one need not genuinely recognize the full implications of these conditions in order to affirm humility as a virtue. Many religious absolutists acknowledge the rightness of a humble attitude, but they envision such humility as part and parcel of their fideism. From this perspective, one has humility toward God, not toward one's beliefs about God. Perhaps one also is encouraged to remain humble in one's relations to other humans, but, again, this is encouraged as a requirement of, but not with respect to, one's religious and moral convictions.

This is certainly not to deny that humility can be adopted in a way that transcends the delimitations of dogmatic frameworks. The neo-Aristotelian (and theistic) philosopher Linda Zagzebski, for example, has formulated a conception of humility within the framework of her 'virtue epistemology' that is highly consonant with certain aspects of the conception of epistemic anxiety that I am offering here.[50] When it is adopted in such a way, humility is certainly a virtuous epistemic stance. But even when humility takes this form, it cannot, in and of itself, fully stand in for anxiety, in the sense I am discussing here, because it does not carry the latter's implication of a creative striving after further and better understandings. That is, even when it takes a virtuous form and underwrites a noncoercive political ethic humility does not, further, underwrite the positive deliberative norms of democratic discourse in the way that epistemic anxiety does so. I can be humbly resigned to my limitations, such that I see no need to—or, perhaps, no point in—striving for further and better understandings. In other words, epistemic anxiety better plays the 'motivational' role that Zagzebski rightly emphasizes in relation to the ethics of belief formation and knowledge acquisition.[51] Moreover, virtuous epistemic anxiety also *provokes and underwrites* humility. So the two do go hand in hand, as I have already suggested. It was not humility alone but, rather, humility founded in epistemic anxiety that helped prompt the modern West's move toward liberalism. The relationship of anxiety to humility is not one of equivalence; it is one in which the former grounds the latter more deeply.

The notion of epistemic anxiety stands as a corrective to the tendency among many religious believers to conveniently ignore the implications of human finitude for religious belief. *Orthodoxism is idolatry*. This is a language that will strike closer to home for many who are not persuaded by the notion of tolerance. The same people who most vociferously hurl the charge of "playing God" at those who extend their technological reach beyond what the former think appropriate are those most often guilty of playing God epistemically, of deifying their own finite, fallible understandings. And this argument leaves little room for strong rebuttal. Even the most conservative traditionalist will not be so brazen as to claim infallibility. Of course, they will claim it on behalf of some person or group of persons portrayed in their religious tradition (e.g., Jesus and the biblical authors), but even setting aside the a priori argument from finitude and granting, hypothetically, the possibility that some person(s) might have possessed infallibility, the problem remains that only another infallible person could inerrantly recognize the infallibility of the first. And no religious tradition of which I am aware licenses such a claim by the practitioner.[52]

Some Potential Challenges to this Perspective

At this point, some readers may object that there is an apparent paradox or self-contradiction implicit in my account of epistemic anxiety and/or in the general liberal principle of noncoercion that I seek to justify through this account. Such an objection might take several different forms. First, there is a formal conception of the (putative) paradox that is as old as the liberalism it is meant to counter. This version of the objection claims that the principle of noncoercion is, if enforced, self-violating, because it requires (or may require) the employment of coercive means in order to prevent actions[53] that are judged to be contradictory to or inconsistent with the principle—for example, the use of law enforcement powers to ensure compliance with antidiscrimination statutes. Traditionally, liberal theorists have responded to this criticism by drawing a distinction between 'substantive' and 'procedural' norms and by arguing that liberal political regulation is purely procedural—and, therefore, substantively 'neutral'—in character.[54]

Thus the liberal prohibition against coercion is viewed by liberals as being categorically different in character from any substantive belief or principle of action that might be enforced contrary to such a prohibition. This difference stems, in part, from the fact that liberalism leaves untouched the individual's right and capacity to believe and to personally act on whatever beliefs she may acquire (through whatever relevant process of belief formation one might identify), so long as she does not violate others' right to this same freedom. Hence the validity of the enforcement of liberal norms is connected to the ineluctable, pragmatic exigencies of social life.[55]

Human beings must socialize across ideological lines,[56] and the only way to do so without enduring endless cycles of violent conflict or arbitrary oppression of some individuals or groups by others is to adopt procedural regulations regarding such socialization that mutually maximize the respective rights to substantive freedom of all members of society. But such mutual maximization of rights requires the minimization of the capacity of any particular substantive viewpoint to intrude on any other. While it is true that the latter form of regulation limits the former (at least for those perspectives that validate intrusiveness), it does so *of necessity*. Thus the complaint against it is what Isaiah Berlin would call a mere "counsel of perfection."[57] Every perspective is limited in the same way and none more so than any other—and this includes the liberal perspective, which is uniquely self-limiting (more on this point to follow). As Charles Larmore puts it, "If just laws serve to check the arbitrary will of others, their impact on our conduct and the prohibitions they impose do not amount in themselves to a reduction in our freedom. By doing away with our vulnerability, they bring into existence a realm of freedom that we would not otherwise have."[58]

Alternatively, one might object that my affirmation of the principle of human fallibility, on which my conception of epistemic anxiety is based—and, therefore, my formulation of the basis of the principle of noncoercion and other liberal norms—is self-refuting because such an assertion of fallibility itself is subject to doubt on its own grounds. In other words, my claim that all human understanding is fallible is also, on its own logic, fallible and, therefore, dubitable. But does this really represent a paradox or self-contradiction? I do not think so because *fallible* is not the same as *false*. I can perfectly well admit that my own conception of human fallibility is, itself, fallible, while maintaining my conviction that it is also true. Indeed, this is the only self-consistent manner in which I can maintain this conviction. I am simply admitting that it is possible that I am wrong about all of this. That does not mean that I *am* wrong. Possibility is not actuality.

However, this particular possibility does have normative implications, which is precisely why—as I noted earlier—I (and other liberals of my type) stop short of seeking to coercively disabuse others of their own absolutist perspectives or their right to live according to those perspectives (within the bounds of mutual noncoercion with others). As I just discussed previously, the claims of liberalism are inextricably linked to the conditions (and necessities) of social life. The enforcement of liberal norms supported by my conception of human fallibility and epistemic anxiety is—consistently with its own logic—self-limiting as well as regulatory. That is, the regulatory reach of this conception of the normativity of liberal norms is limited by its own internal check on the claims of authority, including its own authority. Obviously, this is not to say that I will not attempt by all appropriate means of persuasion to convince others that absolutist understandings are inherently flawed and pernicious, just as I expect that they will attempt to convince me otherwise. I value such dialogue precisely because of my recognition of my own fallibility (indeed, that is the point). Moreover, my obligatory affirmation of the fallibility of my own view is the reason I have deployed various arguments to support my claim regarding the ineluctability of human fallibility vis-à-vis religious beliefs. If I could somehow infallibly prove human fallibility (now, there would be a paradox), then such arguments would be superfluous (and, in the case of the example just given, mistaken).

Finally, one might formulate the objection substantively, rather than formally, by challenging the logic of epistemic anxiety in relation to the very dynamics of belief. This form of the objection might proceed thus: imagine that I hold a set of beliefs that, among other things, implies that I have an obligation to enforce a particular doctrinal orthodoxy by preventing the dissemination of heretical views and, if necessary, to do so coercively. Further, assume that this set of beliefs is at least prima facie rational because it is based on my considered assessment of the relevant evidence. The foregoing account of the normative implications of epistemic anxiety appears, in this case, to require that, given any doubt whatsoever regarding the certainty of my beliefs in general, I must reject as false a specific belief that currently I hold as true on the basis of the preponderance of evidence as I construe it. This seems to be a paradoxical conclusion—and, perhaps, an impossible requirement in practice, given the often-involuntary character of belief formation as a function of evidential consideration.

But this objection misconstrues the relationship of epistemic anxiety to the dynamic of belief that informs our hypothetical absolutist's conviction. My point is that human fallibility itself is an ineluctable element *in* the body of evidence that our erstwhile believer must consider in forming her beliefs in the first place. In other words, epistemic anxiety does not require that she paradoxically find false a belief that she heretofore held to be true on reasonable grounds. Rather, it *calls into question the assumed reasonableness of her belief that she is justified in approaching others coercively* because such a belief necessarily ignores the epistemic implications of the fact of human fallibility. (It is worth emphasizing that my claim is limited to her belief in her right of coercion; she may, in my view, continue reasonably to have faith in her overall belief system, despite her recognition of its fallibility, since there can be no rational obligation to eschew substantive belief in general—because "ought implies can.") So the normative connection between fallibility and anxiety, and, in turn, between anxiety and liberalism, is founded on the very rational obligation to consider all relevant and available evidence in the formation of one's beliefs to which this objection refers.

Hence while I am not putting it forward as part of a systematic epistemological theory, I am treating epistemic anxiety as a dispositional criterion of reasonable belief formation in a manner that is consonant with Zagzebski and other virtue epistemologists' formulation of intellectual virtues such as humility. For obvious reasons, I do not wish to connect my account of fallibility and anxiety to any particular theory of knowledge. Rather, my aim is to present these concepts in a way that is neutral to the controversies of epistemological theory, just as I am aiming to formulate a justification for liberal norms that is neutral in relation to the diversity of substantive worldviews that such norms are meant to mutually accommodate.

Now one might attempt to avoid the implications of the previous line of argument for religious belief by admitting that fallibility is, indeed, an ineluctable condition of human nature and, therefore, a significant evidential factor that must be considered in the formation of rational belief but, also, claiming that *revelation*—when added into the mix of evidential support for a certain set of beliefs—can override the normative implication of fallibility by providing a touchstone of certainty that trumps all reasonable doubt. But as I have already discussed, this position involves a vicious regress because any claim to an infallible, revelatory understanding could only be inerrantly identified as such by one who was, already, also infallible—and therefore without need of such a revelation, in any case. The same logic obviously holds, mutatis mutandis, for any revelatory text, act, and so on. Moreover, with things like texts and acts, issues of interpretation further compound the problem. Hence appeals to revelatory knowledge can validate the claims of faith only when that faith is conditioned by an acceptance of the fallibility of the very "knowledge" provided by—and deciphered from—the revelation in question—that is, only when that faith embraces the virtue of epistemic anxiety. (I will have much more to say about the relation between revelatory authority and epistemic anxiety in Chapters 3 and 4.)

Nor will it do to admit that human fallibility must be considered as one element in the evidential mix but claim that a consideration of the whole of the evidence might still, legitimately, lead one to affirm an absolutist position—if that implies a willingness to coerce others to think as one does or to force them to act in accordance with an ideology they do not share. The implications of acknowledging one's own fallibility must be viewed *categorically*, not as a matter of degree, in relation to one's interactions with others. For there is a categorical difference, morally speaking, between voluntarily adopting and adhering to a perspective or ideology on the basis of one's own fallible construal of the evidence for and against it and forcing someone else to adopt and/or adhere to it contrarily to her own judgment on the matter. It is one thing, to take a currently prominent example, for an individual to suppress and refrain from acting on her own homosexual tendencies on the basis of her commitment to a religious perspective that proscribes them. It is quite another thing for her and other members of her religious community to seek coercively to impose the same proscription on others.

Here is where epistemic anxiety connects with respect for the dignity of the individual. As I indicated in my discussion of Kant in Chapter 1, liberalism certainly depends on such respect, but it also depends—crucially, I think—on the recognition that respecting human dignity requires respecting the right of others to construct, and live in accordance with, diverse conceptions of what contributes to and what derogates from that dignity. And I submit, it is epistemic anxiety, as I have formulated it here, which produces and supports this further recognition. If one could know, *infallibly*, that one's own perspective on any matter of moral judgment were correct, then such knowledge would (at least arguably) override the moral distinction between adopting the requirements of this perspective for oneself and imposing them on others. Without such a guarantee, however, one must respect the right of others to adopt contrary perspectives as a matter of highest principle. In my view, this conception of the implications of fallibilism vis-à-vis the justification of liberal-democratic norms represents a sort of theoretical purification of the logic of Miltonian-Lockean-Millian liberalism. Particularly in Milton and Locke, the justification for tolerance of opposing perspectives is founded on their own particularistic metaphysical commitments in a manner that, it seems to me, is deeply problematic, because it is patronizing. Here I am in-line with the contemporary Rawlsian attempt to offer a justification for liberalism that is not dependent on any particular 'comprehensive' perspective.[59] One person's comprehensive freedom ought not depend on another person's comprehensive certainty.

In sum, tolerance is *not* an "externally imposed mandate" that stifles the spirit of authentic religious belief by holding in check its natural impulse to assert itself over others. Rather, it is an internal requirement of the logic of the religious mentality, which is founded on the recognition of humanity's inadequacy in the face of forces and questions that are larger than us, holding in check what Niebuhr calls "the tendency toward sinful self-assertion."[60] As I will argue further in the next chapter, authentic religious faith does not imply a 'suspension of the ethical'[61] (in the sense of modern liberal norms). For such faith—insofar as it makes even implicit reference to the distinction between the infinitude of its object and the finitude of its subject—necessarily includes recognition of the inadequacy of the individual's understandings and, therefore, should be construed as prohibiting dogmatically motivated action that transgresses contractual liberal norms and freedoms. In other words, genuinely self-reflective faith in something that is believed to transcend the human, eo ipso, implies the normativity of liberal norms, like tolerance.

Tolerance, therefore, is not the foundational virtue of liberalism. Tolerance is derivative from anxiety—psychologically, historically, and theoretically.[62] Anxiety about the limitations of one's own understanding (an inescapable by-product of the erosion of appeals to epistemic privilege that helps define the Enlightenment mentality) is the true sine qua non of liberal democratic culture. In a society in which epistemic anxiety is suppressed, neither tolerance nor liberty can long survive.

Finally, before turning to a closer examination of traditional conceptions of Abrahamic faith in the next chapter, I would like to say a last word regarding the common connotations of the term 'anxiety.' While I have tried to show that there are good reasons for accepting a use of the term that is positive, rather than negative, it should also be clear that the mind-set that I am propounding is a difficult one. The conscious acceptance of anxiety, in the sense I have outlined here, represents the embrace of a higher level of self-responsibility. This is not an easy task nor should we expect it to be. If virtuous attitudes and behaviors came easily, we would all live in near utopias. This is one thing that religious consciousness understands and that liberals have been too reluctant to insist on. Genuine liberal democracy, like genuine religiosity, makes serious, sometimes even unpleasant, demands on its practitioners. We must give something up in order to gain something immeasurably greater—in this case, the ignorant bliss of a self-satisfied understanding in exchange for a society in which people are free to choose for themselves not only how to interpret the world but also how to live in it.

Sartre, at one point, observes that the existentialists' diagnosis of the human condition is rejected "not [because of] our pessimism, but the sternness of our optimism."[63] We live in a world in which only a stern optimism is a credible optimism. Anxiety regarding our inescapable fallibility-in-finitude represents more than a past turning point in human history; it represents the maturation of human consciousness, and maturity, like civilization, has its discomforts. But without an ever-present sense of such anxiety, we fall back into a self-satisfaction (or worse, a nervous bellicosity) that belies the fundamental truth revealed in all the world's great traditions of wisdom: we are imperfect.

Chapter 3

Anxiety, Secrecy, and Authority in the Abrahamic and Liberal Traditions

For the promise, that he should be the heir of the world, was not to Abraham, or to his seed through the law, but through the righteousness of faith.

—Rom 4:13 (AV)

In Chapter 1, I discussed Immanuel Kant's 'positive' conception of human freedom and the way in which this element of his moral and political theory became the basis for far more totalitarian visions of society than Kant himself would ever have endorsed. Within Kant's complex formulation, one contravening element that helped to blunt some of the problematic implications of his conception of freedom was the emphasis he placed on 'public' reasoning. According to Kant, ethical conduct is ineluctably tied to norms of discourse and disclosure. And while Kant's particular delineation of the boundaries between the public and the private is sometimes idiosyncratic or muddled, this general element of his thought has played a defining role in the development of many of the most influential contemporary moral and political theories, in both Anglo-American and Continental philosophy. (I will engage with various forms of contemporary 'discourse' and 'deliberative' theories at some length in Chapter 6.)

As I have also discussed, in Chapter 2, traditional conceptions of revealed religious faith tend to invest the beliefs that proceed from such faith with an *epistemic privilege* that challenges liberal political norms of tolerance, noncoercion, and individual liberty, as well as the public procedures of justification and deliberation that frame the enactment of these norms in democratic societies. Contrary to such traditional conceptions, however, I have argued that these norms are actually *implicit in the internal logic of religious consciousness* and, therefore, that claims to justification or authority that issue from faith in revealed "truths" are *in no way* exempt from the normal rules that govern opinion formation, democratic discourse, and political coexistence among autonomous individuals in modern Western democracies.

No religious narrative more clearly or iconically portrays the seeming conflict between the dictates of public ethical norms and the sometimes contrary commands of 'private' revelatory understandings than the biblical story of Abraham's trial of faith, according to which God personally commands Abraham to violate a fundamental ethical principle and Abraham proceeds dutifully to execute that command:

> And [God] said, Take now thy son, thine only son Isaac, whom thou lovest, and get thee into the land of Moriah; and offer him there for a burnt offering upon one of the mountains which I will tell thee of.
>
> And Abraham rose up early in the morning, and saddled his ass, and took two of his young men with him, and Isaac his son, and clave the wood for the burnt offering, and rose up, and went unto the place of which God had told him.
>
> Then on the third day Abraham lifted up his eyes, and saw the place afar off.
>
> And Abraham said unto his young men, Abide ye here with the ass; and I and the lad will go yonder and worship, and come again to you.
>
> And Abraham took the wood of the burnt offering, and laid it upon Isaac his son; and he took the fire in his hand, and a knife; and they went both of them together.
>
> And Isaac spake unto Abraham his father, and said, My father: and he said, Here am I, my son. And he said, Behold the fire and the wood: but where is the lamb for a burnt offering?
>
> And Abraham said, My son, God will provide himself a lamb for a burnt offering: so they went both of them together.[1]

From a modern point of view,[2] neither the decision to sacrifice Isaac nor Abraham's evasiveness if not outright deceptiveness, in seeking to carry out this command without informing Isaac of his true intentions, can be justified on ethical grounds. Indeed, modern analyses of this story tend to focus attention precisely on the apparent rupture between ethical norms and faithful obedience to God that characterizes Abraham's choice. On this reading of the story, to turn toward the divine is to turn away from 'the ethical,' to repudiate the latter's claim to absolute dominion in matters of conscience and action. Not surprisingly, Søren Kierkegaard provides the consummate articulation of this perspective.[3]

Of course, it is by no means clear that this modern interpretation of the ethical dynamic of Abraham's choice is consonant with the perspective of the story's author(s) or plausibly attributable to Abraham himself (if, in fact, there was such a person). In the biblical version of the story, we see none of the hand-wringing, existentially tortured sense of heroic 'transcendence' of moral intuition and socially validated ethical norms that we find in Kierkegaard's retelling of it. God instructed Abraham to kill his son, and the next day Abraham "rose up early in the morning" and set about his task.[4] If his soul was racked with doubt or internal controversy during the intervening night, we do not hear of it. God having (apparently) spoken to him in an unambiguous way, Abraham has no need to mull over his decision. His duty, as he sees it, is clear and straightforward. For him, religious and ethical obligation converge, rather than diverge, around the command he has been given. His choice, as he likely would have understood it, is not between faith and ethics. Rather, it is between an ethical obedience to God that is informed by faith—as trustfulness that God will not abandon God's prior promise that Abraham will have a multitude of descendants through Isaac—and an unethical and unfaithful resistance to God's command—which would demonstrate a lack of trust in God's promise.

Yet this certainly does not mean that Kierkegaard's analysis represents an interpretive failure, for he realized that we moderns—standing as we do in the bright, revealing light of the Enlightenment's exposure of the epistemic pretension that characterizes claims to absolute authority (not to mention the emergence of psychological explanations of purported revelatory experiences)—must come to our own understanding of Abraham's situation and our own judgments regarding his choice. Abraham's story required reinterpretation in relation to the novel challenges posed by modern thought precisely because these challenges have altered the dynamics of faith in modern life.

As I will argue later, this also does not mean that the implications of 'revealed faith' are different for us than they were for Abraham.

Rather, we have gradually come to understand these implications better, though many still cling to a traditional conception of religious belief that fails adequately to account for this clearer understanding. The general claim around which the discussions in the previous two chapters revolved is that the implicit internal logic of religious belief, including belief in 'revealed religion,' actually supports the very ethical norms of public justification and noncoercion, among others, that we associate with liberal-democratic theory and, more generally, with contemporary philosophical ethics following in the Enlightenment tradition. In this chapter and the next, I will seek further to establish this general claim through consideration of the analysis of Abraham's choice presented by Kierkegaard's pseudonymous persona Johannes de Silentio, in *Fear and Trembling*,[5] as well as Kierkegaard's discussion of the relation of Abrahamic faith to the resolute 'ignorance' of Socrates in this work and elsewhere. Examining these issues with reference to Silentio's analysis of Abraham not only further reveals the problematic underlying dynamic at work in those conceptions of faith that I rebutted in the last chapter, conceptions that are typically asserted within the framework of Anglo-American/analytic philosophy of religion, but also allows me to connect this discussion to a prominent thread in contemporary Continental philosophy of religion, where the Silentian perspective has been taken up as a primary lens for the deconstructive analysis of the dynamics of religion and politics by Jacques Derrida and others who have followed his lead.[6]

Ultimately, I will argue that we must normatively invert Silentio's analysis of the epistemic 'anxiety' that results from modernity's illumination of our finitude and fallibility as human beings. Such anxiety is not a problem to be overcome by a 'leap' into 'the absurd.' Rather, as I have argued in the preceding chapters, it is a *virtuous response* to the inescapable truth of our own limitedness and epistemic inadequacy. Abrahamic faith must be paired with, and conditioned by, 'Socratic anxiety.' *This* is what Athens has to do with Jerusalem.[7]

SILENTIO'S DIALECTIC OF FAITH

In *Fear and Trembling*, Kierkegaard has his pseudonymous author, Silentio, offer a "dialectical lyric" that conceptually juxtaposes the traditional Christian understanding of Abraham's trial with the requirements of modern ethical norms. As in much of his work, Kierkegaard uses the perspective of his authorial persona to highlight the tension between the religious claims and narratives associated with traditional Christianity and the Kantian and Hegelian philosophical concepts and principles that had been adopted theologically by the Danish Lutheran community at the time. Put another way, Silentio relentlessly pursues the implications of the religious valorization of Abraham's choice in order to demonstrate its incommensurability with modern ethics, particularly in terms of the ethical norms of discourse and disclosure, as Kant and, then, G. W. F. Hegel had formulated them.

According to Silentio, from a religious perspective, Abraham's greatness lies precisely in the inexplicable 'absurdity' of his faith and the unshakable firmness with which he holds fast to it. Abraham "had faith and did not doubt; he believed in the preposterous."[8] He believed that God had sent him to Moriah to sacrifice Isaac, and he went there committed to doing so. Yet he also believed that regardless of whatever might happen when he got there, God would make good on his promise that, *through Isaac*, Abraham would become father of a great nation of people—and not merely in some metaphorical sense but, rather, in a concrete and literal way: "Abraham . . . had faith for this life. In fact, if his faith had been only for the life to come, he certainly would have more readily discarded everything in order to rush out of a world to which he did not belong. But Abraham's faith was not of this sort, if there is such a faith at all . . . Abraham had faith specifically for this life—faith that he would grow old in this country, be honored among the people, blessed by posterity, and unforgettable in Isaac."[9]

Thus Abraham had faith in the impossible, which, we are told, is the truest—maybe the only true—form of faith. Abraham embraced "the prodigious paradox of faith . . . that makes a murder a holy and God-pleasing act," while, at the very same time, it "gives Isaac back to Abraham again."[10] This "prodigious paradox of faith," Silentio admonishes his contemporaries, is one that the Hegelian dialectic cannot resolve. It is not a merely apparent paradox that disappears once one attains the putatively higher, more perspicacious perspective of Hegelian philosophical analysis. Despite the Hegelian pretension that has infected the theological discourse of his age, leading everyone to speak of "going further" than faith,[11] Silentio insists that Abrahamic faith *essentially resists* rationalization. Philosophical reason cannot penetrate, disclose, and thereby cancel the paradox of faith, because faith stubbornly extrudes beyond the boundaries of reason. By the logic of its own terms, the rational dialectic cannot encompass Abraham's choice. It cannot explicate him and, then, move on. Hence Silentio tells us, "[F]aith begins precisely where thought stops."[12]

Silentio contrasts Abraham with the familiar figure of the "tragic hero." The latter is one who subordinates some deep—and, under normal circumstances, ethically obligatory—individual desire to the greater good. Setting aside individual attachment, the tragic hero sacrifices that which he or she loves most dearly on the altar of the ethical. Silentio gives as one example of such a hero: Lucius Junius Brutus, founder of the Roman Republic, who sentenced his own sons to death for rebellion.

Normally, a father ought to look after the welfare of his children. He should protect them from harm. But here the circumstances demand a different ethical calculation. Brutus's sons have threatened the fragile new republic. They have placed themselves at odds with the common good and with the law. Brutus's duty as a father is trumped by his duty as consul and judge. Were he to show mercy to his sons that he had not shown the other conspirators, then he would be guilty of nullifying the law, which is by definition dispassionate and universal, and replacing it with his own arbitrary will. Thus he would be reenacting precisely the dynamic that he had heroically fought against in ending the monarchy and founding the republic in the first place. And, of course, as Silentio emphasizes, everyone around Brutus, as he sits in judgment over his sons, comprehends all of this.

Brutus's choice is terrible and magnificent. It inspires awe, and makes one wonder if one could have made the same choice. But it is not mysterious. Everyone can understand Brutus, even if they cannot imagine doing what he did. His actions were thoroughly bound up in the discourse of the law and the expectations of ethical conduct. Moreover, the tragic nature of his heroism is a function precisely of his "resignation" regarding the death of his sons. He has no expectation that their deaths will somehow, miraculously, be overcome. They will not be returned to him. He gives them up with a heavy heart, secure only in his own fidelity to the law.[13]

Abraham, on the other hand, sacrifices the ethical on the altar of faith. Isaac is not just Abraham's beloved son. He is the foundation on which an ethical community is to be built. Isaac *is* the greater good. The very existence of the ethical community that God has promised to found through him is completely dependent on Isaac's survival. From Abraham's point of view, there can be no higher ethical duty than to protect Isaac from harm and ensure that he has the opportunity to procreate. As Silentio explains,

> The tragic hero is still within the ethical. He allows an expression of the ethical to have its *telos* in a higher expression of the ethical; he scales down the ethical relation between father and son . . . to a feeling that is dialectical in its relation to moral conduct . . .
>
> Abraham's situation is different. By his act he transgressed the ethical altogether and had a higher *telos* outside it, in relation to which he suspended it . . . The ethical in the sense of the moral is entirely beside the point. Insofar as [it] was present [on Moriah] it was cryptically in Isaac, hidden, so to speak, in Isaac's loins, and must cry out with Isaac's mouth: Do not do this, you are destroying everything.
>
> Why, then, does Abraham do it? For God's sake and—the two are wholly identical—for his own sake. He does it for God's sake because God demands this proof of his faith. He does it for his own sake so that he can prove it.[14]

It is precisely in passing beyond the bounds of ethical justification that Abraham becomes a 'knight of faith.' He is the exemplar, par excellence, of the 'movement' of faith, which leaps past resignation and seizes on the impossible as inevitable. Of him, Silentio says, "I cannot understand Abraham—I can only admire him." And this failure to understand is not a fault of the author. It is essential to the character of the movement of faith. This movement is categorically nondiscursive. "Abraham . . . *cannot* speak," Silentio explains. "Even though I go on talking all night and day without interruption, if I cannot make myself understood when I speak, then I am not speaking. This is the case with Abraham."[15]

Unlike Brutus sitting in judgment over his sons, in the crucible of his trial of faith, as he raises the knife over Isaac's chest, Abraham does not have even the consolation of knowing that his actions are explicable to others, that his motives can be understood, or that his choice is validated by the assent and honor of the community. Thus Abraham, unlike Brutus, does not feel the support of the community as it bears with him, through its implication in the ethical logic of his choice, the weight of his making of that choice. He alone bears it. He alone is responsible for it. He cannot share that responsibility with the community by referring his choice to the dictates of his ethical relation to the community, because his choice negates that relation.

The community has not received a revelation from God; only Abraham has. Given the epistemological dynamics at work in modern discursive ethics, therefore, the community *cannot*—and could not, even if it were an already existing community—affirm Abraham's faith in the impossible outcome by which he expects to fulfill

God's command to sacrifice Isaac and, yet, to receive him back again just as before. Only if the community were to enter into a relation of faith vis-à-vis Abraham, to invest in him a trust that deifies, to treat him as a god, could it affirm his choice. But then, this would be precisely an affirmation of faith, not an ethical affirmation. Or, put alternatively, the ethics of this affirmation would be premodern and, in Hegelian terms, 'despotic.'[16] That is to say, such an affirmation belongs to the politics of authoritarianism, not those of liberal democracy and republicanism. To display more clearly the political implications of Silentio's analysis, I will turn now to two closely related appropriations of it in contemporary philosophy of religion, Derrida's and that of the Christian philosopher of religion Jonathan Malesic.

Secrecy and Authoritarianism in Abrahamic Faith

In 2006, at the height of the public controversies over both the expansion of governmental secrecy and the role of Christian evangelicalism in the Bush White House, the *Journal of the American Academy of Religion* published an important special issue dedicated to religion and secrecy.[17] In his provocative contribution to this issue, Malesic—drawing also on the work of Derrida—traces the religious logic of Abraham's 'transcendence of the ethical' as formulated in *Fear and Trembling*, with a focus on its applicability in the context of current debates over the role of religion in political discourse.[18] As Malesic observes, the conflict that Silentio describes between the modern ethical imperatives of disclosure and public justification on the one hand and the religious requirements of 'inwardness' and 'radical responsibility,' on the other can be formulated in terms of a fundamental disagreement between philosophical ethics and revealed religion over the normative status of 'secret' claims to authority and any actions that proceed therefrom. Malesic, like Silentio, is not seeking to reconstruct the concept of faith in a way that fundamentally departs from its traditional orientation—as I am seeking to do here. His interest is in describing what he takes to be the inner logic of the traditional concept of faith in Abrahamic religions in the conceptual terms of contemporary philosophical discourse without, thereby, reducing faith (as both Kant and Hegel did) to a subordinate adjunct of philosophical reasoning.

Before I proceed further to analyze (and critique) Malesic and Derrida's respective interpretations and applications of Silentio's account of Abraham's trial, it is important to add a qualification regarding their references to Kierkegaard himself. While Malesic draws no apparent distinction between Silentio and Kierkegaard, it is important to do so since it is by no means certain, so far as I can see, that Silentio's perspective on the gulf between faith and ethics is identifiable with Kierkegaard's own, actual views, whatever they may have been. My own sense is that Kierkegaard employs the character of Silentio in at least a partially ironic mode, with a voice that expresses real ambivalence about a subject that his contemporaries had, he thought, deluded themselves into thinking they understood with perfect clarity. Kierkegaard's oeuvre is among the most complex of the modern era, and Kierkegaard scholars will likely never cease arguing over where to locate the man himself amid his many, sometimes contrary, personae. Thus for the sake of clarity—and since it is not my concern here to enter into the debate regarding Kierkegaard's true authorial intent—in the following discussion, I will refer exclusively to Silentio as the author of *Fear and Trembling* and the views therein expressed.

For his part, Derrida recognizes the importance of Kierkegaard's choice to employ a pseudonym here. However, his analysis of this rhetorical choice—as well as of the symbolism of the pseudonym chosen—leads him, nevertheless, to equate Silentio's perspective with Kierkegaard's. In fact, at one point, he even hyphenates the two names: "Kierkegaard-de Silentio."[19]

As Malesic observes, contemporary philosophical ethics, following Kant, demands disclosure, because secrecy creates a hierarchy of knowledge—and, thus, power—which not only undermines the free exchange of information that enables informed and rational deliberation but also, thereby, threatens the autonomy of those from whom secrets are kept.[20] "Revealed religions," on the other hand, according to Malesic, "are committed to the possibility of a revelation that occurs at a particular time and to a particular person or group." And "because this entails a further commitment to the existence of the individual's inward life that is not accessible to others," Malesic contends, "revealed religions approve of secrecy."[21] This implication follows from the epistemological dynamic involved in revelatory experiences/claims, for the inaccessible inward life in question here is precisely the locus of revelatory experience and, therefore, the warrant for the claims to revelatory—that is, absolute—knowledge that emerge from this experience resides beyond the bounds of discursive justification. No one who does not share directly in the revelation can be made to understand its force; it is inexplicable in abstraction from the concrete subjectivity of its experiential reception as an absolute determiner of belief and commitment. (Note the epistemological parallel with Alvin Plantinga's influential account of Christian knowledge claims as 'basic'—that is, in need of no further justification than the subjectively compelling authority they have for the believer).[22]

That is to say, on the conception of revealed religion reflected in Silentio's analysis of Abraham, the *justification of* a revelation that is transmitted to the 'secret' interiority of the individual self is also 'secret.' It depends only on the self-validating particularity of the individual's (or group's) concrete relation to the divine: Abraham receives instructions from God, but relaying these instructions to another person would not communicate to that person the nature of his faith or the warrant it carries (over against the claims of ethics) because these are ineluctably bound up with the essential 'hiddenness' and 'unspeakableness' of Abraham's covenant with God. As Malesic puts it, "The rules of this covenant are not universal, and so Abraham's justification is secret by virtue of being unsayable; his covenant is so particular and qualifies him as so different from all other human beings that he shares no medium of communication about it." Hence, according to this account, Abraham is freed from the bounds of ethical action through his apprehension of the divine will, precisely because the normative force of the divine will transcends both the possibility and, therefore, the requirement of public justification.[23] (Thus the one principle that seems to transcend the divide between the ethical and the religious in this interpretation is "ought implies can," since it is by this logic that we are told that Abraham is not obliged to share his intent with those involved. Because he cannot do so; it is incommunicable.)

Silentio makes clear that 'faith,' as he conceives it, cannot be achieved in communion with others but only by the individual, qua individual—precisely because it is incommunicable. However, Malesic rightly recognizes that the logic of interiority and secrecy applied to Abraham by Silentio does, in fact, relate to the claims of special knowledge and revelatory justification lodged by—and within—religious groups. Thus while Silentio would not extend to members of such groups the designation of 'knights of faith' on the basis of their collective faith claims, his discussion of the 'movements' of the knight of faith nevertheless parallels and illuminates central characteristics of such communities of faith and their relations to outsiders. When, for example, such communities put forward in the public sphere normative claims that are based exclusively on particularist religious reasons as the basis for coercive political regulations, they are essentially *saying nothing*. That is, their faith-based justifications are discursively vacuous, precisely because they depend on a validation that is, by definition, 'inaccessible' to those who do not share their faith: one cannot be persuaded by these reasons in terms of any criteria of evaluation external to the orbit of their normative acceptance; to be persuaded by such reasons requires relating to them as matters of faith. To put it in the terms of standard contemporary liberal political theory, such faith-based reasons are illegitimate because they cannot be translated into alternative formulations that could, in principle, be persuasive on nonparticularistic grounds.[24] (As I made clear in Chapter 2, I reject the standard liberal conflation, in this context, of 'nonparticularistic' and 'secular.') More specifically, I believe this analysis of the essentially noncommunicative nature of such claims provides the missing framework needed to validate the Rawlsian argument that, as a general rule, religious reasons cannot be accepted by autonomous individuals as the basis for coercive regulations (which is distinct from John Rawls's argument for restraint on the basis of respect for other persons).[25] Rawls himself goes too far, I think, in construing practically all forms of public discourse as properly falling under this prohibition. But at least he does not, like others, single out religious—as opposed to secular—reasons as deserving scrutiny of this sort. With proper modifications the argument from autonomous reason matches up nicely with my account of epistemic anxiety. (I will return to these issues in Chapter 4.)

Following Silentio, Malesic argues that revealed religion—by its very nature—necessarily claims an ethical exceptionalism that obviates the normal requirements for epistemic and moral justification. And this exceptionalism is connected to a divergent notion of 'responsibility.' Whereas modern ethics conceives of responsibility in terms of respect for others' autonomy and adherence to the classic liberal political norms associated with such respect, Abrahamic revealed religion, as explicated by Silentio, conceives of responsibility more 'radically,' in terms of "taking over the autonomy of another person, acting on his or her behalf." Such 'radical responsibility,' Malesic explains, "doesn't keep account or give an account, neither to man, to humans, to society, to one's fellows, or to one's own . . . Such a responsibility keeps its secret, it cannot and need not present itself."[26]

Of course, as both Silentio and Malesic recognize, modern ethical thinking "must condemn" this radical conception of responsibility as an illicit power grab. From an ethical point of view, a secret justification (in this sense) is, by definition, an arbitrary justification—and, hence, no justification at all—because it rests solely on an unverified (and, indeed, *unverifiable*) presumption of self-righteousness by the one who claims its warrant. The questions surrounding the veracity of the revelation—Is it really God, and not 'the demonic,' who has issued these instructions? Is Abraham deluded or even delusional? Has he heard God rightly?—cannot be eluded within the realm of the ethical. Nor can the requirements of public justification and noncoercion meant to address such concerns be ignored without violating one's ethical duty.

But according to the logic of the Silentian analysis, religion, by its very nature and most essential *telos*, validates that which is arbitrary and pernicious from an ethical perspective. On this view, from a religious perspective, Abraham is 'heroic' precisely because he is willing to set aside any (public) question of the justifiability of his intentions and actions. Yet our modern minds must inquire, if Abraham's withdrawal from the requirements of the ethical is justified by his claim to a secret understanding and agreement with God—which requires the presumption of the infallibility of his own belief about what has occurred and his understanding of its implications—from whence does Abraham draw the authority to self-validate this claim?

From an *epistemological* point of view—one that can be said to transcend the distinction between the ethical and the religious, precisely because it frames any statement of, or interpretation regarding, such a distinction—Silentio's description of Abraham's movement of faith embraces a vicious circularity. Abraham—however implicitly and "silently"—lodges the following claim in relation to Isaac: "I cannot communicate my justification to you; for it is 'secret.' Thus, you will simply have to trust that my peremptory appropriation of your autonomy is justified on the basis of evidence that you cannot evaluate because I can not explain it to you." To lodge such a claim goes beyond substituting one's own reason for another's. To lodge such a claim is to wave off reason altogether, solely by the arbitrary fiat of one's own self-idolizing will to power.

Derrida concisely explains the Silentian knight of faith's movement of 'absolute duty,' which negates one's 'ethical duty,' in this way:

> The absolute duty that obligates her with respect to God cannot have the form of generality that is called duty. If I obey in my duty towards God (which is my absolute duty) *only in terms of duty*, I am not fulfilling my relation to God. In order to fulfill my duty towards God, I must not act *out of duty*, by means of that form of generality that can always be mediated and communicated and that is called duty. The absolute duty that binds me to God himself, in faith, must function beyond and against any duty I have.[27]

But here we must remember just what we are so often wont to forget. In real life—as opposed to contrived narratives—it will always be *oneself*, and not 'the Other,' to which one sacrifices one's ethical duty as a Silentian knight of faith. It is *never* to God, per se (whatever that might be), and it is *never* to 'the wholly Other' (if, indeed, that is how God should be understood) to which we *actually relate* in any affirmation or act of faith. It is *always*—at least to some degree—to *our own representation* of the divine that we relate.

Even if God does, in fact, call to me—and I happen to believe that God calls to each of us, in every moment—this call is *always mediated*. It is mediated by the categories and preconceptions that frame my understanding of that to which I attribute whatever call I hear. I may well hear God's voice clearly at times, but I will always hear it through *my ears*. What is more, I may, in any particular case, be mistaken when I believe that it is God's voice and not some other voice—some voice from inside myself, perhaps, or the voice of some false god, some idol that I have set up, or that has been set up for me—that I hear. To pretend otherwise, to assert the privilege of an 'absolute duty' that negates the claims of general duty, of my ethical duties to others, is nothing other than to assert an implicit claim to self-deification. There is nothing heroic in such a claim, or in any act that might proceed from it. It is, to the contrary, an act of existential cowardice, for I hide myself behind the coattails of my representation of 'the Other.' I wave 'the Other' in front of me and pretend that *It* is the actor and I merely the conduit of its activity, the means of *Its* ends rather than my own.

Malesic echoes the logic of Silentio's distinction between the tragic hero and the knight of faith when he claims that "[b]y choosing to be responsible in the sense of always acting in accordance with universal duties, we gain security and certitude." Whereas, he says, "[b]y choosing to be responsible in the sense of becoming responsible *for* others, we risk serious culpability for the consequences."[28] But surely this reverses the true dynamic at work in the choice here presented. While there is, I suppose, a kind of "certitude" to be had in the observance of ethical norms of public justification and noncoercion—namely, the certitude that one has not arbitrarily violated another's autonomy—the price of such assurance is precisely the (at least implicit) recognition of the *impossibility* of absolute, unequivocal certitude on the part of finite and, therefore, fallible[29] human minds.

Just insofar as I am fallible, it is incumbent on me to appeal to some form of external validation of the legitimacy of my thinking on some matter of ethical concern before I act *in a way that affects others*. By following the ethical dictates of disclosure, I express an implicit acknowledgement of my own fallibility and its implications in relation to my moral choices. I show the courage to leave behind the illusory security of self-validation and risk the possibility of finding that I am incorrect—or at least that others think me so. Indeed, in my view, this is the proper understanding of its own warrant at which *liberalism* should ultimately arrive. Derrida, following in the footsteps of the Czechoslovakian philosopher and political dissident Jan Patočka, claims that "Christianity [along with the other Abrahamic traditions] has not been thought right through," that "Christianity has not yet come to Christianity." Similarly, I believe that liberalism has not yet been thought right through. Liberalism has not yet come to liberalism. And this work is one part of my own attempt to think Abrahamic religion and liberalism through together.

To assume "responsibility *for* others," without their free and informed consent, on the basis of a 'secret' revelation, is either to make the morally vicious choice to *gamble* with their lives on the basis of my own desire to fulfill a revelation I admit is uncertain, or to express a self-satisfied—and, therefore, delusional—certainty that I could not possibly be wrong about the revelation I believe that I have received. Delusional because the only way in which such an appropriation of others' autonomy could be (arguably) justified is if it followed from my own *in*fallibility.

As I discussed in Chapters 1 and 2, only if I could infallibly know that I were right could I (perhaps) legitimately override the autonomy of another human being for my own purposes, absent appeal to the regulatory procedures and mutual restrictions of liberal political norms of public justification and democratic decision making. Surely it *is* precisely such an implicit claim to infallible knowledge that characterizes Abraham's actions as presented in the biblical account. Lacking adequate self-awareness about the implications of his own finitude and fallibility in relation to his apprehension and interpretation of his (apparent) revelation, Abraham, therefore, lacks also any sense of epistemic anxiety regarding the accuracy of and warrant for his beliefs. Thus he feels no compunction about appropriating the autonomy of those around him, including Isaac, precisely because he does not suppose that he could possibly be mistaken about what he should do.

Such a delusional certitude is what unites those who use, or would use, political coercion, or even outright violence, to get their way, regardless of where they fall on the spectra of religious and political persuasions. It is basic to the psychology of the terrorist, which manifests this delusion in its most acute and aggressive form. Whether it is a Saudi Arabian Islamist jihadi flying a plane into a building full of people as an attack on "the West," or a Norwegian right-wing Christian who murders those he identifies with cultural pluralism in the name of protecting the West from Islam,[30] it is precisely from the comfortable position of unearned certitude that such terrorists act. The same was true, I should note, of the antireligious left-wing terrorists who followed the path of Leninism throughout the twentieth century. These religious and antireligious terrorists are the truest exemplars of the political logic of 'radical responsibility.'

To be very clear, I do not at all mean to suggest that Malesic himself endorses political violence of this sort (I will comment on Malesic's normative development of his own position in his book *Secret Faith in the Public Square: An Argument for the Concealment of Christian Identity* in the next chapter). I am simply pointing out that *the account of religious responsibility that he endorses* supports such violence, since one can draw no line short of it on the basis of this account. This goes back to a point that I mentioned in Chapter 1, where I noted that the progress away from the employment of violent coercion in the name of religious claims to authority in modern Western history has come only *in spite of* the attitudes and efforts of successive generations of those who maintain a political stance of epistemic privilege regarding their own beliefs. That is to say, the level of coercive moral conformism for which religious critics of political liberalism argue today is somewhat less oppressive than what was argued for by their historic antecedents precisely because liberalism triumphed over those antecedent arguments, making them unviable in mainstream discourse in the contemporary West. This change did *not* come because the basic principles underlying contemporary religious criticisms of liberalism are different from earlier versions of such criticism. To put it even more plainly and pointedly, it seems likely to me that many of the people today who argue for somewhat more moderated versions of religiously justified coercive social orders would have been arguing for less moderated forms of such coercion had they lived in earlier periods of Western history, when liberalism was in its infancy and such arguments had not become widely anathema. Indeed, it only makes sense to think of the entire spectrum of opinions on these issues as having shifted several increments in the direction of tolerance and to worry, therefore, that it could shift back in the other direction, should the traditionalist perspective regain sufficient momentum within the broader social conversation.

As Jeffery Stout has observed, there's been a worrisome resurgence of this perspective among certain overlapping circles of academic and popular theology. (I will say more about these 'New Traditionalists' in Chapter 4.) And this is also one primary reason for concern over contemporary expressions of religious particularism by political figures that cross over from appropriate public self-identification (an important form of disclosure) into inappropriate legitimization of attitudes of moral and epistemological superiority to all alternative perspectives. This sort of violation of the ethic of epistemic anxiety undermines the integrity of public discourse and, ultimately, poses a challenge to the very logic of the political system in which such figures participate. (I will say more about such political expressions of normative particularism later.)

Within the context of liberal–democratic public discourse, the recognition of the full implications of human fallibility that I am identifying with epistemic anxiety represents a metacriterion of reasonableness. Those who do not accept this criterion may be treated as unreasonable precisely because their denial of these implications translates discursively into a refusal genuinely to communicate. Like Abraham, their epistemic self-satisfaction places them beyond the bounds of the discursive community. They relate to that community negationally; therefore, the community has no obligation to treat their claims as deserving consideration.

Derrida—who, near the end of *The Gift of Death*, fundamentally departs from Silentio in a way that Malesic seems to ignore—alludes in passing to the issue of Abraham's self-validation of his claim to revelatory knowledge, when he says, "[Abraham] might claim that the wholly other ordered him to do it, and perhaps in secret (*how would he know that?*), in order to test his faith, but it would make no difference."[31] In an exceptionally clear and concise reading of *The Gift of Death*, Adam Kotsko summarizes Derrida's departure from Silentio thus: "[O]ne stands in relation to every other as one stands in relation to (Kierkegaard's) God: there is no single, privileged 'more other' other who automatically preempts every other."[32]

Had Derrida only lingered a little longer on the implications of his parenthetical question regarding Abraham's claim of a secret transmission from God—"*How would he know that?*"—he might have linked it explicitly to his insight regarding the flat topography of *alterity* and, perhaps, moved somewhat in the direction of the analysis of the logic of faith claims that I am offering here. As Kotsko evocatively puts the matter, "Abraham is playing a game of cards without a trump card."[33] That is, he is "bluffing."[34] What I am adding here is that it is just such a bluff that we find in any and every claim to religious exceptionalism, in the sense in which I have used this term earlier.

But of course, the *foundational* understanding of the epistemic mandate of liberalism to which I am navigating through my own analysis of religious bluffing goes further than Derrida's own commitments would allow him to go. Thus while I agree with Kotsko's Derridean claim that "it would be possible to construe the entire history of responsibility as a history of *bluffing*," I would add the qualification that this applies only to the entire history of responsibility *so far*, for unlike Derrida, I do not believe that we "should conclude that not only is the thematization of the concept of responsibility always inadequate but that it is always so because *it must be so*."[35] As I have already indicated, my goal is precisely to think through religion and liberalism in order to attain a concept of responsibility that *is* adequate (or, at least, to come as close to that ideal as I am able).[36] In my view, therefore, the concept of radical (or 'absolute') responsibility is inadequate not because, as a concept of responsibility per se, "it must be so"; rather, it is inadequate because, as the particular, flawed concept of responsibility that it is, it contradicts the central insight regarding human insufficiency that lies at the root of religious consciousness, ineluctably entangled with our apprehension of the divine, the infinite object to which we contrast ourselves, explicitly or implicitly, in every religious appeal and act.

In this regard, my conception of the mandate and raison d'être of liberal-democratic norms also contrasts with the pragmatist conceptions thereof that have exerted so much influence in American philosophy over the last several decades. Unlike, for example, the defense of liberalism on the grounds of its strength as a shared moral tradition informing American history articulated by Stout,[37] my own defense of liberal norms is grounded in what I take to be a principle of, as Kant would have put it, *transcendental anthropology.* Human fallibility is not a historically contingent fact; it is a transcendental condition of human existence, per se. Any and every moral point of view must take account of this condition, and any and every moral or political claim that imposes on the autonomy of another individual must be subject to some proceduralized recognition of it. In this sense, my understanding of the mandate of liberal democracy is closer to the 'transcendental pragmatism' of the neo-Kantian philosopher Karl-Otto Apel than to the Jamesian-Deweyan pragmatism of Stout or the related—and even more relativistic—'neopragmatism' of Richard Rorty, which is not to say that I do not find William James's and John Dewey's own pragmatist insights useful. Like most thinkers who have been influenced by the 'process' philosophy of Alfred North Whitehead, I prefer the original perspectives articulated by James and Dewey themselves over those offered by the vast majority of those who claim them as antecedents. (More on all of that in Chapter 6.)

For all the flaws of their respective positions in normative terms, in my view, Derrida and Malesic provide important descriptive-analytic clarification to any discussion of traditional Abrahamic faith. Adding contemporary context and conceptualizations to Silentio's original dialectical unpacking of the story of Abraham's trial, they illuminate the traditional conception of faith, while connecting it to the contemporary conversation in a way that highlights its continuing relevance and the challenge it poses to liberal-democratic discourse. The affirmation of, and reliance on, secret justifications (in the sense described earlier) has had a pernicious effect on religious belief and behavior since the first claim to such justification was lodged—long before Abraham went to Moriah. It is the source of the authoritarianism that so often pollutes religious traditions and institutions, from the temporal abuse of the spiritual powers conferred by hierarchies of knowledge and the coercive imposition of "orthodox" beliefs within particular religious communities to the adoption of an attitude of belligerent moral and sociopolitical self-imposition in religious communities' relations with outsiders.

Moreover, this religious validation of secrecy, tied as it is to a sense of "responsibility as taking over the autonomy of another person, acting on his or her behalf," not only parallels but also prompts and reinforces a similar stance in political life, blurring the very line between the ethical and religious realms that supposedly demarcates its province and justifies its claims.[38] If one can claim authority to usurp the autonomy of another individual on the basis of 'secret knowledge,' why not claim such authority over an entire society? If it is heroic to assume sole responsibility for decisions that affect another on the basis of one's own, untested presumption that such responsibility has been delegated to one by a mandate of heaven, how much greater a heroism must there be in presuming to shoulder such responsibility for a nation, or even the world? Surely, given the logic of 'radical responsibility,' the ethics of disclosure must yield before the claims of religion at every level. Constitutions and laws can no more withstand the overriding force of the edicts of divine revelation than can the norms of personal interaction, once this logic is affirmed.

Yet despite a clear-eyed recognition of the underlying threat posed by the Silentian notion of absolute responsibility, Malesic expresses a sort of sympathetic ambivalence toward it and its relation to the contrary claims of modern ethical life. He ends his exploration of the "dilemma" posed by the conflicting understandings of responsibility found in revealed religion and modern ethics thus:

> It may simply be that the question *Fear and Trembling* raises—both for believers and for scholars—can ultimately only be begged. Secrets are sinister. They harm and exploit and arrogantly refuse all criticism. But for Kierkegaard, humans' ability to keep secrets indicates an interior depth to the person who is the site of the religious sphere. On his account, religious individuals practice exceptionalism because religion—the sphere of not only the relation to God, but also of the relation to oneself in inwardness—*is* the exceptional in human life . . . [W]ithout the secrecy of inwardness, there an be no individual, no one for the Kantian tradition's universalism to protect from secrecy's moral harms.[39]

It would seem that we are meant to conclude from this passage that the issue between *ethical universalism*—in the form of respect for norms of public justification and the autonomy of others—and *religious exceptionalism*—in the form of claims that deny norms of public justification and seek to override the autonomy of others—is ultimately undecidable. But we must remember that this conclusion follows only if we accept that the Silentian analysis of the logic of revelation and secrecy expresses not only an illuminating interpretation of *the traditional understanding of Abrahamic faith*—and a powerful metaphorical representation of the 'secret' interiority of the subjective self—but also a representation of the *true inner logic of faith in revealed religion, as such.* That is, it follows only if a certain sort of self-privileging, authoritarian-minded interpretation of how faith ought to be understood and what it requires is, in fact, correct.

Moreover, this conclusion requires us to accept that it is true that, as Derrida puts it, the "irreplaceable singularity of the self,"[40] which is the precondition of responsibility and decision, is dependent on silence, and "as soon as one speaks, as soon as one enters the medium of language, one loses that very singularity."[41] But why should we accept this view of the entrance into discourse? Why should my willingness to discuss a belief or plan of action with others be understood as, eo ipso, an abnegation of my "unsubstitutable" selfhood or the responsibility that flows from it? It is, after all, still—and always—*my responsibility* to draw *my own conclusions* from such dialogue, and *my decision* whether and how to enact those conclusions. Indeed, one may ask, what moment of responsible decision making has any human being ever faced that was not preconditioned by "the medium of language" and the context of social relations to which that medium gives voice?

Before proceeding further, let me be clear that in nothing I have said have I intended to suggest that affirming and acting on a perceived revelation—or the transmitted beliefs that historically emanate from such—is never a heroic choice. It can be, when this choice is made *for oneself and oneself alone.* There is nothing illegitimate or inauthentic about choosing to embrace the implications and consequences of revealed faith *insofar as those implications and consequences do not intrude on the autonomy of others, who, by right—both ethical and religious—must be allowed similarly to choose for themselves.*

It is precisely on this point that Derrida, in explicating the significance of Silentio's analysis, fails to look beyond the horizon of his own immediate interpretive concern. Because he is so focused on making the (perfectly valid) point that Abraham's response to God may be read as a telling metaphor for the responsiveness to *some* 'others' over against *all other* 'others' that characterizes the preferentiality of human relations in general, Derrida fails adequately to account for the ramifications of the *truly* 'other' side of the sacrificial journey to Moriah. For, there, riding along with Abraham as he makes his way to the altar of his own sacrificial singularity, *there sits Isaac,* whose singularity must also be taken into account in our reading of this story. Isaac, whose presence in the story cannot be treated merely in relation to his status as that which Abraham loves and, yet, gives up. The implications of Isaac's autonomy must be factored into our interpretation of the journey to Moriah, or else we all are lost.

Derrida, like Silentio, makes much of Abraham's response to Isaac when the latter asks, "Where is the lamb for the burnt offering?" Derrida tells us, "It can't be said that Abraham doesn't respond to him. He says God will provide . . . Abraham thus keeps his secret at the same time as he replies to Isaac. He doesn't keep silent and *he doesn't lie.*" Or, which is apparently the same thing, "[h]e responds without responding."[42] Later we are told that Abraham, in making his reply to Isaac, "speaks without saying anything either true or false, says nothing determinate that would be equivalent to a statement, a promise or a lie."[43] But this is an untenable reading of their exchange. Abraham knows full well *how Isaac will understand* his reply. This child, having inquired about *the* (literal) *lamb* that he expects to see sacrificed, must surely have thought his father's response indicated that God would provide *just such a lamb*, not that God had previously designated Isaac himself, as the (metaphorical) "lamb," the sacrifice led to the slaughter *in place of a lamb*. Nor does it matter at all whether one agrees with Silentio/Derrida that Abraham does not know—and that he *believes* that he does not know—what will happen on Moriah. What matters is that he knows what his son is asking and how his response to that question will be interpreted.

Abraham lies. It may be lie of omission, rather than commission, but nonetheless a lie, a dissimulation, an equivocation meant to keep the boy in the dark and, thus, unable to protest on behalf of *his own unsubstitutability, his own singularity*.

Isaac, too, has said, "Here I am." It is the "here I am" of the other, the autonomous other, who *deserves a response*. And not a response that is not a response, but a true *disclosure*. If Abraham has an *absolute* duty here, it is as a finite—and therefore fallible—individual encountering another finite individual whose unique subjectivity is also irreducible and, therefore, whose autonomy must be respected.[44]

None of us is, or can definitively speak on behalf of, 'the Other'; we are all merely *mutual others*. Hence the issue of where to draw the line between legitimate and illegitimate appeals to 'secrecy' must be addressed in *both* the ethical and the religious realms. To better see how this can be so in the latter, let us look briefly at how it is so in the former. In doing so, we can also see what it looks like when the traditional Abrahamic perspective invades the liberal–democratic public sphere in a peremptory manner.

Secrecy, Authority, and Legitimacy in Liberal Democracies

Malesic notes Sissela Bok's widely accepted claim that 'privacy' is the only "legitimate form of secrecy" in modern Western-democratic society. He argues, contrarily, that since 'privacy' is distinguishable from 'secrecy' in terms of the *intent* implied by the latter, but not the former, "no form of secrecy is ethically legitimate in the democratic West."[45] But this is not quite true. Both Bok and Malesic take the Kantian criterion of disclosure as *absolute*, allowing no exception (as does Kant, at times). Yet Western political theory has always—if somewhat inconsistently—recognized the reality of *competing goods.* While public disclosure and deliberation regarding the decisions of political authorities is an organizing *ideal* of liberal democracy, even the most "liberal" citizens will typically acknowledge that *some* information relevant to *some* decisions by authorities must and should remain undisclosed.

Indeed, the current, ongoing controversy in this country over the expansion of the realm of state secrecy under the banner of the "war on terror" is generally circumscribed by the fact that (practically) no one in the debate would claim that the government *never* has a compelling interest in classifying certain information. Instead, the debate is over how often, and how much, information should be classified. More specifically, much of the debate is explicitly framed in terms of the *procedures* by which determinations are made regarding what ought to be classified and for how long and under what circumstances it ought to remain so. In other words, the issue revolves around the maintenance of certain—however necessarily limited—requirements of 'public' justification of 'secret' governmental determinations. For example, many in Congress were less upset by the fact that, following the September 11th attacks, the Bush administration initiated certain new forms of domestic surveillance than that it did not seek constitutional and legal validation of these programs through consultation with the appropriate congressional committees and special courts.

Now setting aside the question of whether these members of Congress ought to affirm or condemn the programs at issue, per se, notice that the claim they are lodging is essentially that secrecy may well be necessary, and even desirable, under certain—highly specified and limited—circumstances, but *that determination itself cannot arise merely from the arbitrary fiat of a single individual*, even the president. *This*, I believe, should be understood as the distinctive character of political liberalism: it seeks, insofar as possible, to reconcile the practical necessities of political life with the ethical norms of individual autonomy, public justification, and deliberative democratic decision making—norms that, I am arguing, flow naturally from the recognition of human fallibility. Liberal governments will, in some instances, need to keep secrets, even from their own constituents. But unlike illiberal governments, (bona fide) liberal ones will keep secrets from their own people *only* when not doing so is judged to pose a greater risk, ultimately, to their peoples' autonomy than doing so. Here is the crucial piece: *this judgment about what is best will, itself, be subject to a process of review and accountability that comes as close to compliance with public norms of disclosure and debate as is practically possible under the circumstances.*

Contrarily, President George W. Bush and many of those around him—consonant with Bush's own public constructions of 'faith' in revealed religion, as validating claims to epistemic privilege—consistently demonstrated a determination to evade such norms and stretch the blanket of secrecy to cover as much of their own decision-making processes as possible. Like Abraham, in Silentio's telling, refusing to consult with Sarah or speak forthrightly with Isaac about what he planned to do, the president and his advisers took it upon themselves to coax us up the mountain through silence and obfuscation, secure in their own self-satisfied assumption of the veracity of their vision of the right and the good, rather than to submit this vision to even the limited check on authoritarianism represented by review in the relevant Congressional committees.

The connection between President Bush's self-described "born again," conservative Christian evangelicalism and the rhetorical logic of his now infamous claim, in the face of the emergence of the Iraqi insurgency following the fall of Baghdad (and the mounting casualties to which it had given rise) that he had not "suffered doubt"[46] is obvious and disturbing. It illustrates how the 'heroic' conception of Silentian radical responsibility, once accepted at a religious level, inevitably invades the realm of political life, with tragic and oppressive results. Silentian faith is perniciously *totalizing* in nature precisely because of the claim of ethical unboundedness that Malesic correctly identifies as essential to its character.

Derrida neatly describes the logic of the type of appeal to authority lodged in Bush's rhetoric and implied in his blanket policy of secrecy and expansive claims to presidential prerogative in his gloss on Kierkegaard's "at least implicit and indirect reference to Saint Paul" in his choice of the title for Silentio's work.[47] When Paul advises the Philippians, "Wherefore my beloved, as ye have always obeyed, not as in my presence only, but now much more in my absence, work out your own salvation with fear and trembling," Derrida tells us, "[they] are asked to work towards their salvation not in the presence (*parousia*) but in the absence (*apousia*) of the master: *without either seeing or knowing, without hearing the law or the reasons for the law.*"[48] Derrida continues,

> If Paul says "adieu" and absents himself as he asks them to obey, in fact ordering them to obey (for one does not ask for obedience, one orders it), it is because God is himself absent, hidden and silent, separate, secret, at the moment he has to be obeyed. God doesn't give his reasons, he acts as he intends, he doesn't have to give his reasons or share anything with us: neither his motivations, if he has any, nor his deliberations, nor his decisions. Otherwise he wouldn't be God, we wouldn't be dealing with the Other as God or with God as *wholly other* [*tout autre*]. If the other were to share his reasons with us by explaining them to us, if he were to speak to us all the time without any secrets, he wouldn't be the other, we would share a type of homogeneity.[49]

Here "the master," namely Paul, is positioned as representing a parallel *presence*—and, thus, also, a parallel *absence*—to that of "the Other," namely God. And this is precisely the position in the public mind that is sought by every aspiring authoritarian. To be the one who is not merely "other" but even "Other" is to be the one who "doesn't keep account or give an account, neither to man, to humans, to society, to one's fellows, or to one's own." It is a position that derives it power precisely from a locus of fear and a populace set to trembling.

Just as in the personal realm, in moments of social *abyss*—where the danger appears as that which may overcome us as humans, that which overwhelms us and our *confidence in humanity*, that which makes us feel *the want of power of our own humanity*—we often turn reflexively toward that which (or whom) appears to represent a "higher power," a power that appears beyond the human, to deal with a danger that appears beyond the human. It is in this sense, and this sense alone (the sense of psychological appearances and responses) that the oft-repeated phrase "existential threat" could ever justifiably have been applied in relation to the United States' struggle with international terrorism. The continued *existence* of this nation was never really in doubt, but the rhetoric of such doubt, of such a threat, served those who have deployed it quite well, at least in the short term.

It should be noted that the important issue here is *not* whether Bush, or those around him, *actually believe in* the constructions of faith and revelation that they have offered in public—or the particular claim to a divine mandate of leadership that was made on behalf of Bush himself—as opposed to merely, cynically employing them for political advantage. To be sure, numerous commentators have offered a wealth of anecdotal evidence suggesting that Bush really does hold such views. As Hugh Urban observes, in his systematic analysis of this element of Bush's presidency and its ramifications for American democracy, the Bush administration appeared to "have a fundamental belief in its own divinely guided and exceptional status, one that place[d] it above public scrutiny, congressional oversight, and even international law."[50] Yet, as Urban rightly insists, our ultimate concern should lie less in detailing how Bush, specifically, appealed to traditional notions of revealed religious authority to bolster his own claims to moral and political exceptionalism and more in understanding the general dynamics of such appeals, why they are so often successful, and how to combat them.

Along the same lines, it should be clear that this is not just about the relatively few followers of R. J. Rushdoony out there (of which Bush himself almost certainly is *not* one). No doubt the unwavering support of 'Christian Dominionists' and other, what we may call, 'hardline' Christian voters who responded to his overtly religious rhetoric was central to Bush's presidency. But the support of these groups alone could never have sufficed if the strategy of appealing to particularistic religious constructions of moral and political authority were to succeed—as it did, twice—in a national presidential campaign. It was not just on the "far right" of the American religious spectrum that such appeals (at least initially) found traction as rhetorical justifications, not only for expanded presidential discretionary authority but also for morally particularistic legal and policy positions, such as state and national prohibitions against gay marriage. In this country—and other, established pluralistic liberal democracies like it—religious fundamentalists generally cannot endanger the freedom of others without the complicity of religious moderates.

Accordingly, those of us who wish to see the political power of appeals to 'secretive,' authoritarian conceptions of revealed religious faith diminish *permanently* must attend not only to the political manifestations of such conceptions but also to the underlying—and pervasive—notion of religious truth claims (including especially putatively revealed religious truth claims) as being, in some unique way, epistemically privileged, and to the traditional, 'Abrahamic' conception of religious faith that promotes this notion. Our desiderata include not merely an external critique of this traditional conception of faith but also an *alternative conception* thereof, one that promotes a genuine political liberalism by discouraging epistemic arrogance and self-delusion. And if, as I have argued earlier, political liberalism's stance toward secrecy is *not* best understood as implying a categorical rejection of it but, rather, a mediating and proceduralized insistence on justification and accountability, then we may, correspondingly, ask the following: Is the *proper* stance of revealed religion toward claims to 'secret' justifications best understood not as a categorical affirmation that transcends the requirements of public deliberation and respect for individual autonomy but, instead, a conditional affirmation, one qualified *not* by a lack of commitment but, rather, a repudiation of epistemic self-satisfaction and the coercive attitude of self-projection that it enables? Are the dichotomies between transparency and secrecy, authority and autonomy, false on both sides? Is there, in fact, as I have suggested throughout this work so far, a logic of reconciliation between the respective dictates of liberal political ethics and the religious ethics of faith?

In the next chapter, I will more specifically spell out the implications of my alternative conception of faith, as qualified by epistemic anxiety, in relation to the norms that should govern the discursive and regulatory interactions among disparate individuals and groups within a pluralistic liberal-democratic society. In particular, I will articulate a position within the current debate within liberal political philosophy and theory over the assertion of religious reasons in the context of public discourse related to the creation or maintenance of coercive legal regulations. I will also offer a related formulation of the theological task vis-à-vis liberal-democratic society. And I will return to the figure of Socrates as emblematic of the attitude of fallibilist faith that I am seeking to promote.

CHAPTER 4

FAITH, FREEDOM, REASON, AND RESPONSIBILITY

When the Almighty himself condescends to address mankind in their own language, his meaning, luminous as it must be, is rendered dim and doubtful, by the cloudy medium through which it is communicated.

—James Madison, *Federalist #37*[1]

I have already indicated my own belief that modern ethical norms are consistent with personal choices that affirm the authority of revealed religious understandings *in relation to the individuals making such choices, insofar as these choices do not adversely impact the freedom of others to make similar (or dissimilar) choices freely for themselves.* This simply represents an application to religious belief of the classic liberal 'harm principle,' which was given its consummate formulation by John Stuart Mill.[2] In turn, the harm principle simply represents a properly *interpersonally qualified* expression of the logic of the classic liberal norm of 'negative liberty,' which Thomas Hobbes succinctly defined as "the absence of externall Impediments: which Impediments, may oft take away parts of a mans power to do what hee would; but cannot hinder him from using the power left him, according as his judgment, and reason shall dictate to him."[3] Accordingly, on my view, religious adherents must be free from impediments to their own autonomous affirmation of a religious authority over their belief and behavior, but only insofar as their behavior does not erect impediments to others' capacity (efficaciously) to reject this authority in relation to their beliefs and behavior.

Referencing Hobbes's formulation is apt in the current context not only because he provides such a clear (if abstract) definition of this norm but also because he, famously, goes on to argue that individuals' unrestrained freedom of choice, in the hypothetical 'state of nature,' ought to be voluntarily ceded to an absolute political authority with a mandate to act with broadly coercive power in maintaining social and political order and security, a political 'leviathan.' That is, Hobbes—writing amid the chaotic upheavals of the English revolutionary period—believes that individuals ought to exercise their freedom of choice by choosing submission to an external authority to which they grant the power of discipline, a power they must recognize may, therefore, legitimately be applied to them if they violate the dictates set in place by this authority.

Now, I obviously do not wish to validate Hobbes's own choice of an authoritarian, over a liberal, political order as the proper response to the challenges represented in the classic liberal analysis of freedom (as anarchistic) in the 'state of nature.' But let me now reiterate clearly that I *do* accept the validity of such a choice, freely made, in the context of religious belief and authority. In other words, not only is it legitimate, from a consistently liberal point of view, for an individual to choose to interpret and apply the dictates of a revealed religious understanding, herself, in the context of her own personal opinions, lifestyle, and behavior, but also it is equally legitimate for her to submit herself voluntarily to the authority of some other person's or group's interpretations and applicative judgments regarding such an understanding. Indeed, given that one central problem linked to the very limitations on human perspective that constitute our fallibility-in-finitude is egoism, there can be something profoundly ennobling in the decision to submit one's personal judgment to the external standard represented by such an authority, if made for the right sorts of reasons. (Particularly, such a choice should *not* be made in an attempt to evade responsibility for one's own moral freedom—one cannot be relieved of that responsibility, in any case, since one will always remain responsible for one's choice of evasion, as well as one's ongoing failure to correct that evasiveness.)

Of course, the matter is rarely, if ever, as simple as this. As Hobbes certainly recognized, the concept of the state of nature—which he employed as a heuristic device, not a representation of an actual state of affairs confronting the individual at any given time in her personal history—theoretically obscures the empirical fact that human beings invariably find themselves *already subject to* some authority (or authorities) prior to their own first conscious deliberations regarding personal choice and the principled and pragmatic calculations it entails. This is the issue that Søren Kierkegaard's existentialist successors treat under the label of 'thrownness.'

We are 'thrown' into the world at birth, not choosing when or where we will arrive within the matrix of historical circumstances and cultural understandings that circumscribes and, in large part, defines the field of human choice and action. Therefore, it is misleading to conceive of the choice to "enter into" some mutually obligatory social contract—be it political or religious, or both—as a choice made in the context of unqualified freedom. Indeed, for most of us, the only "entrance" into such arrangements that characterizes our initial sociocultural and/or religious location is the largely unconscious and wholly unchosen event of birth itself. As conscious, choosing beings, we simply "find" ourselves already situated within such a contract—or, more accurately, within a number of overlapping (and sometimes conflicting) contracts. Our choice, then, most often is whether or not to affirm that which already characterizes our social and/or religious relations to authority. The question we must ask is not, "Do I wish voluntarily to construct, with others, a mutually obligatory structure of social or religious life predicated on a particular set of authoritative relations to be codetermined by those from whom it arises?" It is rather, "Do I wish to *remain within* my inherited structure of socially or religiously authoritative relations, or would I prefer to secede from, reform, or overthrow this structure (and, if I choose one of the latter options, what are the possible alternatives open to me)?"

John Locke (somewhat underexplicitly) treats this complication of the issue of entrance into the social contract in terms of the notion of 'tacit consent.' Although Locke's formulation of this issue reflects the contrived character of the background conceit of the state of nature—as well as his own theoretical fixation on the concept (and terminology) of 'property'—it can help to illuminate the logic of the current discussion. According to Locke, "[E]very man that has any possessions, or enjoyment of any part of the dominions of any government, doth thereby give his tacit consent, and is as far forth obliged to obedience to the laws of that government, during such enjoyment, as anyone under it."[4] However, "the obligation any one is under, by virtue of such enjoyment, to 'submit to the government, begins and ends with the enjoyment,'" because, while tacit consent makes one subject to the regulations of the relevant polity, it does not make one a genuine "member" of that polity. "Nothing can make any man so, but his actually entering into it by positive engagement, and express promise and compact."[5]

Though his formulation of the issue mainly focuses on the status of "foreigners" residing within a polity's "dominions," Locke also (at least implicitly) gestures toward the applicability of this logic to the more or less universal experience of finding oneself thrown into a polity through birth when he discusses "inheritance" as one way in which one can find oneself so related to a polity's regulatory authority. Whereas passively accepting the authority of a polity simply by remaining within its borders represents merely tacit consent to being subject to its regulations, the active choice to remain within and affirm the regulatory authority of a polity on a permanent basis can be viewed as a "positive engagement," presumably leading (through whatever relevant procedures and dependent on one's acceptance by the polity in question) to some official form of "express promise and compact." In contemporary terms, this is the difference between holding a visa and formally seeking citizenship.

The difference between the immigrant citizen and the native born individual who has reached the age of political "majority" is simply that as native born the latter need take no extra formalized step for her determination to remain within the bounds of her native polity to count as a promise and compact. She *affirms*, rather than earns, her citizenship through her choice to stay. That it is a choice—and, therefore, that the authority is legitimate in relation to her—is, of course, dependent on her being allowed to leave if she desires to do so. But this is just to say that we are discussing a liberal, rather than an authoritarian, regime.

It is important to note that the form of liberalism that I am embracing here claims only that *the enforcement of* specific legal regulations that arise through the proper sorts of political procedures is just, not that the determination of the consensus of the community through such procedures guarantees the justness of *the regulations themselves*. This is where my conception of the implications of human fallibility points in the direction of the Anglo-American, rather than the Continental, liberal tradition. The latter—which takes its cue from Jean-Jacques Rousseau and develops its logic through the 'unitary' views of rationality offered by Immanuel Kant and G. W. F. Hegel, finding its contemporary consummation in the work of thinkers such as Jürgen Habermas—suggests that (in ideal terms at least) the normatively dispositive character of just procedures extends beyond the legitimacy of the enforcement of the determinations reached thereby, conferring a definitive justness on these determinations themselves, as ethical norms. In other words, (truly) just procedures *guarantee* just outcomes.

Contrarily, the liberalism of the tradition that takes its cue from thinkers such as Hobbes, Locke, and Mill distinguishes sharply between the justness of *the authority of* properly determined social norms within the context of the relevant society and the justness of any given norm (however properly determined) as such. Here, just procedures produce *justly enforceable* outcomes, but these outcomes are not, eo ipso, considered to be substantively just. Why not? Because the procedural coordination of the deliberations of multiple fallible subjects does not somehow magically produce an infallible result. *Fallible but fair*—that is the highest standard to which human communities can legitimately aspire.[6]

As I have already indicated, the justification for applying the logic of such fallibilist liberalism within the context of membership in a religious community, and subjection to its norms, lies in the very logic of religious consciousness and belief. Religion is, perhaps most essentially, a response by finite beings to the reality (or at least the perception) of *that which transcends* our own finitude and the normalization of the perceived implications of the relationship between the former and the latter. The central implications of this relationship rest in the categorical distinction between the finite subject experiencing in a religious mode and the infinite object of such experience—namely, the divine. Moreover, while religions generally seek to effect some reconciliation between the finite believer and the infinite object of belief, no such reconciliation can legitimately be taken to negate the implications of the relevant distinction as long as the believer remains a finite-being-in-the-world.[7] One such implication involves the ineluctably limited and, therefore, fallible epistemic situation of any and every religious believer or group of religious believers—no matter how conceived or organized and regardless of whatever revelatory warrant may be claimed to the contrary.

Accordingly, subjection to the normative claims of a religious community can justifiably be imposed on an individual *prior to* her reaching a sufficient point of personal and intellectual development to be in a position to be held responsible for affirming or denying that authority for herself in a definite way. However, such an imposition cannot legitimately demand or require that which either directly or indirectly effects the negation (or substantive diminishment) of that individual's capacity or opportunity to exercise her autonomy once she has attained the requisite level of maturity. So, for example, while it is perfectly legitimate—and appropriate—for fundamentalist Christian parents to seek to inculcate their children with their own religious beliefs and values, it is *not* legitimate for them to seek, as some have, to prevent their children from developing a capacity for critical thinking that could potentially lead to the abandonment of those beliefs and values by attempting to exempt their children from the critical thinking components of public school curricula[8] or by withdrawing them into a private or homeschool curriculum that purposefully suppresses their capacity for critical thinking. Such a maneuver represents a morally vicious epistemological despotism, which fundamentally undermines the autonomy of those on whom it is imposed.

Epistemological freedom depends on the development of the capacity genuinely to consider alternatives, and such freedom is a foundational human right, one on which many other basic human rights necessarily depend. As the United States Supreme Court observed in its majority opinion in *Board of Education v. Pico*, a case in which the banning of certain books from school libraries was at issue, "[T]he right to receive ideas is a necessary predicate to the recipient's meaningful exercise of his own rights of speech, press, and political freedom."[9] Without the right to be exposed to (and to have the capacity to meaningfully evaluate) contrary perspectives, the adoption of an inherited worldview by a child—and her carrying forward of that worldview into adulthood—will be epistemologically *autonomic* rather than *autonomous*. Moreover, for just this reason, the suppression of a child's capacity to intelligently consider alternatives to her inherited perspective violates the logic of religious faith itself.

To present one's own understanding of the divine and its dictates to one's children *as unquestionable* and, especially, to work to prevent or prohibit the possibility of any questioning of it on their part, is to idolatrize one's own fallible understanding. It is to, in effect, substitute oneself for the divine in the eyes of one's children. One thereby unjustifiably interferes in their relationship not only to their own consciences but also to the divine itself, just as Abraham, in remaining silent, positions himself as not merely an*other* but as *the Other*, as God's stand-in, in relation to Isaac. Such interference represents not a defense but, rather, a subversion of the fundamental relationship between the individual and the divine. To return to Paul, it is worth noting that the most underconsidered part of his aforementioned advice to the Philippians—namely, the phrase "work out *your own* salvation"—might be the most important part of it. Derrida focuses solely on the authority in absentia that is asserted by Paul in this passage. But here, in this phrase, we see a reflection of the responsibility of each individual to inform *her own* religious understanding. The individual must *decide for herself*, not out of certain (or circumscribed) knowledge, but out of the internal subjective requirement of self-determination amid a multiplicity of possible understandings.

Obviously, given this logic, attempts to subject nonadherents to the particularistic moral vision of a certain religious perspective or community do not even have the provisional legitimacy that obtains in the case of children born into such a perspective or community. To recur to Lockean terms, such religious 'foreigners' remain in the state of nature in relation to the perspective or community in question. Moreover, unlike Locke's foreigner in the preceding formulation of tacit consent, such religious foreigners—especially in the context of a pluralistic society such as our own—are in no way beholden to the perspective or community in question through 'enjoyment' of habitation or proprietorship within the 'dominions' of said perspective or community. Thus they owe no allegiance whatsoever to any particularistic elements of its moral vision. It has no legitimate claim on their attitudes or behaviors, beyond the totally generalized interpersonal qualifications on the foreigners' own negative liberty to which they 'expressly' submit as a function of membership in the liberal-democratic polity in which we all cohabitate. That is, so long as they do not infringe on a religious community's right to live as its members see fit (subject to the same interpersonal qualifications), they can in no way legitimately be held to the particularistic moral standards of that community.

The point here, in short, is that a genuinely modern—that is to say, an epistemically and ethically legitimate—conception of faith requires a *different sort* of 'radical responsibility,' not responsibility "for another" but, rather, a greater degree of responsibility *for oneself* and *one's own choices about what to believe*. Such epistemic self-responsibility requires that the believer acknowledge the fallibility of her own belief and, therefore, refrain from attempts coercively to impose it (or its normative dictates) on others. To deny this obligation is to deny one's own fallibility, and to deny one's fallibility is to deify oneself. Surely that is not a responsible form of religiosity.

FAITH, REASONABLENESS, AND COERCION IN LIBERAL-DEMOCRATIC DISCOURSE

As I indicated briefly in both Chapters 2 and 3, the account of faith, fallibility, and epistemic anxiety that I have developed so far has significant implications in relation to the prominent contemporary debate over what role, if any, religious reasons ought to play in the liberal–democratic public sphere. The most widely held view among contemporary liberal theorists is that the deployment of purely religious reasons as justification for coercive political regulations is always illegitimate. On this view, religious reasons, per se, represent a special class that is uniquely problematic vis-à-vis pluralistic liberal-democratic discourse. Thus secular reasons, per se, are given privileged standing, over against religious reasons, as the only sort that may acceptably be deployed in favor of coercive regulations. Critics of this view—who stand within the broader liberal tradition—object that this privileging of secular over religiously informed reasoning cannot be maintained on a nonarbitrary basis. They argue that religious reasons are on par with secular reasons, at least insofar as the latter make substantive reference to controversial metaphysical or anthropological assumptions or claims.[10] Thus according to this view, any prohibition that is applied only to religious reasons represents an illegitimate expression of secular bias rather than a valid principle of discursive impartiality. As should be clear at this point, my own view combines elements of both of these positions.

On the one hand, my analysis of the ethics of secrecy and disclosure (in Chapter 3) provides support for the standard liberal injunction against dependence on religious reasons for the justification of regulations that will impact the autonomy of those who do not share the religious commitments in question. *As an ideal*, good faith political discourse in a pluralistic liberal-democratic society depends on the willingness of all parties to limit the claims they make in relation to others to those that can be 'communicated' (in the Silentian sense of the term). The assertion of normative prescriptions or proscriptions within the public sphere on the basis of claims that *require* prior commitment to a particularistic perspective as the source of their persuasiveness represents an implicit negation of the very concept of liberal-democratic public discourse, per se. Accordingly, religious believers who wish to promote or defend coercive regulations that are consistent with their own normative commitments must be willing—and able—to translate those commitments into nonparticularistic terms. Otherwise, *generally speaking*, it is inappropriate for them to assert the relevant norms as properly binding on other members of society. (I will explain the qualification implied by my use of "generally speaking" here, shortly.)

On the other hand, my analysis (in Chapter 2) of the logic of faith and its cognitive pervasiveness at the level of substantive intellectual and moral commitment suggests that many forms of secular reasoning deserve the same sort of scrutiny, and require the same sort of public restraint, as religious reasons. And here I am not referring merely to those quite obvious instances in which a comprehensive secular ideology, such as Marxism, is logically on par with religious worldviews. Equally suspect should be any assertion that rests (solely) on some particular controversial secular metaphysical or anthropological assertion or presupposition that cannot be translated into propositions that could be found persuasive by others who reject that assertion or presupposition. So, for example, if a particular proposed coercive regulation were unjustifiable on any other grounds than, say, a commitment to 'preference satisfaction utilitarianism' as formulated by the contemporary philosopher Peter Singer, then there is the same obligation to refrain from imposing that regulation on others as there would be were it being justified by, say, Thomistic Christian virtue theory. In such a case, those who would attempt to establish such a regulation on a secular particularistic basis would be enacting precisely the same dynamic of discursive negation that the religious do when they make such a move. Of course, in the case of secular particularistic absolutism, there is no attempt to redirect responsibility for the claim to moral infallibility that is being implicitly asserted onto an external, divine agent. Instead, the claim is issued unabashedly out of the epistemic overconfidence of those who assert the right to coerce. They play the role of God themselves. In this sense, then, Robert Audi is wrong to claim that the presence of religious reasons in the public sphere is uniquely problematic because it creates a situation in which rival religious positions square off in "a clash of Gods vying for social control."[11] Since a secular particularistic claim to normative infallibility involves the direct equivalent of what I have termed epistemic self-deification—here we have "Gods" in a Feuerbachian sense[12]—we can speak meaningfully of the danger of clashes between *either* religious or secular Gods vying for social control. So I am with Audi on the general principle of particularistic restraint, but I am with those, like Audi's longtime religious-liberal foil, Nicholas Wolterstorff,[13] who believe that religious particularism is no more deserving of strict scrutiny when it enters into the public sphere than is secular particularism.

Now at this point, it is crucial to reemphasize that my construal of the implications of human fallibility and the virtue of epistemic anxiety does *not* lead me to assert an absolute prohibition against the invocation of particularistic reasons in all discourse within the public sphere. I have linked my construction of the discursive norms associated with epistemic anxiety to the harm principle, and I have stipulated that I am applying these norms narrowly within the context of discourse regarding coercive regulations that meaningfully impact individual (or group) autonomy—beyond the mutualistic requirements of the harm principle itself—at the level of basic identity formation, self-determination and expression. Nothing in the position I am developing in this work implies the inappropriateness of persuasive argument on behalf of particularistic understandings or norms outside of the context of such directly coercive legal regulation. Indeed, I also agree with Wolterstorff (and others, like Stout[14]) who has argued that the disclosure by participants in public discourse of their own relevant particularistic commitments is often an important component of good faith liberal-democratic conversation. Malesic's Silentian approach leads him to argue for the "concealment of Christian identity" in the public square.[15] His intention in making this argument, which is laudable, is to reduce the tendency/ability of politicians to play on Christianity for political gain and of Christians themselves to identify their faith with the sorts of superficial and, often, consumerist or militarist expressions of it that are most common in contemporary political discourse. He hopes that a diminishment of Christian self-identification in the short-term might allow for a reemergence of it in a more authentic mode in the long term. Yet how much better, and more effective, would it be for Christians (and other religious believers) who share Malesic's concerns to actually make that argument within Christianity public?

However, I believe that Wolterstorff and other liberal critics of the standard view tend to go too far in endorsing the employment of particularistic justifications vis-à-vis issues that cross over in to the realm of coercion that I have just delineated. One reason that Wolterstorff, for example, does so is that he rightly perceives that the Rawlsian conception of the proper content of public reason is too thin to do the necessary work of actual political discourse within a highly pluralistic liberal democracy. But the fact that particularistic reasons will sometimes have to be invoked if public discourse is to be substantive enough to settle all the issues that face any pluralistic liberal-democratic society does not legitimate their invocation as a matter of course. Rather, in my view, particularistic reasons ought to be invoked *only as a matter of discursive last resort* and, even then, only if (1) *they are not being used to justify the sort of coercion I have previously proscribed;* or (2) *the issue at hand cannot be settled without someone being coerced, and there are no nonparticularistic reasons available that could possibly settle the issue.* (The contemporary debate over abortion in the United States provides a good example of the latter circumstance: for at least some of the contending perspectives, the relevant disagreement is over the foundational, metaphysical question of the nature of human existence as related to the status of the fetus, and no one on either side of this disagreement can be persuaded by any argument that does not connect with this metaphysical question in what I am describing as a particularistic manner.)

Jean Bethke Elshtain, in discussing the historical development of the public/private polarization in liberal theory, complains that "although Locke put back into the picture some of the complexity Hobbes had shoved out . . . Locke nonetheless finds in the logic of sovereignty the requirement to privatize that which one holds most dear."[16] She frames the issue as one of religious freedom, which (like Wolterstorff and other religious critics of the standard liberal view) she rightly insists must include a public as well as a private dimension. But, whatever problems there are in Locke's or any other particular liberal theorists' specific demarcations of the bounds of the appropriate expression of religious reasons in the public sphere, it is important to recognize that the motivating logic behind the Lockean push toward political secularization was *not* based on a desire to force the privatization of belief but to *protect the right to privacy as regards belief.* Elshtain focuses attention on those who are curbed in their pursuit of religiously informed visions of the right and the good by the application of Locke's principles, whereas Locke was focused on those who would be coerced if such curbing did not take place. Reorienting our conception of liberal norms to better reflect this focus—as I have tried to do throughout the present work—clarifies why the limitation of one's right to assert metaphysically particularistic claims as the basis for legally coercive laws is acceptable as an unavoidable collateral consequence of the protection of what Supreme Court Justice Louis Brandeis famously called "the right to be left alone—the most comprehensive of rights, and the right most valued by a free people."[17]

Furthermore, it is important to clarify that most liberal theorists do *not* assert the proscription against coercive entrance into the public sphere as one that is primarily legal in nature. Nor am I doing so here. While I favor very robust forms of constitutional guarantees of basic individual rights that, in effect, legislate an absolute modicum of mutual restraint against all forms of particularistic coercion, clearly such guarantees cannot be so exhaustively stipulated as to carry the full burden of restraint on behalf of citizens in a pluralistic liberal democracy. Individual, and particularistic communities of, participants in public discourse must still be called on to voluntarily recognize the implications of their own fallibility within the context of that participation and exercise restraint beyond the legally imposed base modicum. This goes back to my observation in Chapter 2 that when we ask, *in what manner, and within what limits, ought any individual or group seek to assert particularistic, worldview-dependent normative regulations in the context of a pluralistic liberal-democratic society?*, part of the answer should be legal and procedural, but another part must be dispositional.

The approach to the moral dynamic of political regulation in a pluralistic society that I have just outlined will, of course, lead to a significantly greater degree of social libertarianism than most religious believers are currently inclined to support. That is the price of maintaining their own autonomy in good faith. Given the fallibility of any and all of our particularistic knowledge claims, we should have no greater moral fear than that we might impose on others a coercive norm that is, in fact, mistaken. The current debate in the United States over gay marriage provides a powerful and illuminating example of why this is so. Let us imagine, for the moment, that I am a traditionalist Christian who believes that the Bible reveals God's definitive judgment prohibiting homosexuality and establishes as a matter of transcendental anthropology that homosexuality is a freely chosen, rather than a biologically dictated, manner of life. And let us further imagine that I have worked diligently within the public sphere to help ensure that existing legal prohibitions against gay marriage remain in force, thereby maintaining what I view as a consonance between divine and human law. What if I am wrong?

What if God did not intend for those statements in the Bible that repudiate homosexuality to become the basis for such a universal proscription? What if there is no God? What if homosexuality is not (or not purely) a choice but a matter of strong (maybe even definitive) biological inclination? Then I would have played a role in the irreparable mangling of other human lives. I would have prevented other, rightfully autonomous human beings from experiencing important elements of self-determination, fulfillment, and happiness. What could possibly give me the right to take that existential gamble on their behalf?

Here I should note again (as I have acknowledged in Chapters 1 and 2) that my construal of the moral dynamic involved in examples such as this depends not only on fallibilism but also on a commitment to respect for other persons. However, it depends only on an absolutely generic such commitment. That is, I believe my construal of the moral implications of epistemic anxiety is compatible with essentially any meaningful commitment to respect for others. For, given a full recognition of the implications of fallibility, as I have outlined them, what manner of respect for others could deny the moral dynamic I just described? Thus as I have argued at various points throughout this work, epistemic anxiety and respect for other persons are mutually necessary. Neither alone is sufficient as a basis for liberal-democratic norms. But together they form a strong foundation for these norms. I will outline my own comprehensive perspective on the basis for respect in the next two chapters.

Obviously, given all that I have said so far, I am thoroughly unsympathetic toward, and deeply concerned by, the current prominence in certain theological and political circles of what Stout has labeled the 'New Traditionalism.'[18] The wholesale theological reaction against liberal democracy represented by this movement is disturbing precisely because it seeks to undermine the hard-won Western consensus around liberal-democratic pluralism. That said, however, as I made clear in the first section of this chapter, my vision of liberal-democratic pluralism is one in which those who adopt such traditionalism have as much space within which to exercise their own autonomous choice to live according to that perspective as can be provided consistently with the principles I have elaborated. Though I do, of course, hope that the number of those making such choices decreases, rather than increases, over time.

FAITH, AUTHORITY, AND THE THEOLOGICAL CIRCLE

The foregoing conception of the moral dynamic at work in liberal-democratic public discourse implies a corresponding conception of the theological task, as it relates to the world beyond the community of believers. As I mentioned in Chapter 2, Paul Tillich comes the closest of any of the contemporary existentialists to making the shift to a nonproblematizing understanding of epistemic anxiety of the sort I am offering here, and I can clarify my understanding of the place of theology within the context of political society with reference to his existentialist account of the traditional notion of the 'theological circle' in his *Systematic Theology*.[19]

According to Tillich, the circle itself marks the boundary between matters of 'ultimate concern,' which lie within its circumference, and matters of 'preliminary concern,' which lie without. To be within the circle—that is, to be a theologian—is to attend exclusively to matters of ultimate concern. And for the Christian theologian, as such, the authority of the content of the 'Christian message' (particularly as embodied in the kerygma) is absolute. To be outside of the circle, on the other hand, is to turn to matters of preliminary concern, and the "theologian *as* theologian is no expert in any matters of preliminary concern." Hence the authority of theology must not seek to contest with those other authorities whose expertise encompasses matters of preliminary concern insofar as they address themselves to such matters—just as such experts in preliminary concerns have no business claiming authority regarding matters of ultimate concern. As Tillich puts it, "The first *formal* principle of theology, guarding the boundary line between ultimate concern and preliminary concerns, protects theology as well as the cultural realms on the other side of the line."[20]

Yet Tillich also insists that "[t]he ultimate concern is unconditional . . . total: no part of ourselves or our world is excluded from it; there is no place to flee from it."[21] Hence "[s]ocial ideas and actions, legal projects and procedures, political programs and decisions, can become objects of theology." Of course, Tillich immediately adds that this concern with such matters is "not from the point of view of their social, legal, and political form, but from the point of view of their power of actualizing some aspects of that which concerns us ultimately in and through their social, legal, and political forms."[22]

But this qualification is, indeed, purely *formal*, and it is not apparent what protection it actually provides for "the cultural realms on the other side of the line" from theology. For, on this understanding, the theologian—or, more expansively, the faith community associated with some particular theological perspective—may justifiably claim that its authority to adjudicate between various actual or possible social, legal, and political forms with regard to their respective fitness to advance the cause of ultimate concern supersedes the claims of those who approach such questions from the (nontheological) perspective of (what that theologian or faith community considers to be) preliminary concerns. In Tillich's own words, the social, legal, and political may become "bearers and vehicles" of ultimate concern and, therefore, "the medium" through which some faith community seeks to give expression to its own conception of the dictates of ultimate concern—perhaps coercively if necessary.[23]

To be sure, Tillich's intention is not to endorse such an authoritarian view of the relationship of the claims that emerge from within the theological circle to the forms of social, legal, and political life that surround it. However, his own claims, early in *Systematic Theology*, on behalf of the "absoluteness" and "uniqueness" of the "Christian message" can certainly be read as providing support for such a view (he does not repeat these claims elsewhere, but they frame this work, nevertheless). Indeed, if it is true that the claims of ultimate concern are "unconditional," and if it is further true that "trends which are immanent in all religions and cultures move toward the Christian answer"[24] and "Christian theology is . . . *the* theology" and "has received a foundation that transcends the foundation of any other theology and which itself cannot be transcended,"[25] then it would seem to follow that the claims of Christian theology may be presented to the wider social, legal, and political community as unconditional.

The question, therefore, is whether Tillich's thought provides some other, nonformalistic basis for a rejection of such authoritarian presumptiveness. I believe that the answer is "yes" and that the requisite basis lies implicit in the very existentialist character of his framing of the notion of the theological circle. As Tillich observes, "[E]ven the man who has entered the theological circle consciously and openly faces another serious problem. Being inside the circle, he must have made an existential decision; he must be in the situation of faith. But no one can say of himself that he is in the situation of faith. No one can call himself a theologian . . . Every theologian is committed *and* alienated; he is always in faith *and* in doubt; he is inside *and* outside the theological circle."[26] The point here is that the choice made by the theologian—or, for that matter, any adherent (or group of adherents) to a particular theological perspective—is framed by the epistemic conditions that define the context of all human choices as such. Accordingly, as I have argued, no faith-based resolution to the problem of epistemic anxiety can legitimately be taken to remove the underlying source of this anxiety or to cancel the *associated fallibility of the very understanding on which said resolution rests.*

In *The Dynamics of Faith*, Tillich writes that "[t]he term 'ultimate concern' unites the subjective and the objective side of the act of faith—the *fides qua creditur* (the faith through which one believes) and the *fides quae creditur* (the faith which is believed). The first is the classical term for the centered act of the personality, the ultimate concern. The second is the classical term for that toward which this act is directed, the ultimate itself, expressed in symbols of the divine." And, he says, "[t]his distinction is very important, but not ultimately so, for the one side cannot be without the other."[27] However, there is another distinction that is implicit in this formulation, one which *is* of ultimate importance, namely, the distinction between the *true* nature of "the ultimate itself" (whatever that may be) and the *perceived* nature of that ultimate (which is "expressed in symbols of the divine"—symbols that may, perhaps, reflect some truth, but that also will, *necessarily*, reflect the limitations and distortions inherent to all finite and fallible attempts to conceive of and represent the ultimate). Hence Tillich is certainly correct that "[t]here is no faith without a content toward which it is directed. There is always something meant in the act of faith. And there is no way of having the content of faith except in the act of faith." But we must add to this proposition that any and every "act of faith" is performed in the context of fallible finitude.

Therefore, while it is true, in a sense, that in the act of faith "the difference between subjectivity and objectivity is overcome" because the "ultimate of the act of faith and the ultimate that is meant in the act of faith are one and the same,"[28] the implication of this statement must be understood in terms of a psychological unity between the character of the person who acts in faith and the (corresponding) character of that person's ineluctably conditioned and fallible conception of the ultimate, *not* (as Tillich sometimes seems to suggest) as a cancellation of the onto-epistemic alienation of the finite individual from the infinite reality designated by the concept of 'the Holy.'[29]

SOCRATIC ANXIETY AND RESPONSIBLE FAITH

To conclude this chapter and my thematic elaboration of the proper relation between epistemic anxiety and religious faith, I will now return to the notion of *Socratic anxiety* that I briefly mentioned in Chapters 2 and 3, which I have drawn from Kierkegaard's account of 'Socratic ignorance.' In *Concluding Unscientific Postscript*, Kierkegaard's pseudonymous persona, Johannes Climacus, describes 'Socratic ignorance' as a continuous and permanent state of consciousness in which one subjectively commits, with the full force of one's deepest existential concern, to the discomforting proposition that *objective knowledge* of eternal truth is an impossibility for the 'existing individual'—that is, the finite being, who, as finite, can only be related to the eternal in an expression of a paradox.[30]

Socrates, according to Climacus, "held fast with the entire passion of his inwardness" to his acknowledgment of this anxiety-provoking aspect of the human condition, so that his awareness of the uncertainty of objective knowledge served to quicken, rather than deaden, his desire to pursue the very truth that he recognized to be ever beyond his reach.[31] Thus, for Climacus, Socrates's true greatness lies not in any of his particular speculations on the nature of the eternal, nor his debunking of the particular perspectives embraced by his generally misguided interlocutors, but, rather, his grasp of the singularly consequential proposition that "*objective uncertainty, held fast in an appropriation-process of the most passionate inwardness is the truth*, the highest truth attainable for an *existing* individual."[32]

Socrates's life, therefore, represents the paradigmatic exemplification of human existence lived in honest and unwavering recognition of human finitude and fallibility. His is an affirmational response to a negational dynamic. He eschews the false security of the dogmatist without falling into the vacuous nonchalance of the skeptic. Objectively, he has only "the uncertainty; but it is this which precisely increases the tension of that infinite passion which constitutes his inwardness," and "the truth is precisely the venture which chooses an objective uncertainty with the passion of the infinite."[33] Hence, "[t]he Socratic inwardness in existing is *an analogue to faith* [emphasis added]"; for, according to Climacus, Socrates's inward resolution of his objective uncertainty lies in his realization that "subjectivity is truth," and this 'Socratic principle' expresses precisely the formal relation involved in the internal dynamic—'the movement'—of faith.[34]

Yet, for Climacus, this Socratic inwardness remains only "an analogy to faith," not faith manifest in its highest form, because the vision of the eternal truth that Socrates speculatively submits for our consideration, which he has pursued with such courageous vigor, is not itself paradoxical. In other words, the Socratic inward commitment to uncertainty can only be analogized, not equated, to the faith required by Christianity (as Climacus conceives it), because the principle of 'Socratic ignorance' to which it attaches presents merely "an analogue to the category of the absurd," not a true expression of absurdity.[35]

True faith, we are told, must match paradox with paradox. Not just the formal relation of the subject to the eternal but also the content of the eternal as conceived by this relating subject must involve some essential contradiction, some absurdity that is irreconcilable within the logic of existence, by which the subject is bound, qua existing individual, but which is overcome in the passion of inwardness, through which the subject is freed of the bounds of existential logic and taken up into the embrace of the eternal.

Climacus's analysis suggests that, in Silentian terms, Socrates's resoluteness transcends the category of 'infinite resignation' and makes contact with the category of 'faith,' because Socrates, while constantly engaging in the procedure of dialogical inquiry and justification that defines the ethical, nevertheless consistently recognizes the gap between the (apparent) objectivity of ethical convention and the (real) objectivity of eternity—which lies beyond the deliberations of existing individuals and the ethical communities they form.[36] Socrates never confuses the latter with the former, nor presumes naïvely to equate them with one another. Therefore, he never loses sight of the fact that belief in such procedures and conventions is a *choice*, one that springs from an inward passion. Moreover, he chooses not only to *discuss* but also to *believe*: he believes in God, in immortality, and in the ethical as a bridge to both, and he is willing not only to live but also die in accordance with those beliefs. (Here we can see the resonance of Derrida's observation that "[t]he knight of faith . . . accepts his responsibility . . . He decides, but his absolute decision is neither guided nor controlled by knowledge [understood as a purely objective determination of truth]. *Such, in fact, is the paradoxical condition of every decision*: it cannot be deduced from a form of knowledge of which it would simply be the effect, conclusion, or explicitation."[37])

However, precisely because he chooses dialogue, Socrates is *not* a Silentian 'knight of faith.' As I explained in Chapter 3, dialogue is impossible for the knight of faith since the content—and not just the form—of the knight's relation to the eternal must involve a paradox, an absurdity that cannot be expressed, much less resolved, in the context of ethical discourse. Whereas Socrates's defining activity is his pursuit of mutual understanding in dialogue with others, the knight of faith does not attempt to explain himself to others, nor could he if he wished to do so. The knight is, at least with regard to that which matters most, cut off from the universe of discourse. To recur to Malesic's formulation, "[The knight's] covenant is so particular and qualifies him as so different from all other human beings that he shares no medium of communication about it."[38] Accordingly, Climacus tells us,

> When Socrates believed that there was a God, he held fast to the objective uncertainty with the whole passion of his inwardness, and it is precisely in this contradiction and in this risk, that faith is rooted. Now [in the Christian era] it is otherwise. Instead of objective uncertainty, there is here a certainty, namely, that objectively it is absurd; and this absurdity, held fast in the passion of inwardness, is faith. The Socratic ignorance is a witty jest in comparison with the earnestness of facing the absurd; and the Socratic existential inwardness is a Greek light-mindedness in comparison with the grave strenuosity of faith.[39]

But surely Climacus has here reversed the true logic of existential courage and authenticity, as did Malesic in his formulation of the choice between respecting others' autonomy and exercising 'radical responsibility' on their behalf.

To seek some coherent and existentially satisfying conception of divinity and its relation to human life, despite one's recognition of the epistemic limitations of one's own nature; to persevere in this quest, rather than to acquiesce to the defeatism of the skeptic; but never to stop critically reassessing the conclusions that one has drawn and never to bury the epistemic anxiety that naturally attaches to all finite understandings under a delusional claim of infallible revelatory knowledge—*that* is a strenuous way of life. And to devote oneself, passionately, to the task of living out one's understanding of the eternal truth, while constantly disciplining one's inward relation to (and outward advocacy of) it with an awareness of its fallibility, *that* is a form of faith worthy of affirmation. Whereas, to admit the rational incoherence, the paradoxicalness, of one's conception of divinity (and its dictates) and yet to "hold fast" to it (or to hedge the paradox around with the conveniently obscuring notion of 'mystery'), to subordinate (or prostitute) one's reason to one's passion in such a way as to give license to a false certainty, and the self-satisfaction it promotes, is to take the easy route; it is to deny the very conditions of finitude from which the state of anxiety—which is the very occasion of faith—emerges.

With everyday anxieties one may have the opportunity to take actions that not only relieve the feeling of anxiety but even remove or resolve its underlying source. And of course, when this is possible, it is appropriate and desirable to do so. But with the fundamental existential anxiety that frames the relation of the finite existing individual (or community) to the infinite—what I have termed *epistemic anxiety*—the source lies in the essential nature of the individual's (or community's) existence, inextricable as it is definitive. No religious (or any other) understanding, whatever its supposed origin or claims to justification, can remove the conditions of finitude that prompt this anxiety, for any such understanding is necessarily *held within the context of these conditions*, the context of the very existence of its adherents. Thus such anxiety cannot be 'resolved' by claims to infallible knowledge; it can only be obscured and suppressed. Hence understandings that encourage adherents to deny the fallibility of their tenets as a means to resolve such anxiety thereby encourage them to adopt a dangerous delusion—dangerous, like all delusions, precisely because it divorces its adherents from reality, so that the attitudes they form and the choices they make are at least partly the product of a fundamental misunderstanding of their situation.

It should be clear by this point that what I am describing under the heading of epistemic anxiety correlates closely to the fundamental category of 'ontological anxiety' in the existentialist tradition that takes its cue from Kierkegaard. For existentialist philosophers like Martin Heidegger and Jean-Paul Sartre, theologians like Paul Tillich and Reinhold Neibuhr, and psychologists like Rollo May, the ontological anxiety that lies at the root of the existentialist diagnosis of the human condition is unlike other anxieties because it strikes at the heart of the individual's existence. For the finite being, to face the abyss of 'nothingness' is to confront the negation of that being's own existence; and the natural reaction, the *temptation*, is to draw back from this abyss and to seek some barrier between its implications and our lives. Yet, understandable as such a response is on an emotional level, it is inadvisable in practice.

No psychologist will prescribe to the anxiety-ridden that they adopt a self-understanding that denies their finitude by denying the inevitability of their own death. Such a delusion of indestructibility would surely lead those who held it to adopt attitudes and make choices at odds with reality and, therefore, certain, in the long run, to have negative consequences.

A well-adjusted and mature human being is one who has, among other things, assimilated a healthy awareness of her own mortality into her view of the world and her approach to living in it. This means that she does not seek to suppress her underlying sense of ontological anxiety, but nor does she wallow in it. She takes account of the inevitability of her own death, but she does not allow her recognition of this inevitability to paralyze her. Indeed, in such a person, the awareness of the inevitability of her own death has a galvanizing effect; it prompts her to strive to achieve all that she might within the horizon of her own finitude. She does not waste her life away in the idle fantasy that there will always be more time but, rather, pursues her ends with a sober urgency. She is, like Socrates, neither cocksure nor nonchalant.

Similarly, the well-adjusted and mature human being is one who has, also, assimilated a healthy awareness of her own (and everyone else's) fallibility into her view of the world and her approach to living in it. She does not seek to suppress her underlying sense of epistemic anxiety, but nor does she take it as a license not to think. She takes account of the ineluctability of human fallibility, but she does not allow her recognition of this ineluctability to overwhelm her capacity to form opinions and make choices, to live her life. Indeed, in such a person, the recognition of the limits of her own understanding also has a galvanizing effect; it prompts her to seek out and attend to alternative understandings. She does not close herself in a bubble of epistemic self-satisfaction but, rather, opens herself to dialogue and the possibility of transformation. In short, her anxiety is Socratic. And—Climacus's misguided elevation of absurdity notwithstanding—such Socratic anxiety lies at the very heart of authentic faith.

One more quick point about Socrates will provide a nice pivot into the final two chapters. When Socrates came to recognize certain logical absurdities associated with the traditional Athenian conception of divinity, he neither ignored these absurdities nor abandoned the idea of divinity, per se. Instead, he *revised* it. And it is at such revision that I will now aim throughout the remainder of this work.

Chapter 5

Divine Anxiety and the Metaphysics of Freedom

The years like great black oxen tread the world,
And God the herdsman goads them on behind,
And I am crushed by their passing feet.

—W. B. Yeats, *The Countess Cathleen*[1]

In the preceding chapters, my aim has been to promote a generalized reorientation of thinking about religious faith and a related, and even more thoroughly generalized, justification for classic liberal-democratic political norms. While I have developed it in relation to certain tradition-specific philosophical and theological touchstones, I believe that any epistemically self-aware individual could adopt the overarching perspective I have formulated consistently with *whatever* worldview she might hold, so long as coerciveness toward others is not *essential to* that worldview. Moreover, I have given reasons why many worldviews that are often understood as essentially manifesting or underwriting coerciveness need not be understood in that way. I have argued, therefore, that a fully authentic and steadfast acceptance of classic liberal-democratic political norms does not inherently conflict with an equally authentic and steadfast commitment to a particular religious (or, for that matter, nonreligious) worldview. And this is true, I believe, even where the worldview in question involves moral or social prescriptions and proscriptions that will never be legally mandated by any genuine liberal-democratic society of the sort implied by my account of fallibilism and anxiety. Accordingly, I have built my case for the universal validity of classic liberal norms independent of any reference to my own particular philosophical and theological positions on substantive matters of metaphysical or doctrinal concern. In Rawlsian terms, I have tried to offer a justification for political liberalism independent of my own 'comprehensive' worldview.[2]

Yet, as I have indicated at various points along the way, my insistence that the sort of liberalism that is grounded in epistemic anxiety is reconcilable with a tremendously wide range of comprehensive perspectives on reality and human existence certainly does not imply that I have no preference among such perspectives. Nor, obviously, does my commitment to noncoercion in matters of existential and moral significance in any way prohibit me from employing rational, moral, or spiritual *persuasion* on behalf of my own philosophical and theological preferences. Indeed, as I have also indicated, liberal-democratic society depends on a robust persuasive discourse among competing perspectives (more on that in Chapter 6). Moreover, while I wish to see society tolerate any worldview or personal orientation that does not require adherents to transgress liberal-democratic norms, that does not mean that I do not think the world would be better off if fewer people held certain sorts of views and orientations. As I see it, some comprehensive perspectives are preferable to others because either they more naturally align with and support the values and principles of liberal-democratic citizenship, or they offer (in my estimation) a more accurate or coherent view of reality. Of course, if forced to choose between them, accuracy and/or coherence must be the trump criterion of these two, but, not surprisingly, it seems to me that they actually go hand in hand.

In the final two chapters, therefore, I wish to present an outline of a comprehensive perspective that I believe both provides powerful complimentary support to the accounts of faith and of liberal-democratic norms and justification that I have given here and, also, corrects what I take to be serious conceptual problems in alternative philosophical and theological perspectives that currently enjoy wider followings. This will not only allow me to make a case for what I take to be the strongest available positions within a set of relevant—and potentially related—ongoing conversations in systematic theology, philosophy of religion and metaphysics, and political philosophy and theory. It will also give me an opportunity to model how one can navigate between the holding of a particular comprehensive perspective and the acceptance of fallibilism and epistemic anxiety even in relation to that perspective.

In this chapter, I will discuss some doctrinal, metaphysical, and spiritual issues related to traditional conceptions of divine 'omniscience,' the nature of the divine-world relation, and the closely related theological notions of *imago dei* and *imitatio dei*. I will draw on the philosophical work of the late nineteenth and early twentieth-century British-American mathematician, logician, and speculative metaphysician Alfred North Whitehead in offering an alternative to the traditional understandings of these issues. I will also, thereby, provide a very brief introduction to some of the main principles of the contemporary 'process' movement in philosophy and theology that counts Whitehead as its founding figure. (In the last chapter, I will discuss some of the implications of the process perspective in relation to contemporary 'discourse' and 'deliberative'[3] political philosophies and theories.)

I will begin here by turning attention to an underlying doctrinal dynamic within traditional Christian theology that poses a challenge to any effort to reorient thinking about faith in the way that I am attempting to do so. Throughout the preceding chapters, I have discussed and criticized the *problematizing* structure of traditional theological approaches to epistemic anxiety. I believe that one compounding, if not originating, factor in the emergence of traditional theological perspectives on anxiety is the 'classical' conception of God's nature and attributes, which came to dominate Christian theology through its successive phases of Hellenization. In particular, I want to focus on the classical doctrine of divine 'omniscience,' which posits an *eternalistic* conception of divine knowledge and understanding that, in its absoluteness, bears no parallel whatsoever to the limitations on human knowledge that provoke our anxiety. Theologically, the absence of such a parallel represents an implicit challenge to the notion of human beings as imago dei (created in the image of God) and, thereby, negatively shapes the normative requirement of imitatio dei (the imitation, in so far as possible, of the divine ideal that is presented through this image). Partly in response to the challenge of God's supposed epistemic impassability, traditional Christian theology has too often pushed in the direction of an epistemically naïve—and, therefore, arrogant—conception of fideism of the sort I have described at length already. Faith is taken to provide a (humanly unachievable) degree of certainty that justifies attitudes and acts of theological or moral coerciveness toward others, in part because such certainty is seen as a defining characteristic of the God with whom one is reconciled, and whose image one reclaims, through faith.

Open Theism and the Doctrine of Divine Omniscience

In recent years, one important trend in philosophy of religion and theology is an increased interest in the notion of the future as 'open'—that is, undetermined and unknowable. In particular, attention has been focused on the implications of this understanding of the future as it relates to the concept of divine omniscience. The open conception of the future runs counter to the classical conception of God's omniscient understanding—as found in most systematic forms of Jewish, Christian, and Islamic theology—which holds that the future is already determinate and, therefore, fully known from God's perspective. On the classical view, God is *wholly* eternal and immutable; there is no (real) change with regard to God, neither in Godself nor in God's relation to the world. Contrarily, open theists affirm that certain aspects of God are eternal and unchanging—such as God's character—but insist that there are also aspects of God's nature and relation to the world that are *essentially* temporal and changing.

Interestingly, the debate between open and classical theists has been particularly lively in areas of philosophy of religion where Christian evangelical theology mixes with contemporary analytic philosophy. Not surprisingly, the closely related issues of human free will and moral responsibility and the existence and origin of evil are among the primary theological concerns driving this conversation. But fidelity to scripture is also being debated, as classical and open theists each highlight biblical passages that seem to support their respective views, while seeking to reinterpret or deemphasize those that seem to support the opposing view.

In the context of Jewish theology, the open conception of God has made some inroads as well. It has a significant appeal for many of those who view the Holocaust as sufficient counterevidence against the classical conception of God's knowledge, power, and relation to history. It also matches better with many scriptural and some nonorthodox classical rabbinic depictions of God.[4] Open theism is a very tough sell in the context of Islamic theology, however, since Islamic theism rests on scriptural depictions of God's relation to the world that are the most unambiguously *omnicausal* of any found in the Abrahamic traditions.

The main elements of the classical conception of God won out over various rival positions fairly early in the development of

Christian theology. While the scriptures that make up the Hebrew Bible (which would become the Christian Old Testament) sometimes portray God as experiencing events in the created world in a manner that suggests something less than absolute knowledge of the future, most ancient Christian theologians and philosophers—under the influence of both the New Testament authors and Neoplatonism[5]—turned away from the conception of the relation between God and creation as genuinely, reciprocally conditioned by creaturely freedom and, therefore, contingency. Instead, taking it as an important implication of God's 'Lordship' over creation, the early architects of Christian systematic theology adopted the view that the *seeming* nondeterminateness of future events from the perspective of created beings, like us, is merely an illusory product of our finitude. God, as creator and Lord of the world (according to this classical view) must be understood as existing 'outside of time' and, therefore, as being eternally aware of the totality of what we perceive as 'past,' 'present,' and 'future' without any limitation or even (real) distinction between these categories. Accordingly, Augustine of Hippo, who played a pivotal role in establishing the classical consensus, writes of "eternity, which stands still and is neither past nor future, [but] dictates the times that are past and the times that are to come."[6] God, therefore, we are told, creates and knows the world in a state of perfect placidity: "Just as *in the Beginning* you knew *the heaven and the earth* without any variation in your knowledge, so *in the Beginning* you created *the heaven and earth* without any alteration of your action."[7]

Later, this conception of the God-world relation was reiterated and reinforced by the medieval scholastic theologians and philosophers, now under the influence of Aristotle. Thomas Aquinas definitively set the terms of the orthodox Catholic conception of God's relation to the world with reference to the authority of "the Philosopher" and his understanding of God as wholly 'eternal' and 'impassible.' Aquinas concisely summarizes the epistemological implications of this view thus,

> Now God knows all contingent things not only as they are in their causes, but also as each one of them is actually in itself. And although contingent things become actual successively, nevertheless God knows contingent things not successively, as they are in their own being, as we do; but simultaneously. The reason is because his knowledge is

> measured by eternity, as is also His being; and eternity being simultaneously whole comprises all time . . . Hence, all things that are in time are present to God from eternity, not only because He has the types of things present within him, as some say; but because His glance is carried from eternity over all things as they are in their presentiality.[8]

Moreover, in this regard at least, Martin Luther and John Calvin fully concurred with Rome. Indeed, Calvin's straightforward articulation of a 'double'-sided doctrine of the predestination of human souls to heaven or hell merely makes fully explicit the claim to divine omnicausality that was always implicit in the theontological doctrines of the Catholic Church.

Of course, some Christian thinkers have attempted to reconcile absolute divine foreknowledge with real, ontologically independent human agency by denying that God *causes* our future choices, while nevertheless affirming that God *inerrantly knows* what we will 'freely' choose—Luis de Molina among Catholics and Jacob Arminius and John Wesley among Protestants are prominent exemplars of this view. Open theists, however, find such attempts at reconciliation logically unpersuasive and, therefore, reject the classical conception of omniscience, with its claim to perfect divine foreknowledge of the future choices of actual individuals, *in all of its various theological permutations.*[9] According to open theists, such a view of divine foreknowledge is irredeemably inconsistent with any *coherent* and *meaningful* construal of creaturely freedom.

In the context of the current debate between open and classical theists, Molina's formulation of divine foreknowledge has been particularly influential, having been adopted in some form or another by a substantial number of theistic philosophers and theologians working in the contemporary analytic tradition (including representatives of both the Catholic and Protestant traditions). In the third section that follows, I will clarify the terms of the metaphysical debate between open and classical theists, and argue for the preferability of open theism as a metaphysical position, through a contrasting discussion of the Molinist and Whiteheadian positions. Whiteheadian process thought represents a particularly strong form of open theism, with a focus on the ontology of the divine-world relation and creaturely freedom.[10] Whereas Molina follows the classical tradition in affirming absolute divine foreknowledge of all future occurrences, Whitehead insists that the actual course of the future cannot be known, even by God, because it genuinely depends on the free—and therefore never absolutely predictable—choices of future nondivine agents. Before wading into the conceptually dense ontological issues at play here, however, I would like to say a bit more about the theological context to which they relate. This will further clarify the importance of these ontological issues and why it is worth engaging with them here, despite their somewhat technical character.

Divine Anxiety, Faith, and the Image and Imitation of God

While considerable argumentation has been devoted to the logical and ontological issues involved in the dispute between classical and open theists, very little attention has, as of yet, been paid to the implications of open conceptions of God's relation to the world for our theological understandings of faith and of the moral and political claims that religious believers lodge on the basis of their faith. Yet these implications are profound.

An 'open' God is an *anxious* God. To create without absolute knowledge of the actual future is to take a risk. In choosing among real alternatives for creation, God must weigh their respective potentialities, both positive and negative, and, yes, "roll the dice." Such a God can be fully omniscient in the only coherent sense of the term—knowing all that is knowable—and still experience epistemic doubt. Contemplating such a God makes me unashamed to admit my own fallibility. The perfect placidity of the God of classical theology tells a different story. A God untroubled by anxiety instills dreams of dogmatic certainty. And such dreams, all too often, inspire real acts of coercion and oppression.

Here we can profitably refer back to the description of the dynamic of faith and reconciliation with the divine offered by Søren Kierkegaard's pseudonymous persona Vigilius Haufniensis in *The Concept of Anxiety: A Simple Psychologically Orienting Deliberation on the Dogmatic Issue of Hereditary Sin*, which I discussed in Chapter 2. Recall that Haufniensis tells us that the qualitative leap into sin that is described in the story of the Fall from Eden presupposes the capacity for such a leap, which Haufniensis identifies with the presence of *anxiety*, conceived as "freedom's actuality as the possibility of possibility."[11] The "possibility of possibility" is, in turn, identified with the entertainment of alternatives. Where there are no alternatives, there is no freedom, only necessity. Thus Haufniensis says that "innocence is ignorance,"[12] but this is ignorance not in the sense of an absence of knowledge. Rather, it is the absence of the recognition that knowledge can become a basis for *choice*. As Haufniensis puts it, in the state of innocence, "the whole actuality of knowledge projects itself in anxiety as the enormous nothing of ignorance."[13] But, again, this "nothing" is not a mere absence, per se. Rather than a void, it represents a potential opening onto the realm of possibility. Hence the emergence of epistemic self-consciousness—represented by Eve's consideration of the claim of the serpent, as an alternative to God's claim—is an awakening to possibility, and this awakening is the beginning of *autonomous agency*.

Anxiety, then, is the slow but steady, quiet yet terrible, upwelling of the recognition of choice, which comes like a flood from which there is no escape, because one does not notice the rising water until one suddenly looks around and finds it everywhere with no dry pathway out. Haufniensis tells us that angels do not experience such anxiety, precisely because they never step through the opening onto possibility; they never contemplate alternatives to God's will. They are 'innocent' in the sense previously described. They act only according to God's directives. They have no will distinct from the divine will, and thus they are never alienated from God. Accordingly, they have no need of salvation, which is precisely the reconciliation with God that comes through the realignment with the divine will produced by the leap of faith. Only historical beings—those for whom the temporal passage from moment to moment involves choosing among alternatives—require salvation. Historical beings must navigate the dark and dangerous waters of possibility. Angels float above these waters, secure in the serene assurance of necessity.

Haufniensis provides a terminologically modernized but faithful summarization of the implications of the traditional Christian theological perspective when he tells us that for the historical human agent, "[w]hen Salvation is posited, anxiety, together with possibility, is left behind."[14] Here we have the Abrahamic sacrifice of the self, the relinquishment of an individuated, historical relation to possibility in favor of an *absolute relation to the absolute*. In the moment that the movement of faith is accomplished, salvation comes to the rescue like some divine helicopter that plucks the stranded soul from the floodwaters of historical existence. From that point onward, the saved individual witnesses history with angelic equanimity. She relinquishes her relation to possibility; she transcends freedom through an infinitely free choice to relate herself *faithfully* to the absolute, and thereby (we are to believe) she escapes the flood.

Thus as I have discussed throughout this work, the transformative character of salvation that is emphasized in traditional accounts of faith is, at its foundation, epistemic in nature. The spiritual and moral aspects of salvation derive precisely from the state of epistemic realignment with the divine will into which the saved individual putatively enters through faithful relation to the commands of the divine. The crucial point to which I now wish to draw attention is the ineluctable connection between this conception of faith and salvation and the classical conception of divine omniscience and the God-world relation. To figure salvation as reconciliation with the divine, and reconciliation with the divine as an escape from historicity and the dissolution of anxiety, presumes that God's experience (if that term even makes sense here) is serenely ahistorical, without any element of contingency, uncertainty, or anxiety. By subordinating ourselves to (some claimed expression of) the divine will, we become more "like" God, on this account, because this subordination allows us to approximate the all-encompassing certainty and, therefore, existential tranquility of God.

This *indirect* imitational aspect of the dynamic of traditional Abrahamic faith is often overlooked. Linda Zagzebski, for example, sees early Judaism as departing from other ancient near Eastern forms of theism precisely in its shift away from imitatio models of worship, writing that "in the Hebrew Scriptures, human beings become like God, not by imitation, but by following God's commandments."[15] But this formulation presents a false dichotomy. Alternatively, I would say that, according to the Hebraic model, by following God's commandments (in the certainty of faith), one puts oneself in position to imitate the divine. Through one's faith, according to this model, God loans one a measure of infallibility, for one's affirmation of the conception of the good and the right associated with God's commandments is epistemically vouchsafed by its divine origin. One is thus relieved of one's epistemic anxiety and also, therefore, of one's sense of obligation to provide justification for one's faith-based claims in the form of discursive reasons accessible to all, including those who do not share this faith. Hence according to this conception of faith, one becomes—in relation to all normative matters that fall within the scope of one's religious commitments—epistemically godlike, infallible.

But what if God, too, experiences in a historical mode? What if God must deal with contingency and uncertainty? What if God knows anxiety? Then the divine ideal is no longer an image of unconflicted quietude and self-satisfied moral transcendence. Rather than aspiring to banish all doubt and uncertainty from ourselves and adopt a posture of authoritarian 'radical' responsibility in the assertion of our own value judgments, we might instead find a very different sort of existential inspiration in the image of a God who pursues the creative good without the absolute assurance of the outcome of all things.

As a Whiteheadian theist, I reject not only the classical conception of divine omniscience but also the notion of divine 'omnipotence,' per se—which I agree with Whitehead is inextricably bound together with the former. Whitehead discusses the pernicious historical effect of the classical doctrine of omnipotence in *Religion in the Making*, where he comments on Psalm 24, with its triumphal ode to the 'Lordship' of God over the world and human history, observing that "[t]his worship of glory arising from power is not only dangerous: it arises from a barbaric conception of God. I suppose not even the world itself could contain the bones of those slaughtered because of men intoxicated by its attraction . . . The glorification of power has broken more hearts than it has healed."[16] Here, I am adding that the same can be said of the *glorification of certainty* that we find in the classical doctrine of omniscience.

Just as the theological glorification of absolute power combined with the idea—and *ideal*—of imago dei in early Western political thought and history to produce notions of human rulership predicated on coercive (rather than consensual) authority, the glorification of God's absolute knowledge of even the future course of actuality combined with this idea/ideal to help produce a notion of faith that posits its own authority as morally superseding the autonomy of those who disagree. Others may be compelled to obey spiritual and moral dictates that are not of their own free choosing because their freedom to choose otherwise betrays them. They are not simply choosing differently than those who hold this faith, they are choosing "against God" with whom "the faithful" epistemologically identify themselves.

In fact, the classical conception of divine omniscience undermines and denigrates the very idea of the freedom to choose. As Kierkegaard fully understood, even *God is not free* on this view, for if God has absolute knowledge of the definite actual future associated with each possible world that God might create, then it follows that God has absolute knowledge of which possible world is best. Add to this the claim of divine omnibenevolence and it follows, necessarily, that there is one and only one "choice" that God could make regarding which possible world to create. That is to say there would be a 'best of all possible worlds' known to God as such, which would constrain God's choice to the selection of that specific world. And this would not merely be an internal constraint that might be seen not really to be a constraint at all. It would represent a constraint imposed by an external relation to the actual course of affairs determined by the known but (putatively) 'free'—and, hence, ontologically independent—choices of the future agents inhabiting that world. Only by forthrightly acknowledging that the classical doctrines of omniscience and omnipotence render the notion of creaturely freedom absurd can classical theists escape this implication of divine constraint—but then they must also admit that the 'creatures' are not ontologically distinguishable from the 'Creator,' and so therefore their systems collapse into pantheism.

The God of open theism, on the other hand, must take account of the *unknowable choices* of future free individuals, so that the divine creative determination cannot be reduced to a simple calculation of fully known factors leading necessarily to one particular, inescapable judgment. God, on this view, must truly choose and, in doing so, must truly risk. Thus if we further presume a loving God, then we may speak sensibly of *divine anxiety* regarding the course of the future. This anxiety is linked to God's concern for the well-being of God's creatures as related to the not-fully-predictable outcomes of their own and their fellow creatures' free decisions. And this notion of divine anxiety can provide a theological parallel between the human condition and the divine condition, helping to rescue our understanding of the doctrine of imago dei, and our theologies in general, from the temptation toward moral and political coerciveness, religious exclusivism, and intolerance toward all expressions of difference and disagreement.

DIVINE OPENNESS AND THE VIRTUE OF ANXIETY

I have devoted considerable space in the preceding chapters to clarifying my use of the term 'anxiety,' not only differentiating anxiety from other, related notions, such as 'fear' or 'dread'—as do Kierkegaard and his philosophical and theological heirs—but also distinguishing my use of anxiety from the alternative uses to which these other authors put it. In the context of the present discussion, I wish to especially emphasize two points.

First, it is important to recognize not only the sort of anxiety that God might share with us but also the sort that is solely human. This is another reason I have focused attention here on the *epistemic* dimensions of anxiety, whereas so much of contemporary existentialist philosophy and theology has been mainly preoccupied with its *ontic* dimensions. God is neither finite nor mortal. Nothing that is already actual lies beyond the far horizon for God. God need not fear sickness, age, or death. God will never be in danger of experiencing the dissolution of Godself. God cannot sin and, in sinning, become alienated from Godself. Thus God's anxiety is wholly bound up in God's concern for us, whereas we feel anxiety not only for those we love but also for ourselves.

Accordingly, when we contemplate the implications of divine anxiety for our philosophical and theological conceptions of religious faith, we should focus on *concern for others*, as opposed to concern for self. And we must combine this concern for others with an unwavering acknowledgment of not only the analogous but also the *dis*analogous element of the parallel between God's anxiety and ours: God is morally infallible; we are not. God's concern for others relates only to the possibility that they may choose otherwise than God would choose for them and, *therefore*, choose wrongly. Contrarily, our concern for others must relate to the possibility that *we may choose wrongly ourselves*. Thus they must be free to choose otherwise than what we would choose for them.

So while it is perfectly appropriate for the religious believer to understand her own affirmations of faith as being inseparably connected to her fundamental concern for her own way of being-in-the-world, she must always maintain an equally fundamental concern for how her choices about how to act on her faith can affect others, who equally deserve the freedom to affirm or reject her way of being. Not being infallible, she cannot claim the right to act on her faith in ways that will coercively constrain others to think or to live according to the dictates of her conscience, rather than their own.

Second, while my use of anxiety here continues to be connected, to some degree, with the common, psychological use of this term to denote a negatively experienced state of apprehensiveness in relation to some unknown aspect(s) of the future to which the anxious subject relates, I also intend for it to connect with more psychologically *positive* connotations that are associated with certain kinds of future-oriented anxieties that are also fundamental to human life. To take just one example, it is illustrative of the sort of anxiety that I have in mind to think of the complex of feeling that precedes a romantic first-date with someone for whom one has already developed a strong infatuation. This is an anxiety that combines apprehensiveness with excitement, fear with joy. It is an enlivening anxiety. There is the thrill of anticipation of what might be, if all goes well, ineluctably entwined with the trepidation for what might come if it does not. Indeed, the one cannot be had without the other. "Maybe she will return my affection, and we will fall in love," one thinks. "Or maybe I will act foolishly, or bore her, or simply not seem her type, and she will reject me." Whichever may be the case in the end, one must recognize, "I have to risk rejection, if I hope to experience love."

Again, the analogy is not perfect, but I believe that it is just such a sense of invigorating anxiety that implicitly underlies Whitehead's use of 'Eros' as one of the primary descriptors of God's relation to the actual world and its creative freedom. God's love for and engagement with the world and the creatures that inhabit it is at once a joyful desire for the wondrous possibilities that God foresees for us, should we choose the creative path of beauty and love, and an apprehensive anxiety regarding the terrible possibilities that could be realized, should we choose the destructive path of disharmony and hatred. The classical conception of God's 'relation' to the world, as utterly unilateral, is a sterile and empty nothing compared to this picture of God as *genuinely*, *reciprocally* related to the world by way of a real *concern*, based in an absence of surety about the outcomes of things.

Here we see the connection so often invoked in existentialist discourse between anxiety and 'care.' In open theism, there is a real sense to the language of care as applied in descriptions of God's relation to the world, a sense that is lacking in classical theistic invocations of this notion, where appeals to God's so-called 'love' are, in fact, merely affirmations of God's power that are cloaked in obfuscating contortions of language to fit rhetorical aims that undermine the natural meaning of the term. It is no surprise that this classical view has historically promoted equally power-driven conceptions of human relations meant to imitate its view of God's relation to the world: the patriarchic father and husband who lords over his family, the 'absolute monarch' who sits unmoved on his thrown while his people cry out in anguish, the self-righteous moralist who cares more for the supposed sanctity of his own moral conclusions than for the autonomy of his fellow human beings, and so forth.

No, this is not the whole story. There has been much goodwill extended, and many good works done, in the name of the God of classical theology. But often enough those who feel this goodwill and do these good works seem to be motivated by a view of God that, in fact, diverges from that of the theologians who have defined the orthodox doctrines of their churches. The shift to open theism rationalizes the commitment that such believers have to their own intuitive sense that God must be more genuinely relational and caring than can possibly be the case according to the classical view. Rather than a cold and distant God who herds along a preordained passage of years, in which the dignity and preciousness of the individual human life is crushed in passing, as Yeats so evocatively describes it in the quote from *The Countess Cathleen* at the beginning of this chapter, open theism instead offers a vision of a God who truly *lives* with us in each passing moment, experiencing our joys and sorrows along with us with a perfect intimacy of internal relation.

Moreover, when we add a theological appeal to divine anxiety to our conceptions of imago and imitatio dei, we further bolster the religious believer's capacity to exhibit such virtuous epistemic anxiety in her relations with her fellow citizens. She need not wholly shy away from sharing her own perspective within the context of democratic deliberations in the public sphere, but she will always condition her advocacy for her beliefs and preferences with a tolerant humility toward, a sense of respect for, and a degree of openness to others' contrary perspectives, which will prevent her from seeking to impose an aggressive, moralistic will-to-power on them. For she will come to understand the uncertainty that necessarily goes hand in hand with her own fallibility as something to be acknowledged and accounted for, not run away from.

All action involves risk, because all action is relational. We do not make ourselves more like God to the extent that we deny our anxious uncertainty in moments of defining choice. We make ourselves more like God to the extent that we acknowledge this anxiety; accept it as a necessary and appropriate accompaniment to freedom; recognize its normative implications—namely, that we should be humble and noncoercive in our relations to others; and, yet, within the bounds of such humility and noncoercion, display the courage to act despite the impossibility of absolute knowledge that we act rightly. In short, if we wish to live in the image of God, when the flood waters of anxiety press up around us, challenging our sense of absolute security and confidence in our own beliefs, we must stop looking around for some magical exit from history and learn to swim.

WHITEHEAD'S ORGANIC THEISM

Alfred North Whitehead was a towering intellectual figure of the early twentieth century, considered by many of his contemporaries to be a polymathic genius of the highest order.[17] But his thought faded into relative obscurity for several decades, especially in Anglo-American philosophy, as intellectual trends cut against the direction of his late systematic work in speculative metaphysics. His earlier work in mathematics and formal logic had included such celebrated triumphs as his groundbreaking *Treatise on Universal Algebra*[18] and the epoch-making first edition of *Principia Mathematica*,[19] which Whitehead cowrote with his former student Bertrand Russell. He also spoke widely and influentially on topics ranging from the origins of religious consciousness to the philosophical and cultural foundations of education (his book *The Aims of Education*[20] is still considered a classic in the field). But beginning in the 1910s, Whitehead became increasingly disenchanted with the exceedingly narrow and formalistic conception of human understanding that was coming to dominate philosophy in the form of 'logical positivism,' with thinkers like Russell, Ludwig Wittgenstein, and Rudolf Carnap as its standard-bearers. Contra the positivists, Whitehead believed that the emergence of the radically new paradigm of Einsteinian physics called precisely for bold metaphysical speculation aimed at a comprehensive reintegration of the full range of human experience and forms of understanding. Whereas the positivists' program of aggressive reductivism and circular criteria of 'meaningfulness' led them to cavalierly repudiate vast swaths of human experience and expression as nonreferential and empty of cognitive content. By the time Whitehead published his metaphysical magnum opus, *Process and Reality* (1929), the philosophical consensus had turned decisively against the metaphysical enterprise, per se.

Moreover, the fact that Whitehead's metaphysics involves theism led many philosophers at the time to reject it out of hand, often without any serious consideration of the manner in which Whitehead had fundamentally revised the classical conception of the divine to be consistent with scientific naturalism.[21] Hence Whitehead's highly original ontological and epistemological system found only a very limited audience during the middle part of the twentieth century. Though, his ideas were kept alive during this period by a small but dedicated and prolific group of thinkers, especially in the context of philosophy of religion and systematic theology, where they have played a significant role in the broader conversations about issues such as the divine nature, the God-world relation, and interreligious dialogue throughout the past century.

Over the last several decades, however, the Whiteheadian 'process' movement[22] in philosophy and theology—which adopted this label from Whitehead's emphasis on the ontological primacy of dynamic 'becoming,' over against static 'being'—has benefited from a resurgence in interest in Whitehead's ideas. In philosophy, a number of prominent analytic philosophers have come to acknowledge Whitehead as having anticipated some important recent trends in both philosophy and theoretical physics.[23] (Though analytic philosophers in general still tend to assume that no form of theism can be worthy of rational consideration, regardless of how systematically one might be differentiated from the traditional forms of theism that led them to that stance.) There has also been a particularly dramatic increase in interest in Whitehead beyond the Anglo-American analytic community, especially in Continental philosophy. In theology, the growing interest in open theism has expanded awareness of Whiteheadian theism even further.

Metaphysically, Whitehead is an unabashed Platonist. But he formulated a thoroughly revised and highly nuanced form of Platonism, which he contrasted to "the absurd simple-mindedness of the traditional treatment of Universals."[24] I obviously cannot offer a full explication, much less defense, of Whitehead's ontology here. But I will attempt to say enough that the appeal of his view on these issues, from my perspective, will become apparent. Any account of divine omniscience that seeks to preserve the meaningfulness of the notion of creaturely freedom must make sense of the categories of 'contingency' and 'possibility' (two categories that go hand in hand and that make no sense in the context of any deterministic conception of the universe, including, I will argue, one in which the totality of actual occurrences is known eternally by God). Thus in the present context, the important thing is to briefly but clearly indicate the strength of Whitehead's interconnected accounts of possibility, freedom, and divine omniscience and to contrast these with the weakness of even the most sophisticated forms of classical theism represented here by Molinism.

Whitehead's thought is notoriously difficult to explicate concisely, in no small part because of the (appropriately) idiosyncratic nature of his terminology. In attempting to formulate a revisionary metaphysics that would reflect the changed nature of the scientific understanding of space, time, and physicality that resulted from the Einsteinian revolution, Whitehead felt the need to break away from traditional metaphysical categories and concepts, which carried with them the associations and assumptions of the now outdated Newtonian—and in many cases even Aristotelian—physics. In some cases, he adapted existing terms, while giving them new connotations. In others, he invented new terms to capture ideas that had little or no precedent in previous metaphysical discourse. Moreover, his own use of terms, in some cases, changed over time, as he worked to refine his system. By the time he articulated the mature version of this system in *Process and Reality*, he offered a more or less fully elaborated conceptual scheme and vocabulary that requires significant study to assimilate (which was another barrier to wider reception of his work at the time of its production). In the following summary explanation, I have tried to limit the number of unfamiliar terms to those directly relevant to the issues at hand and necessary for a proper understanding of Whitehead's views on these issues. Also, rather than engage in detailed exegesis of these terms, I have tried to provide just enough exposition to give the unfamiliar reader a sense of what is going on in Whitehead's thought—enough, I hope, to make the general ideas comprehensible, as they relate to my own program in this chapter, without requiring the reader to come to any definitive conclusion regarding the final worth of Whitehead's system.

Whitehead's conception of God is 'dipolar,' combining elements of transcendence and immanence. The 'primordial' nature of God is God's eternal aspect, which transcends and provides the foundation for the actual world of temporal and physical occurrences. Here we have God as the explanatory factor required to make sense of the basic ordering of the actual world. God's primordial nature takes the place of the Platonic realm of forms, as the storehouse of potentiality. It is because of the divine primordial determination that there is a particular cosmic order, an actual universe of a certain form and constitution, rather than merely an indeterminate multiplicity of unrealized possible universes: "Viewed as primordial, he is the unlimited conceptual realization of the absolute wealth of potentiality. In this aspect, he is not *before* all creation, but *with* all creation."[25] Thus Whitehead rejects the classical doctrine of *creatio ex nihilo*. God does not create reality in (or from) a void. The divine creative act is conditioned by the character of the potentiality to which it relates. Moreover, God's nature itself is conditioned by the character of this relation, which is the primordial expression of the underlying metaphysical character of all relations. So "God is not to be treated as an exception to all metaphysical principles . . . He is their chief exemplification."[26] Nor does God "freely choose" to create a world, as in classical theism. Creativity is essential to the divine nature and necessary to the complete realization of the divine entity, per se, which exists in 'organic' relation to the world: "[A]s primordial, so far is he from 'eminent reality,' that in this abstraction he is 'deficiently actual' . . . His feelings are only conceptual and so lack the fullness of actuality."[27] Aseity is *not* an attribute of this God. *All* entities, including God, exist in the mutual dependency of co-relation, according to Whitehead's organic conception of reality. This is an implication of his absolute metaphysical generalization of the principle of relativity.

Accordingly, God also has a 'consequent' nature that is paired with the primordial nature. Here we have God as participant in every act of temporal becoming, living in and through the experiences of the actual entities that come to populate the world that emerges from God's primordial determination. "Thus, by reason of the relativity of all things, there is a reaction of the world on God. The completion of God's nature into a fullness of physical feeling is derived from the objectification of the world in God."[28] This consequent aspect of God is temporally 'everlasting,' rather than eternal, and God as consequent experiences in a temporal mode, for temporality is *not* an illusion of finitude. It is ineluctably basic to the actual existence of any conceivable nondeterministic universe whatsoever.

God presents to each actual entity the range of possibilities relevant to it in any given moment, and the actual entity chooses for itself which possibility to instantiate in that moment—just as God chose from among the primordial range of possibilities in ordering the world of which the entity is a part. Thus God provides each moment of temporal actuality with the necessary ontological link to the eternal content of primordial possibility, and each moment of temporal actuality, in turn, contributes—positively or negatively—to the divine experience by concretely manifesting some particular possibility, as opposed to any other. There is, therefore, an essential, continuous, and everlasting organic feedback loop between God and the world. The "reaction of the world on God" that results from the actualization of *this*, rather than *that*, available possibility in any given moment, is twofold: There is the determination of which possibilities remain, and which have been foreclosed, for subsequent moments in the relevant chain of actualizations, which thereby determines the objective content of God's relation to the next moment in that chain. And there is the intrinsic value—either positive or negative—that God derives from the experience of the actualization. Something new is added to the divine life by every new moment of actuality.

God's relation to the world is, therefore, 'pan*en*theistic': God is immanent in the world, and the world is immanent in God. Unlike simple pantheism, panentheism does not *identify* God and the world. Their organic relation is precisely that, a relation. But though they are distinguishable, they are not separable. As Whitehead puts it, "[I]n respect to the world, God is everywhere. Yet he is a distinct entity. The world (events in it) has a (specific) locus with reference to him, but he has no locus with reference to the world. This is the basis of the distinction between the finite and the infinite. God and the world have the same locus."[29] Also, the nonidentity of the actual entities with God goes hand in hand with their freedom to choose otherwise than God would have them choose, when they are confronted with the possibilities that God presents to them. God cannot overrule the freedom of any individual actual entity anymore than God can interrupt the metaphysical order of which God is, necessarily, a part. This is Whitehead's answer to the problem of evil. God does not create—nor voluntarily "allow"—evil. Evil is an inescapable by-product of creaturely freedom, and creaturely freedom is a metaphysical necessity.

POSSIBILITY, ACTUALITY, AND THE GOD-WORLD RELATION

Elsewhere, I have argued at length for an understanding of 'possibility' that embraces a robust version of Whitehead's conception of the potential qualities and characteristics that collectively constitute the *formal* basis for the range of possible states of affairs.[30] I should note, here, that process thinkers are divided between those who affirm Whitehead's inclination toward a strong form of Platonism and those who follow Charles Hartshorne in rejecting this particular aspect of

Whitehead's ontology. Describing my own, maximalist Whiteheadian position is useful here because of the contrast I wish to make with Molinism. But the larger theological point about God's relation to the future toward which I am working through this description is one that Hartshorneans would also generally accept, mutatis mutandis.

Whitehead conceives of the potential forms of actuality as interrelationally codeterminate. Rather than maintain the misleading terminology of 'universals,' Whitehead labels these possible formal characteristics of actual states of affairs 'eternal objects,' signifying, among other things, their status as the discretely individuate-able (i.e., determinate) constituent elements of the conceptual content of the divine understanding. Their determinateness is a function of their interrelationally constituted objective status within the context of the infinite imaginative-synthetic capacity of the primordial divine apprehension of possibility. Accordingly, as a function of God's perfectly inclusive 'entertainment' (i.e., active apprehension and consideration) of this interrelationally determinate totality of possible formal characteristics, God eternally 'envisages' all possible states of affairs in their abstract potentiality.[31] As Whitehead puts it in *Religion in the Making*:

> God, who is the antecedent ground of transition, must include all possibilities of physical value conceptually, thereby holding the ideal forms apart in equal, conceptual realization of knowledge. Thus, as concepts, they are grasped together in the synthesis of omniscience . . .
>
> He is complete in the sense that his vision determines every possibility of value. Such a complete vision coordinates and adjusts every detail. Thus his knowledge of the relationships of particular modes of value is not added to, or disturbed, by the realization in the actual world of what is already conceptually realized in his ideal world . . . [T]hese ideal forms are not realized by him in mere bare isolation, but as elements in the value of his conceptual experience. Also, the ideal forms are in God's vision as contributing to his complete experience, by reason of his conceptual realization of their possibilities as elements of value in any creature. Thus, God is the one systematic, complete fact, which is the antecedent ground conditioning every creative act.[32]

In explaining the existential status of these 'ideal forms' (a terminology he soon dropped in favor of 'eternal objects'), Whitehead importantly offers a modal distinction between 'existence' and 'actuality.' (Hartshorne is rightly credited with clarifying this distinction and the related terminology, but it is clearly present already in Whitehead's work—more or less explicitly so by the time he completed *Process and Reality*.)

According to Whitehead, the eternal objects exist, but they are not actual. Generally speaking, for Whitehead, the term 'actuality' designates the temporally successive flow of *concrete events* (in which *some* eternal objects come to be manifested, as matters of fact) and the *concrete entities* that constitute these events.[33] (Whitehead's is an 'event ontology,' so the distinction between *events* and *entities* should be read fluidly here.) More specifically, as I will further explain momentarily, to be actual is to exercise choice among alternatives. Eternal objects and the possibilities constituted by their relations are the alternatives from which the actual emerges through the efficacy of choice, and 'concreteness' here refers to the finality of this choice. The alternatives, in themselves, are ontologically nonconcrete or 'abstract' and, therefore, nonactual, because there is no finality in the realm of the eternal. Only by participating in the temporal, as 'ingredient' in the formal composition of actual entities, do these eternal alternatives attain concreteness and, thereby, causal efficacy. Nevertheless, there is, on this account, a meaningful sense in which eternal objects and the possible states of affairs they support can be designated as 'existent' in a real, ontological way, prior to concrete temporal manifestation. Which is to say, among other things, that actuality does not emerge from sheer nonbeing. The ancient principle *ex nihilo nihil fit* is foundational in Whitehead's thought. Choice does not operate in an ontological vacuum. The alternatives are *real*. But only one alternative in any given moment of becoming will be actualized through the decision of the entity that becomes itself in the form of that alternative (I will explain what this means shortly).

Crucially, Whitehead treats the respective distinctions between abstractness and concreteness and indeterminateness and determinateness as both conceptually and ontologically separable. Taken as such, 'eternal objects' are abstract because their collective 'subsistence'[34] in the divine primordial envisagement of possibility is both logically and ontologically prior to their concrete manifestation as ingredient elements in actual states of affairs (if they are, in fact, ever so manifested). Yet they are also ontologically determinate existential units because there is both an internal and external logic of individuation for each discrete possibility as a function of the exhaustive imaginative-synthetic capacity of the divine primordial apprehension in which all eternal objects are corelationally ordered and 'graded' according to their respective moral-aesthetic values for realization. As Whitehead puts it, "[T]he differentiated relevance of eternal objects to each instance of the creative process requires their conceptual realization in the primordial nature of God . . . Such a primordial superject of creativity achieves, in its unity of satisfaction, the complete conceptual valuation of all eternal objects . . . By reason of . . . this primordial valuation of pure potentials, each eternal object has a definite, effective relevance to each concrescent process [i.e., the process of becoming of each and every actual occasion]. Thus possibility which transcends realized temporal matter of fact has a real relevance to the creative advance [of actual affairs]."[35]

To employ a term that was much in vogue in British philosophical discourse during Whitehead's formative years as a student at Cambridge, the eternal objects exist as the 'ideational' content of the divine mind. And just as you or I can entertain an ideational conception of some possibility with quite distinct clarity—its 'abstractness,' qua anticipatory idea, notwithstanding—so, too, can God entertain the eternal objects and their respective relations to one another as abstract yet determinate possibilities for actualization in the world. Indeed, whereas only some small portion of the ideational content in my mind ever attains the clarity of precision associated with distinctly and thoroughly conceptualized possibilities, in the divine mind all envisaged content is clearly and distinctly conceptualized.

Whitehead is also a *panexperientialist*,[36] and he rejects the classical ontology of 'enduring substances.' His technical term for the concrete things through which some determinate possibilities come to be manifested in the world is 'actual occasions.' Whitehead, generally speaking, uses this term as interchangeable with the more colloquially transparent term 'actual entities.' But the use of 'occasion' is meant to emphasize the dynamic character of the basic units of actuality, as opposed to the static character of Cartesian/Newtonian 'substances.' These occasions are momentary in nature. Enduring things and persons are constituted of series of such occasions that are bound together across time through a chain of particularly intimate internal relations, by which shared characteristics are transmitted through successive moments in the "life" of the series. Per the relativity principle, in the unity of its final 'satisfaction' as a concrete addition to the universe of fact, each actual occasion microcosmically reflects the entire universe, according to its own unique, 'subjective form.' The occasion's subjective form is derived from (1) its particular situatedness within the cosmic nexus of mutually conditioning actualities; (2) the contribution of God to its formation, in the provision of available possibilities for it; and (3) its own final causal power, which it exercises in its selection of one of these possibilities for instantiation. Whitehead terms the process of becoming through which occasions pass on their way to completed actuality 'concrescence.' These atomic units of concrete experience are the fundamental constituents of the actual universe. With the completion of its concrescence, the actual occasion attains a finality that both satisfies its personal 'subjective aim' (its choice about what to be and do in the world) and defines it as a concrete datum for all subsequent actualities. Whitehead gives this final product of becoming a double name, signifying its twofold status as satisfied actual occasion, with its own intrinsic existence and value, and as settled causal factor relevant to the concrescences of other occasions. He calls the final actuality the 'subject-superject': "The ultimate metaphysical principle is the advance from disjunction to conjunction, creating a novel entity other than the entities given in disjunction. The novel entity is at once the togetherness of the 'many' which it finds, and also it is one among the disjunctive 'many' which it leaves; it is a novel entity, disjunctively among the many entities which it synthesizes. The Many become one, and are increased by one."[37]

Each such occasion uniquely embodies the ultimate metaphysical category of 'creativity'—which is the more basic ontological notion on which the more specialized concept of 'freedom' rests for Whitehead. "Creativity is the universal of universals characterizing ultimate matter of fact . . . [It] is the principle of *novelty*. An actual occasion is a novel entity in the 'many' which it unifies." For Whitehead, "This Category of the Ultimate replaces Aristotle's category of 'primary substance.'"[38]

Human beings, in Whitehead's thought, are not essentially different, in kind, from other entities. Rather, occasions of human consciousness—which are actual entities that emerge from the organic complexity of our bodily systems, as synthesized and transmitted via our brains—differ from other forms of actual occasions in degree, representing higher-grade examples of a monistic ontological schema that is consistent throughout the entire continuum of actual entities. In his Lowell Lectures of 1925, later published as *Science and the Modern World*, Whitehead criticizes modern Western philosophy for accepting two "inconsistent presuppositions" as fundamental to its worldview: "A scientific realism, based on mechanism, is conjoined with an unwavering belief in the world of men and higher animals as being composed of self-determining organisms."[39] Whitehead rejects the arbitrary division of reality that posits one world of value and final causation and one world of moral vacuity and determinism. However, unlike so much of contemporary philosophy, with its widespread acceptance of Weberian 'disenchantment,' Whitehead rejects the division not by divesting humans of their essential value and freedom but rather by investing the rest of reality with an analogous status.

To be clear, in Whitehead's panexperientialist ontology, the term 'experience' is used in an utterly basic, generic sense to denote a locus of 'feeling,' which is the subjective reception of the causal efficacy of the past as intrinsic to the constitution of the emerging actual occasion. (This notion of causal efficacy replaces the purely extrinsic conception of efficient causation in mechanistic forms of naturalism.) In this generic sense, the term does not carry any necessary connotation of *high* forms of experience, such as consciousness, which emerge only at the far end of the spectrum of organic complexity. 'Feelings' may be 'physical' or 'conceptual' (or a complex mix of the two), and, where feelings attain sufficient organic complexity, they become the basis for *thoughts*. But at the lower end of the scale of complexity (which includes the vast majority of actual entities in the universe), the synthesis of feeling attains no threshold of self-awareness. By way of illustration, consider an amoeba being prodded by a sharp microscopic instrument. As one watches the amoeba react to the stimulus by retreating from the instrument, one could quite meaningfully say, "It felt that," without thereby implying any conscious awareness on the amoeba's part.

Also, Whitehead does not attribute even experience in this most basic sense to objects such as rocks or chairs, which are merely amalgamations of simple actual entities, not organic 'societies' of actual entities that, through their social organization, constitute higher, more complex entities. An example of the latter is the human body, where simple actual occasions are 'socially ordered' into cells, and cells are socially ordered into organs, and organs are socially ordered into systems, and so on. But Whitehead does insist that any full-fledged actual entity—from a simple electron to an emergent moment of human consciousness—is an 'occasion of experience,' by which he means a (partially) self-ordering unit with an internal life constituted by the integration of a complex of feeling through the exercise of some measure (even if relatively negligible) of *final causal power of self-determination*. This exercise of final causation in the self-integration of every actual occasion is the expression of creativity, by which the occasion synthesizes its inheritance of past causal influences with its reception of forms of possibility from God, in order to construct itself as a subject-superject. There are, for Whitehead, no "vacuous actualities"[40] of the sort described by René Descartes and Isaac Newton. To repeat, *every completed actual occasion, in some meaningful ontological sense, represents a manifestation of choice*, even if the choice in question is a merely reiterative one—as will nearly universally be the case with 'primitive' actualities (such as electrons, which endure across series of occasions through simple inherited patterns transmitted through internal repetition).

Thus all actual occasions make determinations in relation to the eternal objects selected for inclusion in their 'subjective aims,' as an integral part of their respective processes of becoming. But these are determinations in a different sense from how I have previously used that term, in discussing the determinateness of the eternal objects themselves. A becoming actual occasion makes a determination (i.e., a *decision*) among already determinate (i.e., *definite, discrete*) possible alternatives for actualization.[41] The occasion's determination of its own concrescent subjective-superjective character—that is, its formal self-constitution and effective presentation of itself to the world—through its (relatively) free choice among the definite alternative possibilities available to it, does *not* add any further determination to the formal constitution (i.e., defining characteristics) of the alternative that it selects. (In this sense, Immanuel Kant is correct that "existence is not a predicate.")[42] The occasion's decision simply clothes the occasion itself, as a settled actuality, in the determinate form of the chosen alternative. Hence while the transition of a complex of eternal objects, representing a possible form for a concrescent actual occasion, from merely 'subsistent' abstract potentiality to manifestation in actuality is, definitively, the product of a determination, this determination does not impact the character of the relevant eternal objects nor of the possibility they constitute.

CREATURELY FREEDOM AND DIVINE FOREKNOWLEDGE

Speaking narrowly in terms of the character of future possibilities as they exist in the divine primordial imagination,[43] the position that I have outlined so far is consistent with the Molinist conception of divine foreknowledge. Both Molinism and Whiteheadianism (as I have developed it here) claim *precise*[44] divine foreknowledge of all possible states of affairs—and, therefore, all possible choices that might be made by the possible individuals that populate those states of affairs. However, as I indicated earlier, the Molinist and Whiteheadian conceptions of divine 'omniscience' diverge sharply over the issue of the openness of the future, in relation to the status of the future choices of actual individuals (and the actual choices of future individuals). Molinism holds that God knows not only all possible choices that any given future individual might make in any possible future in which that individual participates but also which of these possible futures will come to be and which choices that individual will actually make when they do. Contrarily, Whiteheadianism denies that God's foreknowledge encompasses not only what *might* be but also what *will* be the case in the future (except in the most utterly general terms and in relation to that which follows necessarily, rather than merely contingently, from the present state of affairs).

I have already indicated some theological reasons to prefer the Whiteheadian view, based on the impact that such a shift toward divine openness might have on Abrahamic conceptions of faith. Whiteheadian open theism meets the first criterion that I gave for preferring one comprehensive view of reality over another at the beginning of this chapter: it more naturally aligns with and supports the values and principles of liberal-democratic citizenship as viewed through the lens of epistemic anxiety. Now the question is whether it also meets the second criterion: Does Whitehead's view of the relationship between the divine primordial synthesis of possibility and the actual course of affairs in the world provide a more coherent understanding of reality than does classical theism? Obviously, I believe the answer is "yes." More specifically, I will now argue that the Whiteheadian perspective is preferable because it provides a more coherent and satisfactory account not only of the concept of creaturely *agency* but also—and which in my view essentially comes to the same thing—the conditions of creaturely *identity*. That is, it seems to me that the Whiteheadian perspective succeeds—where the Molinist perspective, like all versions of the classical perspective on these matters, fails—in making sense of the cluster of fundamental onto-epistemic characteristics and functions associated with 'selfhood' at the creaturely level.

Luis de Molina was a Spanish Jesuit, Scholastic theologian, and contemporary of Luther and Calvin who became a central figure in the doctrinal controversy over the reconciliation of divine grace and human liberty within the Catholic Church that ran parallel to Rome's external clash with the reformers. Molina was influenced by the new Renaissance humanism, and he sought to articulate an understanding of the God-world relation that would uphold human free will less ambiguously than did the standard Augustinian-Thomistic model, in his estimation. He, therefore, rejected the Augustinian conception of the *eternal presence* of all actual states of affairs in relation to the divine, which he saw as irreconcilable with any meaningful notion of human freedom or moral responsibility. However, being wed to the overall classical conception of the divine nature associated with Thomism, he did not wish to establish the reality of human freedom at the cost of absolute divine foreknowledge and immutability. So he required an alternative basis for God's sure knowledge of the actual course of the future.

Molina found this basis in the notion of divine 'middle knowledge' (*scientia media*), which was also being propagated at the time by his influential older, Portuguese contemporary Pedro da Fonseca. (It is unclear whether Molina inherited this notion from Fonseca or developed it independently. Fonseca uses the term *scientia mista*.) Molina further developed this notion and articulated a systematic formulation of it in his *Liberi Arbitrii cum Gratiæ Donis, Divina Præscientia, Providentia, Prædestinatione et Reprobatione Concordia*,[45] a work that sparked a firestorm of protest from traditionalist defenders of Augustinian eternalism but survived a decade-long papal inquiry without formal rebuke (ultimately, the Vatican took no side in the dispute, simply forbidding both sides from accusing one another of heresy).

'Middle knowledge' is so labeled because it straddles the traditional distinction between God's 'natural knowledge' (which Molina calls *scientia naturalis*)[46] and God's 'free knowledge' (*scientia libera*)[47] that had been established by Aquinas. Molina's understanding of God's natural knowledge corresponds closely to Whitehead's conception of the divine primordial envisagement of all possibility, prior to the divine primordial determination. This is God's eternal contemplation of possibility qua possibility. It (logically) precedes the issuance of God's creative decree. Moreover, since the content of God's natural knowledge is necessary, in the metaphysical sense, it is independent of God's will, or 'prevolitional.' It, therefore, constitutes an internal or essential limitation on the divine will, since God cannot will anything contrary to (i.e., absent from) this totality of the possible.

God's free knowledge, on the other hand, is God's knowledge of what God wills. It is, therefore, contingent and 'postvolitional.' It depends on the choices that God makes about what to create, so it might have been different from what it is, had God chosen differently than God in fact did. The content of God's free knowledge is analyzable as a comprehensive set of existential propositions of the form "*it is the case that p*"—because God's will is also eternal, the modal 'tenses' of temporality do not apply (to paraphrase Aquinas, God knows all such propositions in their 'presentiality'). According to Augustine and Aquinas, God's free knowledge encompasses the totality of actual occurrences, per se. For Molina, however, this equation of the content of the free knowledge with the actual is the locus of the classical theistic problem of evil and human responsibility.

Whereas his traditionalist opponents were satisfied to found God's decrees of predestination and reprobation regarding individual human souls on these two types of knowledge alone, Molina perceived that such an approach clearly implies a form of divine omnicausality that is irreconcilable with human freedom and responsibility. If God can infallibly decree which souls are bound for heaven and which for hell based solely on God's knowledge of what is possible and what God wills to be so, then the fate of each soul is wholly dependent on the divine will. There is, in such an account, no room for any *meaningful* reference to the role played by the will of the person whose soul is in question. (Molina, like Whitehead, holds that only a 'libertarian' conception of freedom is meaningful.) Thus Molina posits middle knowledge as a third type, which stands between the natural and the free and combines characteristics of each.

According to Molina, God knows the character and dispositions of every possible contingent being so perfectly and exhaustively that God can *inerrantly predict* what each such being will (or would) *freely do* in every possible set of circumstances in which that being might ever participate. This infallible predictive knowledge obviously depends on God's natural knowledge in that it is necessarily indexed to the totality of possibilities constituting the natural knowledge. It is also like God's natural knowledge in that it is independent of God's will. But it is not reducible to an aspect of God's natural knowledge, since the natural knowledge is, by definition, strictly neutral to the distinction between which possibilities will and which will not be actualized, whereas the middle knowledge, by definition, includes both conditional and counterfactual propositions.

Thus God's middle knowledge is also like God's free knowledge in that it is concerned with matters of contingency. Moreover, since, on this account, the contingencies of future creaturely conduct are (putatively) dependent on the noneternal determinations of creaturely volition, actuality is genuinely, essentially temporal in character, even for God. To put it in analytic terms, the addition of middle knowledge introduces *de re* temporal modalities into the divine epistemic economy. Whereas the all-determinative propositional content of Augustinian free knowledge is logically reducible to the present tense in every respect, middle knowledge is irreducibly tensed.

In other words, contra Augustine and Aquinas, according to Molina, God knows the future not because the future is already 'present' for God but, rather, because God perfectly foresees that which is *not yet present* even for God. So like Whiteheadianism (and unlike Augustinianism), Molinism seeks to establish an irreducible distinction between any given possibility 'x_p' that is primordially envisaged by God qua possibility, and the actuality 'x_a' that corresponds to that possibility as manifested in the course of events qua actuality. (In the Augustinian, account, since there is no substantive ontological criteria of identity by which one can differentiate an actuality known by God as eternally present in God's free knowledge from that actuality as temporally manifested in the world, $x_p = x_a$.) However, since, on the Molinist view, in any given situation one particular possibility is *guaranteed* to be actualized, in the course of events, it is unclear how one can, ultimately, escape the reductive identification (both formally and substantively) of any given x_p/x_a in their/its (verbally distinct) 'possible' and 'actual' modes.

The problem here lies precisely in Molina's hybridization of 'natural' and 'free' characteristics in his conception of middle knowledge. For it makes a muddle of the distinction between necessity and contingency and ignores the most basic logical implications of each of these categories in relation to the distinction between God and the world, per se. One way to clarify this problem is to observe that irrespective of its own claims about the status of middle knowledge, if Molinism is correct that God has infallible detailed knowledge of the course of the future, then, from the point of view of God, all true existential propositions, as such, must be understood as *necessary* propositions. In fact, given such an understanding of divine foreknowledge, there can be no contingent existential propositions whatsoever from God's perspective—only necessarily true and necessarily false existential propositions—precisely because propositional contingency in this case would imply that there is no guarantee as to which putatively contingent proposition would actually turn out to be true, in the course of events. Hence we must ask, if the propositional content of God's knowledge of the future is *eternal* and no future decision by any actual agent could *conceivably* turn out otherwise than as is known eternally by God, then what sense can there be in labeling the truths to which God's middle knowledge refers 'contingent'?

Indeed, so far as I can see, if God is conceived of as being eternally and infallibly prescient, it follows that the content of God's prescience *must* be eternally actual. For if this were not the case, then (as Molina recognizes) God's eternally prescient vision of the course of actual events would not be a *sufficient condition* of the actualization of that course of events, as envisaged by God in aeternum. But then the actual course of the future would be dependent on some factor outside of Godself—which would in turn imply that God's foreknowledge could *not*, in fact, be infallible—since the truth of any existential proposition held eternally by God would be a function of some factor not present in God's eternal relation to the proposition in question. (This is, of course, one of the main lines of arguments that Augustinians have used to counter Molina's view within the context of the classical theistic consensus.)

Thus only if God's envisagement of the future is, in and of itself, a sufficient condition of the actualization of the content of that envisagement can God's foreknowledge be infallible—which is why the classical conceptions of divine omniscience and omnipotence are logically inseparable. And if God's foreknowledge *is* a sufficient condition of the actualization of this eternally apprehended envisagement of the future, then the future itself must be understood *as a function of* the divine faculty of envisagement by which the eternal determination (i.e., the primordial 'synthesis') of all possible and actual states of affairs is constituted. But this further implies that, as an *aspect of* the eternally envisaged future, the (apparent) 'freedom' of the (apparent) 'individuals' that populate the divinely foreknown actual states of affairs is wholly reducible to this temporally transcendent function of divine understanding. As I have already indicated, such an implication removes the basis for not only the notion of genuine creaturely agency but also any substantive differentiation of the identity conditions of the (formally) individuated objective elements of the divine envisagement and the identity conditions of the (apparent) subjective individual agents to which these objective elements of the eternal divine synthesis correspond from a temporally relative point of view.

In other words, Molinism fails adequately to conceive of and account for individual agency—and, therefore, fails to offer any coherent criterion of identity to differentiate between creatures and Creator—because the *actual freedom* of such individuals is not reducible to a merely *formally possible* plurality of contrary alternatives in God's anticipatory apprehension. Put alternatively, the merely formalist understanding of 'libertarian freedom' embraced by the Molinist conception of divine middle knowledge is neither morally nor ontologically satisfactory, because it (unintentionally) implies a strict (and incoherent) pantheism—just as Augustinianism does.

As I have already indicated, according to Whitehead's understanding of the metaphysically basic character of subjective freedom, the expression of 'creativity' in the formation of the actual occasion's 'subjective aim' is a *substantive*, rather than merely formal, element of the ontological event of concrescent becoming (indeed, creativity *is* the ontological 'substance' of the becoming event), for Whitehead agrees with Plato and Locke that *to be* an actual individual is *to exercise power*. There can be no merely passive, or purely receptive, actuality. And for Whitehead this point further implies that *to choose* is to exert an influence on the character and constitution of one's environment (both local and total). It is to do real work in the world, to reshape—in accordance with one's choice, and in proportion to the efficacy of that choice—the conditions of reality as related to the context and scope of the choice at hand.

Certainly, receptivity is involved in the process of choosing. The agent must choose from some given set of possible alternatives for it. On Whitehead's account, as I previously discussed, these alternatives are 'felt' by the concrescing subject as elements in 'the many,' which are the received, 'superjective' environmental conditions that are presented to the emergent subject through the efficient causal efficacy of the past actual agents, whose own prior choices have defined the environmental context of the concrescing subject's alternatives for self-actualization. But even this receptive aspect of the subject's becoming is not wholly passive, for the subject actively *re-presents* this 'many' to itself as a function of its very subjectivity—which is emergent from, but (definitively) not identical to, the objectivity of its antecedent causal circumstances.

To be clear, this is not 'representation' in the sense developed in the work of Descartes, Locke, and other, pre-Kantian 'representationalists,' but in the sense that one finds under the label of 'synthesis' in Kant's treatment of the 'spontaneous' unity of 'transcendental apperception' as a function of the activity of the faculty of understanding in the constitution of the individual's experience—and, in an important sense, as the constitutive faculty of the individual's personhood as such.[48] According to Whitehead, Kant's account of "an act of experience as a constructive functioning" represents a seminal moment in modern philosophy and one of the most important insights in the entire history of philosophy.[49]

To have (or, rather, to *be*) a *self*, Kant tells us, is to *actively* synthesize—that is, to re-present to oneself the data of one's experience. The transcendental synthesis of the understanding is not only a conceptual explication of the coherence of the experiential field containing the objects of empirical 'appearances.' For Kant, it is also a fundamental principle of personal identity. This principle is taken up by Whitehead under the concept of 'concrescence,' which I discussed earlier, and developed ontologically in a much more satisfactory way—and in a way that sheds light on the underlying ontological problem with Molinism (and every other form of classical theism).

The first thing to observe is that for both Kant and Whitehead the activity of 'synthesis' or 'concrescence' that constitutes the emergent unity of personal experience for the subject is, eo ipso, the intersection of ontological and epistemic conditions of selfhood at which personal freedom is located in their respective systems. For Kant, the transcendental synthesis effected by the understanding necessarily functions in accordance with the universal, and deterministic, 'laws of empirical advance,' insofar as it is, by definition, a synthesis of objects of empirical appearance, which can appear in no other way than in accordance with these 'laws.' However, as a *transcendental* function of human subjectivity, this synthesis is also, by definition, an activity of the noumenal self (i.e., the hypothetical *soul*, as the 'transcendental object' grounding the possibility of empirical subjectivity), which—again, by definition—cannot be conceived of in terms of any dependence on the laws that regulate merely 'apparent' (i.e., empirical) objects. Thus one may, I think, justifiably read into Kant's account the proposition that both the coherence of empirical experience and the existence of the subject of such experience (as a real, individuated personal entity) depend on the intervention into the process of the unfolding of antecedent causal conditions of an active determination of self-constructive consciousness that transcends the mere amalgamation of the effects of those causal conditions at the physical locus of their convergent valences.

Indeed, what we see in this part of the *Critique of Pure Reason*,[50] it seems to me, is Kant (somewhat unreflectively) developing the fundamental underpinnings for an ontology of serially ordered occasional selfhood. The problem is that Kant fails to perceive the full implications of this potentially epoch-making shift and, therefore, attempts to graft this revolutionary insight about the self-constructive character of each moment of empirical subjectivity onto a traditional enduring-substance conception of the noumenal self. And, thus, his system lapses into incoherence.

In other words, Kant articulates a *serial-atomic phenomenology* that fundamentally contradicts the logic of traditional enduring-substance ontology—to which he clings, rather than taking the next logical step and resolving the contradiction in favor of a serial-atomic ontology of temporal endurance. Hence he fails to see that his insight regarding the necessarily active—that is, *agential*—character of selfhood implies the essential incoherence of ontological determinism (and so, it seems, have most contemporary analytic philosophers, the majority of whom have, in one way or another, maintained Kant's nonsensical notion of the 'symmetricality' of time).

It remained, therefore, for Whitehead to recognize and develop the full implications of Kant's insight. Whitehead saw clearly that freedom—or, more precisely, 'creativity'—must be *immanent within*, rather than transcendent of, the temporal order of subjective experience. This is why Whitehead's insistence on the substantive character of the act of creativity as constitutive of the actuality of the concrescent subject—as that which is required to manifest an *abstract* determinate possibility in the *concrete* superjective determination of a concrescent actuality—is so crucial to the ultimate coherence of his account of creaturely freedom.

On the Whiteheadian view, God's primordial envisagement of the eternal possibilities for actualization that are relevant to some future individual's choice in a given situation does not (indeed, cannot) include knowledge of which will in fact be actualized (assuming that the given situation itself is realized in the course of actual events), precisely because such knowledge would imply that the apparent 'freedom' of the individual in question is logically reducible to a merely formal component of God's temporally transcendent imagination, rather than being the very substantive essence of the contingent temporal process of concrescent becoming that constitutes the actual individual as such. Thus, according to Whitehead, the relevant possibilities in the divine primordial apprehension are known only qua possibilities, each of which has *some* relative probability of actualization—and, thus, none of which can be *identified with* the actual outcome, qua actuality. This understanding preserves both the logical and the ontological distinction between the identity of the subjective-agential determination of the individual through its exercise of its own creative freedom and the identity of any and every particular primordially envisaged possibility (including whichever one of these the individual does, in fact, actually manifest).

Kant's system also provides a useful point of comparison in the current context because it manifests Augustinian eternalism in its critical-hypothetical appeal to the notion of a noumenal or 'intuitive' (i.e., divine) intellect and in its treatment of the *real unity* underlying the apparent temporal diversity of all past, present, and future phenomenal objects and states of affairs, which defines 'actuality' in Kant's system. G. W. F. Hegel recognized and seized on this implication in Kant's thought in his reframing of phenomenal reality as the deterministic unfolding of the eternally predetermined dialectical representation of the one, all-encompassing noumenal reality of 'the Idea'—which is (at least by implication, if not Hegel's intent) the only being that is really 'real' in his system. William James offered a wonderfully concise formulation of the implied character of reality that corresponds to the Kantian and Hegelian—and, I would add, the Molinist—perspective with which he became so deeply disenchanted, namely, that it represents "one vast instantaneous co-implicated completeness."[51]

In Kantian terms, the classical notion of infallible divine knowledge of the future implies the mutual identity of the faculties of 'imagination' and 'understanding' in God. So God's eternal envisagement of all possible and actual states of affairs represents what we may term a 'metaphysical synthesis of *intuitive* apperception,' whereby all reality is not merely perceived but actually *constituted*, as such. (The Whiteheadian view for which I am advocating also supports the notion of a metaphysical synthesis of apperception, but not one that is 'intuitive' in the Kantian sense referenced here.)[52] Hence the classical conception of God implies that actuality, including apparently futural actuality, is defined by—indeed, can coherently be defined *as nothing other than*—the eternally self-constitutional, and logically 'simple,' unity of the divine consciousness. Therefore, God is all in all and responsible for all. And we are merely aspects of this utterly deterministic "coimplicated completeness," with no freedom whatsoever in any meaningful sense.

Moreover, as I mentioned earlier in this chapter, in relation to Kierkegaard's critique of Hegel, if God knows, prior to deciding what world to create, what every actual outcome of whatever decision is made would be, then one must ask whether God's own decision about what world to create can be understood as a "free choice." After all, if God has perfect knowledge of every detail of the respective futures associated with every possible world, then God must surely have perfect knowledge of the total moral worth respectively associated with each possible world. Given the notion of divine omnibenevolence (which, presumably, the Molinist will not wish to abandon), it therefore follows that there is one and only one choice that God could make consistently with God's own character. Since, as I have previously mentioned, there would be a particular 'best of all possible worlds' that would be known to God as such before God's decision to create, and, therefore, would surely constrain God's 'choice' to the selection of that specific alternative. (In this sense, then, the classical 'free knowledge' is not really 'free.') Whereas, since Whitehead's God must factor in the unknowns represented by the actual choices of future free individuals, the divine creative determination cannot be reduced to a simple calculation of fully known factors leading necessarily to one particular, inescapable judgment.

In short, the implicit pantheistic consequences of the classical conception of divinity can only be avoided through a revision of this conception that breaks with its claim to infallible divine foreknowledge of the actual course of events (as well as the logically corollary claim of divine omnipotence). Only if creaturely freedom is understood as the essential, substantive characteristic that differentiates temporal actuality from eternal ideality—such that it cannot be logically reduced to, nor adequately represented in terms of, the formal constitution of the order of eternal ideality—can we maintain the logical and ontological distinctions between Creator and creatures, as such, without which the notion of 'free will' (on both sides of this distinction) is rendered nonsensical.

Whiteheadian Metaphysics and Political Libertarianism

Finally, before moving on to discuss the connections to be made between the foregoing account of free will and the God-world relation and contemporary deliberative democratic theory, I would like to note one important aspect of the relevance of this account in relation to my own appeal to 'classic liberal' political norms throughout the present work. In Chapter 1, I indicated that my own construal of the logic of these norms does *not* run in the direction of political 'libertarianism,' as that term is typically employed in both its classic and contemporary systematic constructions. My explication of Whiteheadian *metaphysical* 'libertarianism' here clarifies several, related reasons why this is so.

Generally speaking, libertarian political thought presupposes a reductively atomistic view of the individual. Politically, socially, and economically, the libertarian self is characteristically constructed as having merely external, transactional relations with others. Particularly in its crasser (and, sadly, currently more popular and influential) forms, libertarianism, therefore, asserts an unsustainably simplistic conception of individual 'independence' as the highest virtue, value, and desideratum of human life. Moreover, libertarian political theories tend to take little or no account of the differences in the existing conditions under which different individuals live and the ways in which these differences either constrain or enable individuals, creating inequities of freedom that would be magnified, rather than eliminated, were the current political order to be replaced with a libertarian regime. Thus political libertarianism tends to be associated epistemologically and morally with 'rational egoism' and economically and socially with laissez-faire capitalism.

Whiteheadian ontology also conceives of the individual—the actual occasion—as atomistic. However, as I have already made clear, Whitehead's atomic individual is thoroughly *relational* in its constitution as such. For Whitehead, all independence is founded on *inter*dependence. In the moment of decision, the individual occasion stands alone, but it does so within, and among, definite relationships and limitations that both supply and circumscribe the context of the decision and the self-actualizing agent's freedom to choose. Also, because the experiences of others are, quite literally, the building blocks from which the emerging individual is formed, there is no absolute separation between individuals, as such, despite their atomic character. The experiential value—positive or negative—realized by past actual occasions becomes part of present occasions, and these present occasions will, in turn, become part of future occasions. Whitehead treats this fundamental mutual relevance and participation of actual entities in and for each other under the category of 'internal relatedness.' And this metaphysical generalization of the notion that we are constituted by our environment provides an ontological basis for a 'social' conception of selfhood and value.

While past and present conditions are not entirely determinative of the future, they do delimit the standpoint and potential satisfaction of each actual entity. In the context of political and social ethics, this distinction between relative and absolute freedom is vital. The human agent is free to choose. Yet her choices are ineluctably conditioned by her personal past and social antecedents, including her assimilation of—and standing relative to—the history, values, and norms or her community. She is—in the most thoroughgoing sense—embedded within a web of historical, social, cultural, economic, and political conditions that must be accounted for in any analysis of what freedom means for her and how it can best be promoted and protected. If one really wants to maximize freedom for all—rather than just for those who already are in a position to take advantage of their privileged standing in the present order—libertarian deregulation of society is decidedly not the way to go.

Whitehead never substantively engaged with political theory in a way that clarified his own specific commitments beyond a general appreciation for modern Western liberal democracy in a broad sense. He does offer a sustained discussion of the emergence and development of this modern Western perspective in *Adventures of Ideas*, and much has been made of the fact that at one point in that discussion he says, "Now the intercourse between individuals and between social groups takes one of two forms, force or persuasion. Commerce is the great example of intercourse by way of persuasion. War, slavery, and governmental compulsion exemplify the reign of force."[53] It is tempting, of course, to read the strikingly unambiguous (even naïve) characterization of "commerce" as being categorically opposite coercion and the classification of governmental compulsion alongside war and slavery, as indicating a strongly libertarian sensibility. But the overall context—not only in this work but also in Whitehead's total opus—makes clear, I think, that Whitehead would include the voluntary association of mutually empowered and legally equal citizens in a liberal democratic order as falling under what he means by "commerce" in the "enlarged sense" in which he employs this term, which he says "involves every species of interchange which proceeds by way of mutual persuasion."[54] What he means in this passage by "governmental compulsion," I think, is any *despotic* exercise of political authority, as I have defined that term in Chapters 3 and 4. On my reading, therefore, Whitehead was not endorsing libertarianism in the sense of the view I have just criticized. (And if he was, then I would be quite willing to say we should depart from him in that regard.)

It is also interesting to note, in the current context, the consonance of the libertarian ideal of selfhood with the classical conception of divinity. Ironically, one finds this correlation even in explicitly atheistic forms of libertarianism, such as Randian Objectivism. Take, for example, Ayn Rand's famous description of the fully actualized human individual in her Objectivist novel *The Fountainhead*, where her egoistic protagonist, Howard Roark opines that "[t]he creators were not selfless. It is the whole secret of their power—that it was self-sufficient, self-motivated, self-generated. A first cause, a fount of energy, a life force, a Prime Mover. The creator served nothing and no one. He lived for himself . . . The basic need of the creator is independence. The reasoning mind . . . demands total independence in function and in motive. To a creator, all relations with men are secondary."[55]

Here we see the insidious power of the classical conception of God as an imitational ideal that so infiltrated Western consciousness and culture that it persists even in places where the idea of God, per se, has been repudiated. Whether Rand was positing this ideal in a sort of Feuerbachian mode or was simply unconscious of the source of her attachment to it, the moral viciousness of her vision is revealing because it unabashedly embraces and makes explicit implications of the classical conception of God that are logically inescapable, even if many believers find ways to moderate these implications (and thereby cast doubt on their own attachment to this conception).

CHAPTER 6

PROCESS METAPHYSICS AND DEMOCRATIC DELIBERATION

Reason is inexplicable if purpose be ineffective.

—Alfred North Whitehead, *The Function of Reason*[1]

IN THE LAST CHAPTER, I MADE A preliminary case for Whiteheadian process metaphysics as a 'comprehensive' perspective that offers powerful complimentary support for the sort of perspective-neutral fallibilist justification of liberalism that I formulated in the first four chapters. I also argued that it corrects certain problems with classical metaphysics and theology. In this final chapter, I will more specifically connect the process perspective to current conversations in political philosophy and theory regarding the proper form, character, and conditions of public 'deliberation' among diverse political conversants.

As I have noted previously, fallibilism needs to be connected to respect for persons to complete the warrant for classical liberalism. Each participant in the public sphere should enter into it with her own comprehensive perspective supplying the basis for respect and with the epistemic anxiety occasioned by an authentic recognition of her own fallibility moderating the temptation to equate such respect with the assertion of the particularistic elements of her own perspective. As long as an individual (or group) within the public sphere affirms *some* basis for respect for other persons—and this basis is not intrinsically connected to an ethic of moral coercion—her (their) perspective is reconcilable with fallibilist liberalism, as I have developed it here. But as I also noted in the last chapter, some perspectives better support both fallibilism and liberalism than others. This is also true in relation to the basic presuppositions and principles at work in contemporary deliberative theory, where it seems to me that the various comprehensive perspectives—that is, metaphysical (or antimetaphysical) doctrines—that have been adopted by most deliberative theorists actually undermine, rather than support, their affirmations of a deliberative ethic.

As I develop the following outline of a deliberative conception of respect for persons based on the comprehensive perspective of process metaphysics, I will also note where I am moderating or conditioning my claims on behalf of the process perspective because of the dictates of epistemic anxiety. In some respects, my adoption of the overarching fallibilist position I have developed in this work has significantly shifted my own understanding of my process-oriented commitments. Indeed, this chapter is a substantively revised and expanded version of an essay I published in the journal *Process Studies* several years ago, and the significant revisions and additions I have made here almost entirely relate to this shift.[2]

Over the last two decades process thinkers have very self-consciously sought to engage an ever-wider range of topics and interlocutors in order to demonstrate the relevance of process thought to issues in all the various spheres of human concern. One focus of increasing attention is the relevance of process ideas to issues in political and social theory and practice. Coincidentally, over the last two decades a prominent movement has emerged from within political and social theory to which, I believe, process thinkers would do well to address themselves more systematically. We may profitably refer to this movement—which has deep roots in nineteenth- and early twentieth-century American democratic and social thought—as 'deliberative theory.'[3] It is a fairly broad movement that has become quite well developed in a relatively short time and now receives much attention from philosophers,[4] political scientists[5] and historians,[6] rhetoricians,[7] education theorists,[8] and even neuroscientists[9]—not to mention civic organizations, academic and private institutions and enterprises, and so on.

Since I am, once again, bringing together groups of thinkers who may not be overly familiar with one another's work, I will begin by providing a very brief, taxonomic overview of the main types of deliberative theories and the central issues with which they are concerned. I will, then, indicate a number of points on which I believe that there can be productive discussion between process and deliberative theorists, particularly noting issues with regard to which process metaphysics and ontology provides strong support to fundamental assumptions, ideas, and practices endorsed (or presupposed) by deliberative theory. Once again, my aim here is not to propose a specific process theory of deliberation. Rather, I will indicate a number of substantive points on which process thought can provide needed theoretical support for deliberative theory, as well as how, generally speaking, a process theory of deliberation might bring together elements of each of the main types of existing deliberative theories. (For this reason I have included substantial bibliographical information in the notes to the text.) As I will try to show, there is much ground for common cause between these two groups of thinkers.

CONTEMPORARY DELIBERATIVE THEORY

The notion of 'deliberative theory' in a very broad sense of the term can be traced back at least to ancient rhetorical theory (especially Aristotle's), as well as to classical republican political thought—though the pronounced socioeconomic elitism of classical republicanism is at odds with the strong neopopulist impulse of most contemporary deliberative theory. Here, however, I am using the term more narrowly to denote a particular constellation of ideas and positions in—or related to—recent American political and social thought and practice that focus on the connection between models of deliberative communication and the values and norms of democratic society. Though it would not be wholly inaccurate to view contemporary deliberative theory as an American outgrowth from Continental 'discourse theory,' especially as developed by German thinkers like Jürgen Habermas and Karl-Otto Apel[10]—an outgrowth that has, in many cases, been significantly filtered through the influence of John Rawls' later work[11]—this view would represent only a partial one. For one thing, deliberative theory is significantly more heterogeneous than discourse theory (more on that momentarily). For another, deliberative theory typically incorporates peculiarly American notions of democratic society and education—it owes as much, at least, to Dewey as to Habermas. As suggested earlier, deliberative theory in the United States has been, from the beginning, highly *practical and populist* in its emphasis. The theoretical development of deliberative thought by political philosophers and theorists has proceeded hand in hand with its practical development (and evaluation) by advocates (and critics) in political science, public policy, education theory, and so on.

Current deliberative theory, especially as it relates to democratic theory, takes as one of its primary conversational starting points a group of influential works that appeared almost simultaneously in the mid- to late 1990s, including Amy Gutmann and Dennis Thompson's *Democracy and Disagreement*, Seyla Benhabib's *Democracy and Difference*, and James Bohman's *Public Deliberation: Pluralism, Complexity, and Democracy*, among others. Gutmann and Thompson's book, especially, garnered a wide range of scholarly response and has helped set the terms of many of the major debates about, and within, deliberative theory.[12]

However, one must be careful not to over generalize when speaking of deliberative theory. Philosophically speaking, the movement contains a number of significant, and significantly diverse, strands. This is true even if one focuses more narrowly on deliberative theories of democratic political society (and all the rest of deliberative theory—of education, as a rhetorical model, as a historical lens, and so on—relates in some way to democratic theory). Loosely speaking, one might identify four primary types of deliberative theories of democratic discourse: (1) *liberal theories*, which typically stress the traditional liberal 'public' versus 'nonpublic'/'private' distinction and primarily procedural conceptions of justice;[13] (2) *virtue theories*, which focus on the development and cultivation of deliberative 'dispositions' as a means of democratic character formation;[14] (3) *hybrid liberal/virtue theories*, which, as the term suggests, seek to bring together the notions of procedural norms and virtuous attitudes and patterns of behavior—and which, therefore, typically make more direct reference to concrete deliberative models, situations, and practices;[15] and (4) *agonistic* (or *difference*) *theories*, which stress the irresolvability of certain fundamental perspectival differences or disagreements, often relating to issues of group identity (e.g., race, gender, religious affiliation).[16]

Liberal deliberative theorists may or may not agree with Rawls' repudiation of the attempt to provide comprehensive justifications for liberal principles in his later work, but they almost invariably agree with his use of the public/nonpublic distinction to mark out a public-political space for deliberative discourse that does not privilege—or perhaps even reference—any particular religious or philosophical worldview. In this regard, liberal deliberative theorists are largely in line with liberal political theorists more generally, and a basic presupposition of this perspective is that democratic justice is (primarily) procedural in nature: just outcomes proceed (perhaps necessarily?)

from just deliberative procedures. Hence the liberal deliberative theorist claims that whatever substantive *injustices*—as opposed to, say, *inequalities*, which may or may not be considered unjust[17]—currently exist in American political society are primarily the result of unjust electoral and decision-making procedures. The task of political theorists is, therefore, to offer systematic suggestions about how to correct or improve these procedures. The challenge for these liberal deliberative theorists is the same as for liberal theorists of the standard model discussed in Chapter 4: to produce a substantively neutral proceduralist conception of deliberation that is not too "thin" to do the work required of political discourse in a modern democratic society. In this context, the challenge particularly relates to the formulation of perspective-neutral criteria of good faith deliberation and reliable opinion/knowledge formulation robust enough to be meaningful.

Virtue-oriented deliberative theorists, on the other hand, may or may not agree with Alasdair MacIntyre's famous claim that there is no way in which to show that one 'tradition' (i.e., historical sociocultural and political nexus of norms and practices) is objectively superior to others, but they all agree that it is the widespread existence of virtuous 'dispositions,' not the formal correctness of certain procedural norms and practices, that ultimately creates and sustains just political and social conditions.[18] Thus, according to this view, political and social theorists ought to maintain a broad focus on the cultivation of such dispositions among citizens, rather than a narrow focus on the reformation of particular existing political procedures. To be sure, deliberative virtue theorists expect that, where necessary, virtuous citizens will attend to the injustice of political procedures, but the point is precisely that better citizens make for more just political processes, not the other way around. Of course, this normative inversion raises its own questions. As the title of MacIntyre's influential work *Whose Justice? Which Rationality* indicates, virtue theorists must face not only the question of whether there are ultimately nonarbitrary reasons for preferring certain culturally contingent matrices of virtue over others but also whether a virtue-based understanding of justification is sufficient to warrant a nonarbitrary commitment to genuinely deliberative discourse as a sociopolitical norm.[19]

Hybrid deliberative theorists,[20] such as Gutmann and Thompson, mix the liberal concern for just procedures with the virtue theorists' concern for character formation and proper dispositional attitudes. There is typically a strong emphasis on historical and/or constitutional norms (both procedural and dispositional), as well as on the educational and civic transmission of such norms. Hybrid theorists often carve out more nuanced positions in relation to problem cases and scenarios by offering middle-way alternatives between the respective interpretations and responses of liberal and virtue theorists. Such theorists typically value the practical benefits of dispositional inculcation just insofar as such inculcation supports and protects the existence and application of traditional liberal norms. Methodologically, then, hybrid theorists tend toward a somewhat casuistic approach, but their casuistry is, so to speak, Aquinian in nature: rather than seeking to discover the proper principles of conduct through an examination of case studies, hybrid theorists use complex or problem cases to work out and demonstrate the proper application of liberal principles that are already taken to be *universally*—or perhaps *constitutionally*—foundational. Obviously, one can imagine a multitude of possible hybrid positions, with diverse proportions and emphases in their respective admixtures of liberal and virtue conceptions. As I noted in Chapter 2, such a hybridization is precisely what I have formulated in this work, through the connection between the universalism of my analysis of human fallibility and the dispositional character of my description of virtuous epistemic anxiety.

Finally, 'agonistic'—or 'difference'[21]—deliberative theorists focus attention on the irreducibly conflictual character of deliberative (and especially democratic) discourse. On the one hand, agonistic theorists differ from liberal theorists in that they reject the latter's diremption of 'public' and 'nonpublic' belief and discourse, and of 'civil society' and the 'state.' On the other hand, they differ from virtue theorists in that agonism emphasizes the modes and means by which diverse groups (and individuals) encounter one another through the divisive lens of difference, which is related to their respective and competing claims and dispositions, rather than the modes and means of transmission by which such claims and dispositions (i.e., 'identities') are constructed and maintained. Agonistic theory, therefore, includes the methodological treatment of what is today generally (and often hostilely) labeled 'identity politics,' but it also generalizes its claims beyond the misleading confines of such a narrow label, recognizing all interest groups as identity groups and rejecting the implicit exemption of majority groups from this description. Agonistic theory claims to offer a 'thicker,' more complex and nuanced understanding of deliberative engagement and mutual respect. Interestingly, agonistic theorists tend to recognize and even, in a way, appreciate the classical *conservative* conception of politics as essentially constituted by power relations between groups. Thus such theorists may view even their own particular normative commitments—to the principle/virtue of 'tolerance,' for example—as a function of ultimately arbitrary (or perhaps 'instrumental' or 'pragmatic') preference, rather than any overarching and universal moral foundation. Given process metaphysics' strong focus on the conditional character of freedom, as related to the social conditions—in the most inclusive possible sense of this term—under which every actual entity becomes, any process theory of deliberative democracy will also need to make significant appeal to the insights of agonistic models.

In spite of the very real and important differences that I have just outlined, we are justified in considering 'deliberative theory' as a single overarching movement because all these groups of thinkers share certain fundamental commitments. Since there is such diversity regarding proper modes and means among deliberative theorists, it may be best to view their commonalities in terms of *aims*. All deliberative theorists, of whatever stripe, are committed to the notion that *communication of the proper sort* (i.e., open and honest, noncoercive, nontendentious, and so on) is fundamental to the creation of a better, more just society—and that, since we are essentially communicative beings in any case, we might as well communicate in a manner that maximizes justice and utility. Understanding, sponsoring, and supporting such communication is, therefore, central to the common goal of deliberative theorists to enable citizens to engage in a more productive conversation with one another.

The ideal deliberative society would, in a sense, represent a localized actualization of what Apel has called the ideal 'communication community.'[22] Both Habermas and Apel, in somewhat different ways, define the 'right' and the 'good' as that which, hypothetically, would be agreed on by the consensus of an indefinitely extended community of rational discussants engaged in a fair and open discourse on whatever relevant issue.[23] Of course, not all types of deliberative theorists accept the underlying moral-epistemological claim in this view. Some would say instead that ideal discourse would aid in the *discovery* of, but would not itself determine, what is right or good. Others would say that the 'right' and the 'good' are relative to instrumental or pragmatic considerations that are essentially historical, not 'ideal.' But they, too, view deliberative communication as essential—as the most effective and appropriate way of bringing such considerations to light and determining their relative significance.

Thus, deliberative theorists also share a common concern with the incapacity (and/or unwillingness) of many Americans to competently participate in anything resembling such an ideal discursive process. Accordingly, they bemoan the manifest failure of both the government and the corporate media as supposed conduits of social and political discourse, and of the educational system as one important venue in which citizens (and future citizens) are trained to value and engage their own discursive capacities. Here we see the deep imprint of John Dewey's conception of the nature and function of social interaction and democratic discourse on contemporary deliberative theory. In *Liberalism and Social Action*, Dewey writes, "The crisis in liberalism is connected with [a] failure to develop and lay hold of an adequate conception of intelligence integrated with social movements [as] a factor giving them direction."[24] If we substitute 'democracy' for 'liberalism' in this formula—a substitution that seems consonant with Dewey's rather expansive definition of the latter term,[25] then we have a wonderfully concise statement of the underlying logic of deliberative theory.

Dewey discusses the various permutations that the notion of 'liberalism' has undergone in the first part of the aforementioned work, but, from his own perspective, the idea of 'liberalism' fundamentally signifies the prioritization of "the free play of intelligence" as a creative force in society.[26] Once human intelligence is freed from artificial cultural constraints and dogmatic presuppositions, Dewey believes that it will naturally seek a progressive development (and equitable distribution) of the material and intellectual conditions of 'liberty.' But Dewey rejects the one-sided identification of liberal freedom with purely individualistic, 'libertarian' conceptions of rights and the good, as is apparent in his list of "the ideals of liberalism": "the conception of *the common good as the measure of political organization and policy*, of liberty as the most precious trait and very seal of individuality, of *the claim of every individual to the full development of his capacities*."[27] And 'intelligence' is not, according to Dewey, merely a "ready-made possession of individuals," a "native endowment unaffected by social relationships,"[28] but, rather, a dynamic social process of discovery, evaluation, accommodation, and cooperative exchange. Hence the creation of a society in which every individual has the most expansive range of personal autonomy possible depends not on a libertarian regulatory minimalism but, rather, the recognition and provision of the conditions necessary for all individuals, equally, to be able to develop and employ the 'capacities'—both epistemic and material—required for the exercise of genuine autonomy.

Though registered in the context of the early 1930s, Dewey's lament that "[t]he inchoate state of social knowledge is reflected in the two fields where intelligence might be supposed to be most alert and most continuously active, education and the formation of social policies in legislation"[29] resonates strongly for the contemporary deliberative theorist. Regardless of whether they frame their principles from a 'liberal,' 'virtue,' 'hybrid,' or 'agonistic' perspective, deliberative theorists share Dewey's fundamental concern that "[t] here does not now exist the kind of social organization that even permits the average human being to share the potentially available social intelligence. Still less is there a social order that has for one of its chief purposes the establishment of conditions that will move the mass of individuals to appropriate and use what is at hand."[30]

Generally speaking, therefore, deliberative theorists seek the realization, in some form or another, of what Dewey called a "planning society." Such a society is open, flexible, responsive, and highly ethical. It is also a society in which the notion of 'education' is generalized onto all social and political action and interaction, a society in which *the learning process* is coincident with *the social process* as such.[31] The political philosopher and educational theorist Alan Ryan has coined the term "educating society" in order to indicate the expansive pedagogical element in this Deweyan conception of civil society, observing that "[a]n educating society is one that tries to maximize the intelligence and perceptiveness of all its citizens, while recognizing that we do not naturally divide into teachers and taught, and that there is no curriculum laid up in a pedagogical heaven."[32] The qualifications at the end of this statement are, of course, crucial. Where many deliberative theorists—and I—part company with Dewey is on his overly expansive endorsement of "[a]pproximation to the use of scientific method of investigation and of the engineering mind in the invention and projection of far-reaching social plans."[33] From my own fallibilist perspective, when Dewey turns in this direction, he tends quickly to lose sight of the primacy of individual liberty and begins to equate the common good more with the achievement of consensus and, in some cases, the production of "far-reaching social plans" that are too particularistic in terms of the values they exhibit to stand the scrutiny of the sorts of limiting criteria for liberal regulation that I linked to epistemic anxiety in Chapter 4.

This important qualification notwithstanding, clearly, the Deweyan understanding of a self-consciously deliberative society requires a more robust conception of democratic discourse than is provided by 'liberalism' in the narrow sense of libertarian individualism. Dewey also demonstrates the 'hybrid' character of his position when he claims that "the primary . . . responsibility of a liberalism that intends to be a vital force . . . is first of all education, in the broadest sense of that term." He observes, "Schooling is a part of the work of education, but education in its full meaning includes all the *influences that go to form the attitudes and dispositions (of desire as well as belief), which constitute dominant habits of mind and character*."[34] Besides the connection made here between liberal goals and the inculcation of virtuous "attitudes and dispositions," this formulation also illustrates the ambitious character that continues to permeate contemporary deliberative theory. Dewey calls not merely for a revitalization of American democracy but, rather, a fundamental reconstitution of it. Though not all contemporary deliberative theorists go this far, they all share a common conviction that American democracy and public discourse is fundamentally flawed, distorted, or broken in some way and that fixing it will require at least some systemic change.

Here, again, we must be careful not to exaggerate the commonality between different sorts of deliberative theories. One might argue, for instance, that agonistic deliberation—even in an ideal form—suggests something more like a "negotiating society," rather than a planning society. After all, if social and political deliberation is ultimately defined by the collision of diverse interests, then it will be the negotiation of (and between) such interests that dominates such deliberation. But this point, though accurate as far as it goes, is also misleading. There is no reason that a sufficiently "thick" view of social and political "planning" cannot incorporate the negotiation of diverse interests as one of its central features—as well as one of its primary *ends*. Indeed, it is hard to imagine successful social or political planning that did not do so. Moreover, the fact that a theorist emphasizes the fundamental role of difference in social and political discourse and decision-making in no way implies that this theorist does not value some level of overarching sociopolitical unity and collaborative efficiency and effectiveness. In fact, Dewey shows a typically forerunning sensitivity to precisely these points, and demonstrates effectively how the hybridization of deliberative theories can encompass agonistic, as well as liberal and virtue models when he writes, "Of course there are conflicting interests; otherwise there would be no social problems. The problem under discussion is precisely *how* conflicting claims are to be settled in the interests of all—or at least of the great majority. The method of democracy—inasfar as it is that of organized intelligence—is to bring these conflicts out into the open where their special claims can be seen and appraised, where they can be discussed and judged in the light of more inclusive interests than are represented by either of them separately."[35]

Thus if we can take Dewey's formulations as fairly representative of the issues that continue to concern deliberative theorists today (and I believe we can), then we can see that there is at least as much that unites as divides such theorists.

Process thought, too, is an umbrella term that embraces a number of diverse positions and perspectives whose differences stem from a deeper, underlying foundation of common principles and convictions. Hence I will also focus here on those fundamental elements of the process perspective that share a wide, consensual support among process thinkers, as they relate to those fundamental elements of deliberative theory that share a wide, consensual support among deliberative theorists. Naturally, to the extent that these two groups become more acquainted with one another, various parallels and connections of a more specific character will become apparent between particular forms of process thinking and particular forms of deliberative theory. And of course, particular process thinkers will already be disposed to favor one or the other of the various types of deliberative theory, based on factors that may, in some cases, have more to do with their own sociopolitical perspectives and commitments than the type of process thought with which they personally identify.

When compared to either classical (e.g., Madisonian) or nineteenth- and *early* twentieth-century American deliberative theory, contemporary deliberative theory is notably underdeveloped with regard to the metaphysical presuppositions of its claims and values. Classical American deliberative democrats widely shared a common set of baseline presuppositions regarding the normative anthropological and cosmological bases for their theories. Though this was significantly less true by Dewey's time, even in the first decades of the twentieth century it was still widely considered a respectable occupation of one's mental energy to pursue such bases. Today, however, the general—though by no means universal—acceptance of the Weberian dogma of 'disenchantment' among deliberative theorists has tended to dissuade them from pursuing metaphysical justifications for their epistemological and methodological principles.[36] And the combination of this disenchanted perspective with a deep (and admittedly reasonable) suspicion of the role of religious belief in sociopolitical and educational contexts—especially among 'liberally' minded deliberative theorists—has largely prevented the systematic formulation of the metaphysical bases of deliberative principles and values (on the common supposition that the search for such bases is either impossible, nonsensical, or unnecessarily divisive).

Like any political and social perspective, however, deliberative theory necessarily implies, and depends on, metaphysical premises, even if they remain unacknowledged. For example, every form of deliberative theory implicitly depends on a suppressed metaphysical premise to the effect that *genuine* 'deliberation' *is possible*. Hence deliberative theory is necessarily inconsistent with any form of complete determinism: completely determined entities cannot genuinely 'deliberate.' Moreover, even if we choose, rhetorically, to employ the terminology of 'deliberation' in a deterministic theoretical context, such usage cannot support the claims of deliberative theory, per se, because deliberative theory depends on the supposition that deliberative reflection is—or at least can be—*efficacious*. This is precisely the point of the quote from Whitehead at the top of this chapter. As he puts it, "Reason is inexplicable if purpose be ineffective."

Similarly, all types of deliberative theory, from the most naïve liberal idealism to the most cynical agonistic instrumentalism, presuppose some conception of objective 'truth'—even when they verbally deny any such conception. As the political historian and 'hybrid' liberal-republican James Kloppenberg has observed in relation to historical analyses of deliberative rhetoric, "At the level of methodology, some historians have dismissed ideas as mere smokescreens for interests. [Yet] the very notions of 'manipulation' and 'misleading' [to which they refer] themselves rely on contrasting standards of sincerity and veracity that conceptions of language as purely instrumental appear to undercut."[37] In what follows, therefore, I will suggest various ways in which I believe process ontology and epistemology can provide an ideal foundation for the central theses and commitments of contemporary deliberative theorists.

THE DELIBERATIVE SELF IN PROCESS THOUGHT

As I just noted, the very sensicalness of deliberative theory, at both the descriptive and normative levels, depends on the reality of *choice*. If one does not, and *cannot*, really make choices, then deliberation—in any meaningful sense of the term—is impossible. Moreover, making a choice—in any meaningful sense of the term—implies the possibility of having chosen otherwise (no thinkers in the history of philosophy or theology have made this principle more central to their reflections than Whitehead and Charles Hartshorne[38]). It makes no sense whatsoever to say that I have chosen to do 'x,' if the causal conditions preceding my action were sufficient to *guarantee* that 'x' is what I would do. Nor does it make a difference whether these fully determinative causal conditions are identified with the activity of an omnipotent and omnicausal 'providence' or an impersonal and mechanistic (and, therefore, temporally symmetrical) 'natural order'; either way, all agency has been stripped from the individual. Deliberation, like history, is nothing but a shadow play without agency. Indeed, deliberation is nothing other than one manner in which agency, either individual or social, is exercised (hence the natural relationship between *pragmatism* and the form and function of deliberative democratic discourse in Dewey's thought).

Thus strong determinism, in whatever form, is inherently antithetical to deliberative theory, which means that such theory requires the support of a nondeterministic ontology. After all, what could be more evident than that genuine cognitive freedom depends on genuine ontological freedom. To put it rather simplistically, I cannot do that which I cannot do. Whatever is ontologically impossible can only be experientially illusory. So unless one wishes to 'decide' (and, yes, there's a contradiction here) that all deliberation, both personal and collective, is mere appearance and without substance or effect, then one must find an ontological perspective that validates freedom—real, robust, irreducible freedom. Fortunately, process thinkers have spent the better part of a century marshalling and refining their arguments for such a validation.

As I discussed in the last chapter, freedom, according to process thought, is built into the very nature of things, at the most fundamental level. Both Whitehead and Hartshorne conceive of the ultimate constituents of reality as intrinsically self-determining entities. They both fully generalize the principle of relativity in their ontologies, so they recognize that the individual is necessarily conditioned by those aspects of its environment that locate and help to define it as the particular, unique individual that it is. As Whitehead puts the matter, "[T]here is no such fact as *absolute* freedom; every actual entity possesses only such freedom as is inherent in the primary phase 'given' by its standpoint of relativity to its actual universe."[39] Yet there is always a remainder of choice in the equation of identity: "[H]owever far the sphere of efficient causation be pushed in the determination of the components of a concrescence [of an actual entity,] . . . beyond the determination of these components there always remains the final reaction of the self-creative unity of [this entity as it subjectively synthesizes] the universe."[40]

This ontologically robust, yet situationally qualified, conception of freedom validates elements of liberal, virtue, and agonistic deliberative theories. First, it strongly affirms the reality of individual moral autonomy and responsibility on which liberalism is necessarily predicated. Second, it provides a powerful ontological model for conceptualizing habit formation—as the genetic transmission of accrued inclination across moments of serial personhood and from person to person in social interaction—which supports the MacIntyrean concern with the inculcation of deeply and widely rooted positive civic dispositions as necessary to maintain the stability of deliberative-democratic norms and attitudes (the profound—one hopes, temporary—breakdown of which is currently causing so much needless strife and suffering). Finally, the sensitivity of process ontology to issues of situational constraint and coercion provides a ready-made metaphysical vocabulary in which to frame the central insights and claims of agonistic theorists: citizens cannot be adequately conceived of in abstraction from their cultural-social-economic identities, since these identities are linked to cultural, social, political, and material conditions that both inform and delimit their capacities for autonomous participation in democratic discourse.

Moreover, the concept of freedom that is validated in process thought is intrinsically deliberative in character. The individual, as actual entity, becomes itself through a process of discrimination that significantly parallels that which defines discursive deliberation. Speaking in general, simplified terms: First there is the reception of data. Next comes the gradation and selection of received data as more or less relevant to the determination to be made by the concrescing entity. Then there is a consideration of the whole—the unity of contrasting facts, perspectives, values, and alternatives presented as data—through which the emerging agent seeks to constitute itself as a decisive f/act adding itself to the causal matrix of the world from which it has emerged. The self-constitution of the actual occasion is a response to its own evaluation of a set of facts that are presented to it already clothed in the prior determinations and valuations (the 'feelings') of the entities that preceded it. In Whitehead's terms, this actualized response is the agent as 'superject,' and through its status as a new objective fact in the world, this self-determination of the entity in question becomes a datum to be appropriated and responded to by future agents who undergo the same process. Insofar as the formulation of the concrescing entity's 'subjective aim,' the expression of this aim in the self-constitution of the entity as actualized fact, and the transmission of the newly actualized entity's particular determinative and valuative judgment(s) to other entities for whom it is relevant are all coincident with one another, we have an agential conception of selfhood that is predicated on the formulation and communication of informed perspective.[41] What ontological account of selfhood and activity could be more inherently deliberative than this?

History (in an absolutely generic, nonanthropocentric sense) is an endless succession of discursive moments. Reality is communicative. Indeed, for process thinkers, the world *is* an indefinitely extended 'communication community' (though hardly an 'ideal' one). To *become* (anything) is to *deliberate*, and to *be* (anything actual) is to *decide*. But since decisions are only final for the specific occasions that they constitute, the onto-deliberative process is never ending. The human self, being an 'enduring' individual, fundamentally composed of a series of deliberative moments, is a sort of discursive community in itself, embedded within larger discursive communities of multiple human selves (groups, societies, cultures, etc.), embedded within the inclusive discursive community that is the universe. Thus the end of any deliberative moment is a beginning (or part of a beginning) for countless others. Process panexperientialism *is* deliberative theory as ontology.

THE NORMATIVITY OF PERSUASION IN PROCESS THOUGHT

Obviously, whatever form it takes, deliberative theory is fundamentally committed to the value of persuasive, rather than coercive, discourse and behavior. As I argued in Chapter 4, genuine deliberation, per se, is predicated on an ethic and methodology of persuasion; coercive discourse and action is inherently nondeliberative. Thus the coherence of deliberative theory, particularly in its normative role, depends on a foundational and thoroughgoing affirmation of persuasion as the proper mode of relation in social and political communication and decision making. Ideally, this affirmation will not stop at the metaperspectival level of fallibilism but will add to the dispositional virtue of epistemic anxiety further layers of commitment to deliberative attitudes and practices based in participants' respective particularistic commitments. And it is difficult to imagine a philosophical or theological perspective that takes the normativity of persuasion as a mode of relation more seriously, or grounds this value more deeply, than process thought. Indeed, persuasive communication and action is not merely an epistemic and moral value for process thinkers; it is a basic ontological characteristic of the nature of reality—and a metaphysically necessary one at that. Even God, according to process metaphysics, cannot override the final freedom (however delimited) of the individual occasion to choose its own final 'subjective form' as a self-actualizing response to its onto-epistemological situation.

Another closely related value that has emerged in various forms within the framework of deliberative theory is that of 'listening.' Obviously, an ethic of genuinely open and attentive listening represents a necessary correlate to the norm of persuasive (rather than either coercive or *merely superficial*) discourse. After all, one cannot have an informed or productive dialogue without attentive listening by all parties involved. And, of course, the notion of listening often carries with it a connotation of sympathetic presence that easily spills over into a normative conception of social and political relations that emphasizes the possibility of transformative discourse. This strand of deliberative theory is represented by thinkers like Benjamin Barber, who describes the ethic of listening thus: "I will put myself in [my interlocutor's] place, I will try to understand, I will strain to hear what makes us alike, I will listen for a common rhetoric evocative of a common purpose or a common good."[42] This perspective has much in common with the ideal of transformational discourse put forward in John Cobb's seminal work *Beyond Dialogue* and picked up as a major theme in subsequent process philosophy of religion and moral and ethical theory. Indeed, Barber's talk of "creative consensus" would be very much at home within a process-oriented discussion of the possibilities of transformative listening. (Though, from my perspective, it is important to subordinate consensus seeking to the preservation of individual autonomy, whenever and wherever these two values are irreducibly in conflict with one another.)

Of course, not all deliberative theorists are so sanguine about the power of attentive listening in political discourse. The political scientist Susan Bickford, a particularly sophisticated agonist, has called attention to the limitations on empathetic openness imposed by the real—and irreducible—differences between diverse perspectives in political discourse in her study of *The Dissonance of Democracy*:[43]

> Political listening is not primarily a caring or amicable practice, and I emphasize this . . . because "listening" tends immediately to evoke ideas of empathy and compassion. We cannot suppose that political actors are sympathetic toward one another in a conflictual context, yet it is precisely the presence of conflict and differences that makes communicative interaction necessary. This communicative interaction—speaking and listening together—does not necessarily resolve or do away with the conflicts that arise from uncertainty, inequality, and identity. Rather, it enables political actors to decide democratically how to act in the face of conflict, and to clarify the nature of the conflict at hand.[44]

Thus while one may certainly (and I believe rightly) lodge a moral claim in favor of empathetic attention to the "other," it is equally important to recognize that deliberative listening need not presuppose either a conciliatory or a compromising attitude. What is of primary importance in political deliberation is that we genuinely *understand* one another, so that our deliberations are informed in an authentic way. (This point represents a sort of flip side to the characterization of authentic liberal political discourse I gave in Chapters 3 and 4. Disclosure and attention are mutually necessary.)

Process ontology and epistemology provides substantial grounds for an ethic of listening within the framework of deliberative social and political practices. As I have already discussed in relation to the deliberative conception of the self in process thought, process ontology grounds the creative self-construction of individual perspective and personality on the emerging subject's consideration of the data and aims presented to it by the world and God. Just insofar as the onto-epistemological vantage point from which the self emerges is essentially constituted by the influx of the in*formative* data offered to the self by the universal matrix of corelation within which the self is framed, 'listening' (in a broadly generic sense) is *not* an *optional* aspect of one's relation to others. But of course, as Bickford reminds us, there are different *kinds* of 'listening': some are more genuinely engaged—and, therefore, more deliberative—than others, and process thought has always recognized this fact. Hence much of process moral theory concerns itself in one way or another with the norm of truly attentive listening.[45]

The overarching norm of persuasive discourse under which process thought frames its notions of listening also connects to the fundamental commitment to a general epistemological principle of fallibilism consistently demonstrated by both Whitehead and Hartshorne, both in their respective methodological approaches and their various moral reflections. Even in the midst of an argument for the possibility of identifying 'necessary' metaphysical truths, for example, Hartshorne is careful to note, "If a truth is unconditionally or categorically necessary, it is explicable as inherent in all coherent thought about experience. *[But] this does not mean that it is self-evidently certain; for we have no godlike clarity of this sort. We have to explore possible theories to discover which best retains its intuitiveness under attack and helps us in the attempt to formulate a coherent system of abstractions on the nonempirical level . . .*"[46]

And the fallibilist justification for persuasive discourse and deliberative listening also connects with the very different, late-Chicago School version of process thought represented, for example, in Bernard Meland's *Fallible Forms and Symbols*, where all philosophical and religious truth claims (including those of process ontology and epistemology) are framed as provisional, speculative conceptions that require constant confrontation with a diversity of experiential perspectives. Of course, Meland saw himself as trying to recover Whitehead's own sense of the tentative character of human understandings, which he (fairly or unfairly) believed had been betrayed by what he saw as the overly literalistic character of the process project as taken up by the likes of Hartshorne, Cobb, and Schubert Ogden.[47] Thus another virtue of engaging with deliberative theory from a process perspective is that such a focus clarifies and reaffirms the historically pluralistic character of process thought by emphasizing its openness to development and correction in light of new experiences, perspectives, evidence, and so on.

FALLIBILIST LIBERALISM AND THE 'METAPHYSICAL TELOS' OF CREATIVITY

Generally speaking, process thinkers reject the Rawlsian notion that we can dispense with comprehensive justifications for liberal norms. Process thinkers (almost universally) believe that at least some human values are also, in some meaningful sense, *cosmic values*—that is, values with objective status and import beyond the framework of contingent human cultural understandings and aims.[48] To the extent that a process thinker affirms basic liberal norms, therefore, she is likely to do so in a comprehensive fashion, with appeal to a metaphysical foundation. Hence as I indicated at the beginning of this chapter, my project here shifts me somewhat away from the prevalent approach to political philosophy among process thinkers. However, as I have tried to show over the course of the last several chapters, my fallibilist approach to the justification of liberal-democratic norms is wholly reconcilable with—indeed, it requires the complement of—some nondespotic comprehensive perspective, on which the principle of respect for persons is founded for the individual participant in liberal-democratic discourse.

Moreover, precisely because the ultimate metaphysical category in process thought—the "universal of universals,"[49] according to Whitehead—is 'creativity,' the comprehensive foundation on which the process perspective's moral and political commitments rest is one that essentially validates and affirms pluralism and tolerance as grounded in what Franklin Gamwell has called the 'metaphysical telos' of the 'maximization of creativity' as the foundational criteria of just social forms.[50] Such maximization clearly depends on great latitude of personal autonomy, embedded within a social framework that enables and supports the individual, even as it seeks to leave her alone with respect to her own proper sphere of self-determination.

In sum, then, the parallels between the necessary basic presuppositions and principles of deliberative theory and the tenets of process thought are striking and suggest the possibility for sustained and fruitful dialogue between these two groups of thinkers. As a well-developed (and multivalent) set of sociopolitical models, deliberative theory offers process thinkers a structure for thinking about fundamental issues in social and political philosophy that meshes nicely with our own general ideas regarding the constructive applicability of process thought in these arenas. Conversely, as a well-developed (and equally multivalent) set of onto-epistemological principles and descriptive formulas, process thought offers deliberative theory a much-needed basis for its central claims and assumptions. This chapter represents only a beginning to a dialogue between process and deliberative theorists, while, I hope, demonstrating the promise that such a dialogue presents in relation to the continued development and justification of both of these perspectives.

NOTES

CHAPTER 1

1. Stephen Macedo, "Charting Liberal Virtues," in *Virtue*, ed. John W. Chapman and William A. Galston (New York: New York University Press, 1992), 215.
2. Samuel P. Huntington, *The Clash of Civilizations and the Remaking of World Order* (New York: Simon & Schuster, 1996).
3. See especially, Richard Dawkins, *The God Delusion* (Boston: Houghton Mifflin, 2008); Sam Harris, *The End of Faith: Religion, Terror, and the Future of Reason* (New York: W. W. Norton, 2004); and Christopher Hitchens, *God Is Not Great: How Religion Poisons Everything* (New York: Twelve Books, 2007). Among the New Atheists, Daniel Dennett is notable for offering a somewhat less dogmatic and more open-ended critique of religion; see *Breaking the Spell: Religion as a Natural Phenomenon* (New York: Viking Press, 2006).
4. Terence Ball, ed., *The Federalist: With Letters of "Brutus"* (Cambridge: Cambridge University Press, 2004).
5. Widely attributed to Voltaire, but probably of later origin.
6. Søren Kierkegaard, for example, writes, "Not for a single moment is it forgotten that the subject is an existing individual, and that existence is a process of becoming, and that therefore the notion of the truth as identity of thought and being is a chimera of abstraction . . . not because the truth is not such an identity, but because the knower is an existing individual for whom the truth cannot be such an identity as long as he lives in time" (Kierkegaard, *Concluding Unscientific Postscript*, trans. David F. Swenson and Walter Lowrie [Princeton: Princeton University Press, 1941], 176).
7. To be sure, the recognition of the epistemic limitations imposed by human finitude predates the modern turn. Augustine of Hippo and Thomas Aquinas, for example, both explicitly discuss the limits of human understanding in such terms, but they apply the recognition of such limits only *within* the context of accepted Christian dogma, not *in relation to* this dogma itself.
8. There were, of course, dissenters from the Enlightenment cult of reason, David Hume chief among them, but I am speaking here of the general character of Enlightenment thought, and it is notable that, for example, Hume's status and influence among his contemporaries was minor, compared to what it is today.
9. See especially Rudolf Bultmann's *The New Testament and Mythology and Other Basic Writings* (Minneapolis: Augsburg Fortress Publishers, 1984); Reinhold Niebuhr's *The Nature and Destiny of Man* (Louisville: Westminster John Knox

Press, 1996); and Paul Tillich's *Systematic Theology* (Chicago: University of Chicago Press, 1951).

10. Isaiah Berlin, "Two Concepts of Liberty," in *The Proper Study of Mankind: An Anthology of Essays*, ed. Henry Hardy and Roger Hausheer (New York: Farrar, Straus and Giroux, 1998), 191–242. The essay was first published in 1953.
11. One such attempt that also provides important clarification of the complexities and ambivalences that one finds in Kant's work is Samuel Fleischacker's *A Third Concept of Liberty* (Princeton: Princeton University Press, 1995).
12. Charles Larmore, *The Autonomy of Morality* (New York: Cambridge University Press, 2008), 177.
13. Berlin, *The Proper Study of Mankind*, 224n1.
14. Jean-Jacques Rousseau, "On the Sovereign," in *Classics in Political Philosophy*, 3rd edition, ed. Jene M. Porter (Englewood Cliffs, NJ: Prentice-Hall, 2000), 412.
15. Johann Gottlieb Fichte, *Johann Gottlieb Fichte's Sammtliche Werk*, ed. I. H. Fichte, vol. 4 (Berlin: Verlag von Veit, 1845–46), 436.
16. Franklin Gamwell, *The Divine Good: Modern Moral Theory and the Necessity of God* (San Francisco: Harper, 1994), 182.
17. Søren Kierkegaard, *Fear and Trembling: Dialectical Lyric*, in *Fear and Trembling/Repetition*, ed. and trans. Howard V. Hong and Edna H. Hong (Princeton: Princeton University Press, 1983).

CHAPTER 2

1. Søren Kierkegaard, *The Concept of Anxiety: A Simple Psychologically Orienting Deliberation on the Dogmatic Issue of Hereditary Sin*, trans. and ed. Reidar Thomte and Albert B. Anderson (Princeton: Princeton University Press, 1980).
2. Kierkegaard, *Concept of Anxiety*, 29.
3. Ibid., 32; emphasis in original.
4. Kierkegaard, *Concept of Anxiety*, 42.
5. Ibid., 37.
6. Ibid., 44.
7. Ibid., 49.
8. Ibid., 53.
9. Rudolf Bultmann, "Sermon on Lamentations 3:22–41," in *This World and the Beyond: Marburg Sermons*, trans. Harold Knight (New York: Scribner's Sons, 1960), 236; emphasis mine.
10. Rudolf Bultmann, *New Testament and Mythology and Other Basic Writings*, ed. Schubert M. Ogden (Philadelphia: Fortress, 1984), 28.
11. Reinhold Niebuhr, *The Nature and Destiny of Man* (Louisville: Westminster John Knox Press, 1996), 182.
12. Ibid., 183.
13. Ibid., 182.
14. Kierkegaard appreciatively refers to the German theologian Franz Baader's recognition of "the misunderstanding of conceiving temptation one-sidedly as

temptation to evil . . . , when temptation should rather be viewed as freedom's 'necessary other'" (*The Concept of Anxiety*, 39–40n*).

15. Niebuhr, *Nature and Destiny of Man*, 183.
16. Kierkegaard, *Concept of Anxiety*, 42–43.
17. Kierkegaard, "Historical Introduction," *Concept of Anxiety*, xiii.
18. Niebhur, *Nature and Destiny*, 185. As Niebuhr points out, Heidegger recognizes a "distinction between *Angst* and *Sorge*," a distinction that points toward a more positive conception of the function of anxiety (183–84n4).
19. Ibid., 183.
20. Ibid., 185.
21. Hence Kierkegaard's claim that angels, whose wills are infallibly attuned to the divine will (so that they cannot 'posit sin'), have neither anxiety nor, therefore, freedom—and, therefore, "an angel has no history" (*The Concept of Anxiety*, 49).
22. Heidegger, echoing Kierkegaard, for example observes that "[t]he existential meaning of anxiety is such that it cannot lose itself in something with which it might be concerned. If anything like this happens in a similar state-of-mind, this is fear, which the everyday understanding confuses with anxiety . . . Fear is occasioned by entities with which we concern ourselves environmentally. Anxiety, however, springs from Dasein itself" (Heidegger, *Being and Time*, trans. and ed. John Macquarrie and Edward Robinson [San Francisco: Harper & Row, 1962], 394–95).
23. Thanks to Troy Dostert and Vivian Wang for bringing Marcus's view to my attention. See George Marcus, *The Sentimental Citizen: Emotion in Democratic Politics* (University Park: The Pennsylvania State University Press, 2002).
24. Marcus, *Sentimental Citizen*, 7.
25. Ibid., 108ff.
26. Ibid., 140ff.
27. In light of recent events, Marcus's claim that "[t]he ability of the government and of social and economic elites to dictate the news, to present a common and united front, to demand and gain deferential acceptance from the populace has never been weaker" (*Sentimental Citizen*, 2) will, I think, sound naïvely credulous to most informed observers.
28. Marcus, *Sentimental Citizen*, 63n15. I am using the term 'cognitive' here in the common sense of conscious thought, which Marcus rightly distinguishes from the technical neuroscientific use of the term, which includes reference to all forms of 'information processing' in the brain, including the 'unaware and inarticulate' functioning of 'emotion systems.'
29. Ibid., 101.
30. Ibid., 102–3.
31. Steven Luper, *Existing: An Introduction to Existential Thought* (Mountain View, CA: Mayfield, 2000), 7.
32. Jean-Paul Sartre, *Being and Nothingness*, trans. Hazel Barnes (New York: Washington Square, 1966), 76.

33. See Søren Kierkegaard, *Concluding Unscientific Postscript*, trans. David F. Swenson and Walter Lowrie (Princeton: Princeton University Press, 1941), 180–88.
34. Ibid., 188. See also, Søren Kierkegaard, *Fear and Trembling*, in *Fear and Trembling/Repetition*, trans. and ed. Howard V. Hong and Edna H. Hong (Princeton: Princeton University Press, 1983), 42, 69.
35. David Hume, *Dialogues Concerning Natural Religion, and the Posthumous Essays*, ed. Richard H. Popkin (Indianapolis: Hackett, 1980).
36. Ibid., 6.
37. Ibid., 69.
38. Ibid., 6–7.
39. As Thomas Aquinas—prefiguring liberalism in his defense of monarchy—says in *De regno, ad regem Cypri*, "It is not possible for individual human beings to attain all things . . . through their own reasoning. It is therefore necessary for humans to live in a multitude, so that one might help another and different ones might be occupied in finding out different things" (Thomas Aquinas [and Bartholomew de Lucca], *On the Government of Rulers*, trans. James M. Blythe [Philadelphia: University of Pennsylvania Press, 1997], 61).
40. John Milton, *Of Education, Areopagitica, the Commonwealth*, ed. Laura E. Lockwood (Boston: Houghton Mifflin, 1911), 31–141.
41. John Locke, *A Letter Concerning Toleration* (New York: Prometheus Books, 1990).
42. John Stuart Mill, *On Liberty*, ed. Gertrude Himmelfarb (London: Penguin Books, 1974).
43. As Marcus points out (*Sentimental Citizen*, 27), the thinker from the early era in liberal theory who perhaps most profoundly and straightforwardly espouses a fallibilist justification for liberal freedoms from too pervasive moral and social regulation (and, in so doing, anticipates the direction of very late modern and early postmodern arguments) is James Madison. See, for example, *Federalist* #37, in *The Federalist: With Letters of "Brutus,"* ed. Terence Ball (Cambridge: Cambridge University Press, 2004).
44. John Hick, *Faith and Knowledge*, 2nd ed. (Ithaca: Cornell University Press, 1966), 11.
45. J. Budziszewski has a wonderfully succinct discussion of this point in his brief essay "Religion and Civic Virtue," in *Virtue*, ed. John W. Chapman and William A. Galston (New York: New York University Press, 1992), 49–68.
46. William James offers a properly encompassing definition of faith as "belief in something concerning which doubt is still theoretically possible" ("Rationality, Activity, and Faith," *The Princeton Review* 58 [July–December 1882], 70).
47. Hick, *Faith and Knowledge*, 15.
48. Budziszewski notes that Christian thinkers as far back as Tertullian have defended tolerance of diverse views. Tertullian, for example, "suggests that 'it is the law of mankind and the natural right of each individual to worship what he thinks proper'" (Budziszewski, "Religion and Civic Virtue," 55).
49. John Calvin, *Institutes of the Christian Religion I-II* (Philadelphia: Westminster Press, 1960).

50. Linda T. Zagzebski, *Virtues of the Mind: An Inquiry into the Nature of Virtue and the Ethical Character of Knowledge* (New York: Cambridge University Press, 1996), 155–60, 223–30, and throughout. See also, Robert C. Roberts and W. Jay Wood, *Intellectual Virtues: An Essay in Regulative Epistemology* (New York: Oxford University Press, 2010).
51. Zagzebski, *Virtues of the Mind*, 165–96. My conception of the virtuous stance of epistemic anxiety actually combines elements that Zagzebski distributes between her categories of 'humility' and 'courage,' which mediate one another in her system. Roberts and Wood embrace a similar dynamic of mediation between these two categories in *Intellectual Virtues*. In both cases, it seems to me, the existential dynamic of anxiety hangs implicitly in the background as the psychoanthropological basis for the attitudes and postures adopted by the authors.
52. In a sense, some forms of Buddhist enlightenment (such as the 'satori' of the Zen master) might be taken as counterclaims on this point, but (setting aside questions of the proper interpretation of such states) it is important to notice that even here there is an explicit recognition that the content of such a cognitive infinitude is, if it exists, necessarily incommunicable (at least in discursive terms).
53. I am using the term 'actions' here in a way that *excludes* reference to thoughts and (most forms of) speech. I favor allowing private individuals and groups as wide a latitude as possible with regard to the formulation and communication of their own beliefs, right up to the point where such latitude becomes problematic in a concrete way in relation to the equal sociopolitical enfranchisement and liberty of other individuals and/or groups. That is to say, I would *not* endorse any governmental intrusion into nonpublic spaces—such as the home, church, or meeting hall—aimed at restricting, for example, the transmission of racist attitudes and opinions among family members or citizens engaged in voluntary association. Nor would I endorse the restriction on public speech intended to communicate such attitudes or opinions (so long as it were engaged in peacefully). I *would*, however, endorse governmental action to prevent such individuals and/or groups from imposing their views on others, for example, through their introduction into public school curricula or enactment in discriminatory laws.
54. Obviously, there can be (and are) controversies over procedural norms, just as there are over substantive norms. Indeed, liberal theorists have proposed many diverse, and sometimes inconsistent or contradictory, formulations of liberal procedural norms, but this does not invalidate the distinction between the two.
55. Where most contemporary liberal theorists have gone wrong, in my view, in accepting John Rawls's argument in his later work that liberalism—in the shadow of Weberian disenchantment—must dispense with any attempt to provide a foundational warrant for the normativity of its proceduralist neutrality (see Rawls, *Political Liberalism* [New York: Columbia University Press, 1993]). Since, once they are enacted, the liberal principles attain a uniquely unchallenged regulative status, it is incumbent on the principled liberal to offer a

substantive argument as to their normative validity, which is precisely my aim in this paper. Nevertheless, as I am arguing here, I believe that the foundational warrant proposed should be neutral to the differences among divergent 'comprehensive' perspectives, and I believe that my construction of epistemic anxiety here meets this requirement as well.

56. This, indeed, seems to be an inescapable fact of human social existence. There probably never has been a society that exhibited unqualified ideological homogeneity, and, even in highly homogeneous and insular societies, history has shown that disagreements are inevitable in the long stretch of time. Whether differences emerge out of purely ideological concerns or in conjunction with other factors, such as social, political, or economic interests, orthodoxism can mask but not indefinitely contain them.
57. Isaiah Berlin, "Two Concepts of Liberty," in *The Proper Study of Mankind*, ed. Henry Hardy and Roger Hausheer (New York: Farrar, Straus and Giroux, 1998), 224.
58. Charles Larmore, *The Autonomy of Morality* (New York: Cambridge University Press, 2008), 173.
59. See Rawls, *Political Liberalism*.
60. Niebuhr, *Nature and Destiny of Man*, 183.
61. Søren Kierkegaard, *Fear and Trembling: Dialectical Lyric by Johannes De Silentio*, trans. Alastair Hannay (London: Penguin Books, 1985).
62. Stephen Macedo observes that "liberalism may temper or attenuate the devotion to one's own projects and allegiances by encouraging persons to regard their own ways as open to criticism, choice, and change, or simply as not shared by many people whom one is otherwise required to respect" (Macedo, "Charting Liberal Virtues," in *Virtue*, ed. John W. Chapman and William A. Galston [New York: New York University Press, 1992], 215). What is missing here, however, is a recognition that the basis for regarding one's "own ways" in this manner or being "required to respect" the ways of others is circular if it is simply referred back to tolerance as a metanorm. Tolerance itself requires grounding in the bedrock assumption of human fallibility and the correlated virtue of anxiety, which pushes one to maintain a critical stance toward one's own ways and to remain open to learning from those of others.
63. Jean-Paul Sartre, *Existentialism and Humanism*, trans. Philip Mairet (London: Eyre Methuen, 1973), 42.

Chapter 3

1. Gn 22:2–8 (AV).
2. Here I am using 'modern' in a narrow sense, implying, among other things, a contrast to 'postmodern'. As represented by Jacques Derrida, some postmodern philosophy has turned back toward the valorization of nondisclosure. See discussion in the following notes.

3. Søren Kierkegaard, *Fear and Trembling: Dialectical Lyric*, in *Fear and Trembling/Repetition*, ed. and trans. Howard V. Hong and Edna H. Hong (Princeton: Princeton University Press, 1983), 1–123.
4. Gn 22:2–3 (AV).
5. Søren Kierkegaard, *Fear and Trembling: Dialectical Lyric by Johannes De Silentio*, trans. Alastair Hannay (New York: Penguin Books, 1985).
6. Jacques Derrida, *The Gift of Death* (Chicago: University of Chicago, 1996).
7. See Tertullian's *De praescriptione* (in trans. and ed. S. L. Greenslade, *The Library of Christian Classics V: Early Latin Theology* [Louisville: The Westminster Press, 1956]), where he famously poses the question.
8. Kierkegaard, *Fear and Trembling: Dialectical Lyric by Johannes De Silentio*, 20.
9. Ibid.
10. Ibid., 52–53.
11. Ibid., 7.
12. Ibid., 53.
13. Ibid., 57–58.
14. Ibid., 59–60.
15. Ibid., 113.
16. G. W. F. Hegel, *The Philosophy of History* (Amherst, NY: Prometheus Books, 1991), passim 104–8.
17. *Journal of the American Academy of Religion* 74, no. 2 (2006).
18. Jonathan Malesic, "A Secret both Sinister and Salvific: Secrecy and Normativity in Light of Kierkegaard's *Fear and Trembling*," *Journal of the American Academy of Religion* 74, no. 2 (2006), 446–68.
19. Derrida, *Gift of Death*, 58.
20. Malesic, "A Secret both Sinister and Salvific," 448.
21. Ibid., 447.
22. See Chapter 2.
23. Malesic, "A Secret both Sinister and Salvific," 458.
24. Prominent exemplars of this view include Robert Audi, Jürgen Habermas, John Rawls, Stephen Macedo, and Martha Nussbaum.
25. See Paul Weithman's "John Rawls's Idea of Public Reason: Two Questions," *Journal of Law, Philosophy and Culture* 1, no. 1 (2007), 47–67, for a clear explication of the two distinct arguments at work in Rawls's late theory.
26. Ibid., 461–62.
27. Derrida, *Gift of Death*, 63.
28. Malesic, "A Secret both Sinister and Salvific," 462.
29. Finite beings are nonomniscient beings. I would argue that this is definitional. Certainly it is not practically disputable (since only another omniscient being could inerrantly verify a claim to omniscience). And not being omniscient, we are fallible. This, too, I think is definitional: without the absolute guarantee that one has overlooked nothing, misconstrued nothing, and so on, it remains always possible that one is wrong.
30. Here, I am referring to Anders Behring Breivik, who confessed this as the reason for his attack on a liberal political youth camp in Norway in July 2011.

31. Derrida, *Gift of Death*, 85; emphasis mine.
32. Adam Kotsko, "The Sermon on Mount Moriah: Faith and the Secret in *The Gift of Death*," *The Heythrop Journal* 49, no. 1 (2008), 44–61.
33. Ibid., 52.
34. Ibid., 53.
35. Derrida, *Gift of Death*, 26; emphasis mine.
36. For more on my view of the nature and implications of "transcendental conditions of human existence," see my *Deep Empiricism: Kant, Whitehead, and the Necessity of Philosophical Theism* (Lanham, MD: Lexington Books, 2007).
37. Jeffrey Stout, *Democracy and Tradition* (Princeton: Princeton University Press, 2004).
38. Derrida goes so far as to say that Silentio's analysis cannot provide "a concept of the ethical and of the religious that is of consequence; and consequently [he] is especially unable to determine the limit between the two orders" (*Gift of Death*, 84). This point, and its central import to Derrida's own treatment of responsibility in the final section of *The Gift of Death*, is strangely absent from Malesic's discussion.
39. Malesic, "A Secret both Sinister and Salvific," 465–66.
40. Derrida, *Gift of Death*, 41ff.
41. Ibid., 60.
42. Ibid., 59; emphasis mine.
43. Ibid., 74.
44. It's worth noting that in some early Islamic sources, when the son (sometimes it is Isaac, sometimes Ishmael) asks, "Where is the lamb?," Abraham (Ibrahim) actually explains the situation truthfully and asks for the boys opinion about what course of action he (Abraham) should take (see Norm Calder, "From Midrash to Scripture: The Sacrifice of Abraham in Early Islamic Tradition," in *The Qu'ran: Formative Interpretations* [London: Ashgate Publishing, 1999].
45. Malesic, "A Secret both Sinister and Salvific," 449–50. See also Sissela Bok, *Secrets: On the Ethics of Concealment and Revelation* (New York: Pantheon, 1982).
46. Bob Woodward, *Plan of Attack* (New York: Simon and Schuster, 2004), 420.
47. Derrida, *Gift of Death*, 56.
48. Ibid.; emphases mine.
49. Ibid., 57.
50. Hugh Urban, *The Secrets of the Kingdom: Religion and Concealment in the Bush Administration* (Lanham, MD: Rowman and Littlefield, 2007), xii.

Chapter 4

1. James Madison, *Federalist #37*, in *The Federalist: With Letters of "Brutus,"* ed. Terence Ball (New York: Cambridge University Press, 2005), 172.
2. See John Stuart Mill's *On Liberty*, ed. Gertrude Himmelfarb (New York: Penguin Classics, 1982).

3. Thomas Hobbes, *The Leviathan*, ed. C. B. Macpherson (Middlesex: Penguin Classics, 1975), 189.
4. John Locke, *Second Treatise of Government*, in *Two Treatises of Government and A Letter Concerning Toleration*, ed. Ian Shapiro (New Haven: Yale University Press, 2003), 153.
5. Ibid., 154.
6. The reader familiar with Isaiah Berlin's famous essay "Two Concepts of Liberty" will recognize the influence of that work here. For a fuller discussion of the relevance of Berlin's distinction between 'negative' and 'positive' conceptions of individual autonomy to my own construction of 'liberalism,' see my article "Liberalism, Faith, and the Virtue of 'Anxiety,'" *Faith and Philosophy* 24, no. 4 (2007), 385–421. I might also add here that it seems to me that part of the reason that Derrida himself is, ultimately, just as unable as Søren Kierkegaard, Friedrich Nietzsche, Martin Heidegger, Jan Patočka, and Emmanuel Levinas to break out of the circular loop of a certain "European" history of responsibility and see, beyond this circle, another possible concept of responsibility is that he, too, in some way "still follows the Kantian tradition of pure ethics" (Jacques Derrida, *The Gift of Death* [Chicago: University of Chicago, 1996], 92), not as a tradition that he affirms, but as *the* only tradition in relation to which he situates his alternative.
7. As Adam Kotsko (echoing Climacus in Søren Kierkegaard, *Concluding Unscientific Postscript*, trans. David F. Swenson and Walter Lowrie [Princeton: Princeton University Press, 1941], 176).) observes, "The quest of . . . the Danish Hegelians to complete 'the system' is *not only* impossible given the status of the human subject as existing—it is also an attempt at usurping the place that rightfully belongs to God alone" ("The Sermon on Mount Moriah: Faith and the Secret in *The Gift of Death*," *The Heythrop Journal* 49, no. 1 [2008], 50).
8. Probably the most famous example of this is found in the case of Mozert v. Hawkins County Board of Education, 827 F.2d 1058 (6th Cir. 1987). In 1983, several fundamentalist parents and students sued the Hawkins Co., Tennessee, Board of Education to prevent the students from being required to read a set of texts that illustrated diverse worldviews, claiming that exposure to views contrary to those of their religious upbringing would undermine their First Amendment right to the free exercise of religion. In 1987, the U.S. Court of Appeals for the 6th Circuit overturned an earlier district court ruling in favor of the plaintiffs and affirmed the School Board's authority to maintain such a curricular requirement.
9. Board of Education v. Pico, 457 U.S. 853 (1982). The court quoted Madison in support of this contention: "[A] people who mean to be their own Governors, must arm themselves with the power which knowledge gives" (James Madison, *The Writings of James Madison*, vol. 9, ed. Gaillard Hunt [New York: G. P. Putnam's Sons, 1910], 103). My assertion here is that the truth of this statement applies not only in the context of political but also of existential self-government (i.e., moral autonomy).

10. Prominent versions of this critique have been offered by Michael Perry, Philip Quinn, and Nicholas Wolterstorff.
11. Robert Audi, *Religious Commitment and Secular Reason* (New York: Cambridge University Press, 2000), 103.
12. See Ludwig Feuerbach, *The Essence of Christianity*, trans. George Eliot (New York: Harper Books, 1957).
13. See Robert Audi and Nicholas Wolterstorff, *Religion in the Public Square: The Place of Religious Convictions in Political Debate* (Lanham, MD: Rowman and Littlefield Publishers, 1996).
14. See Jeffery Stout, *Democracy and Tradition* (Princeton: Princeton University Press: 2004), chap. 3.
15. Jonathan Malesic, *Secret Faith in the Public Square: An Argument for the Concealment of Christian Identity* (Grand Rapids: Brazos Press, 2009).
16. Jean Bethke Elshtain, *Sovereignty: God, State, and Self* (New York: Basic Books, 2008), 128.
17. Olmstead v. U.S., 277 U.S. 438 (1928).
18. Stout, *Democracy and Tradition*, 2ff.
19. Paul Tillich, *Systematic Theology*, vol. 1 (Chicago: University of Chicago Press, 1951), 6, 8–15.
20. Ibid., 12; emphasis mine.
21. Tillich, *Systematic Theology*, 12.
22. Ibid., 13.
23. Ibid., 13–14.
24. Ibid., 15.
25. Ibid., 16.
26. Ibid., 10.
27. Paul Tillich, *The Dynamics of Faith* (New York: HarperCollins, 1957), 11–12.
28. Ibid., 12.
29. As Kierkegaard observes, "Not for a single moment is it forgotten that the subject is an existing individual, and that existence is a process of becoming, and that therefore the notion of the truth as identity of thought and being is a chimera of abstraction . . . not because the truth is not such an identity, but because the knower is an existing individual for whom the truth cannot be such an identity as long as he lives in time" (*Concluding Unscientific Postscript*, 176).
30. As with Johannes de Silentio, I will, for the present purposes, maintain a clear distinction between Climacus and Kierkegaard.
31. Kierkegaard, *Concluding Unscientific Postscript*, 180.
32. Ibid., 182.
33. Ibid.
34. Ibid., 183–84.
35. Ibid., 183.
36. Thus Climacus's analysis of Socrates's position in relation to the various 'movements' extends and completes Silentio's treatment of him. Silentio writes, "If faith is no more than what philosophy passes it off as then Socrates himself already went further, much further, rather than the converse—that he didn't

come that far. He made the movement of infinity intellectually. His ignorance is the infinite resignation" (Søren Kierkegaard, *Fear and Trembling: Dialectical Lyric by Johannes de Silentio*, trans. Alastair Hannay [New York: Penguin Books, 1985], 97). But as Climacus indicates, Socrates both does and does not stop at 'ignorance.' He accepts the limitation of his understanding, as an existing understanding, but he nevertheless pursues 'truth' and, indeed, is willing, if not eager, to lay down his life in this pursuit.

37. Derrida, *The Gift of Death*, 77; emphasis mine.
38. Jonathan Malesic, "A Secret both Sinister and Salvific: Secrecy and Normativity in Light of Kierkegaard's *Fear and Trembling*," *Journal of the American Academy of Religion* 74, no. 2 (2006), 458.
39. Kierkegaard, *Concluding Unscientific Postscript*, 188.

Chapter 5

1. W. B. Yeats, "The Countess Cathleen," in *Poems* (London: T. Fisher Unwin, 1895), 156.
2. For Rawls, a 'comprehensive' justification is one that references either metaphysical or transcendental-anthropological premises, as his own argument in *A Theory of Justice* did. Comprehensive justifications necessarily correspond to 'comprehensive views'—that is, overarching religious or philosophical worldviews—and, therefore, according to Rawls, violate the public/nonpublic distinction and the 'neutrality' of liberal norms in relation to such views, by introducing nonneutral substantive premises into public (political) discussions, which Rawls believes must take place separately from all such premises. See John Rawls, *Political Liberalism* (New York: Columbia University Press, 1993), 12–14, 38, 135, 175, 374.
3. I will clarify the distinction between these two closely related movements in Chapter 6.
4. For a good introduction to the connections between process philosophy and theology and Judaism, see Sandra B. Lubarsky and David Ray Griffin, eds., *Jewish Theology and Process Thought* (New York: SUNY Press, 1996).
5. I use this term broadly here, in a manner that is neutral to scholarly distinctions between the ideas of the pre-Plotinian followers of Plato and the specific school of thought initiated by Plotinus.
6. Saint Augustine, *The Confessions of Saint Augustine*, trans. Rex Warner (New York: Mentor, 1963), 265.
7. Ibid., 284.
8. Thomas Aquinas, *Summa Theologica*, vol. 1, trans. Fathers of the English Dominican Province (New York: Cosimo Classics, 2007), Q.14, A.13.
9. From the perspective of open theism, the elements of the Molinist/Arminian/Wesleyan view that distinguish it from the standard classical view are far less significant than the elements that unite it and the standard view. Thus I will refer to both as rival *forms of* classical theism. (Substantively speaking, the

Molinist, Arminian, and Wesleyan views are essentially indistinguishable with relation to the relevant issues at hand here.)

10. I use 'creaturely' here, rather than the more narrow 'human,' because, as I will discuss later, Whiteheadian process metaphysics posits degrees of freedom throughout the spectrum of actual entities.
11. Søren Kierkegaard, *The Concept of Anxiety: A Simple Psychologically Orienting Deliberation on the Dogmatic Issue of Hereditary Sin*, trans. and ed. Reidar Thomte and Albert B. Anderson (Princeton: Princeton University Press, 1980), 42.
12. Ibid., 37.
13. Ibid., 44.
14. Ibid., 53.
15. Linda Zagzebski, *Divine Motivation Theory (New York: Cambridge University Press, 2004)*, 190.
16. Alfred North Whitehead, *Religion in the Making*, ed. Judith Jones (New York: Fordham University Press, 1996), 55.
17. U.S. Supreme Court Justice Felix Frankfurter, for example, wrote, "From knowledge gained through the years of the personalities who in our day have affected American university life, I have for some time been convinced that no single figure has had such a pervasive influence as . . . Alfred North Whitehead . . . a thinker whose philosophic speculations were mostly beyond the capacity of those whom he touched" (from Frankfurter's tributary essay "Alfred North Whitehead," in Alfred North Whitehead, *The Aims of Education and Other Essays*, 2nd ed. [New York: Mentor Books, 1949], 7). Similarly, Gertrude Stein famously wrote in *The Autobiography of Alice B. Toklas* that Whitehead had caused the "little bell" in her head that told her she was in the company of genius to ring, as it had done before only in the presence of Picasso (Gertrude Stein, *The Autobiography of Alice B. Toklas* [London: Penguin Books, 2005], 78).
18. Alfred North Whitehead, *A Treatise on Universal Algebra with Applications* (Cambridge: Cambridge University Press, 1898).
19. Alfred North Whitehead and Bertrand Russell, *Principia Mathematica*, 3 vols. (Cambridge: Cambridge University Press, 1910–13).
20. Alfred North Whitehead, *The Aims of Education and Other Essays* (New York: The Free Press, 1929).
21. Perhaps the most clear and concise explication of Whiteheadian naturalism can be found in David Ray Griffin's *Reenchantment without Supernaturalism* (Ithaca: Cornell University Press, 2001).
22. Nicholas Rescher, one of the most esteemed contemporary representatives of the broader process tradition—and one who has expressed considerable appreciation for Whitehead's thought—offers an illuminating discussion of the relation of Whiteheadian-Hartshornean process philosophy and theology to the broader tradition of process thought and the place of both in the contemporary scene in "Process Philosophy," Stanford Encyclopedia of Philosophy, last modified January 9, 2008, http://plato.stanford.edu/entries/process-philosophy/.

23. For a good overview of the connections, see Timothy E. Eastman and Hank Keeton, eds., *Physics and Whitehead: Process, Quantum and Experience* (Albany: State University of New York Press, 2003).
24. From a letter Whitehead wrote to Charles Hartshorne, who served as Whitehead's graduate assistant at Harvard and went on to become widely recognized as the second founding figure of the contemporary process movement, published in Hartshorne's collection of critical-appreciative essays (Charles Hartshorne, *Whitehead's Philosophy* [Lincoln: University of Nebraska Press, 1973], xi).
25. Alfred North Whitehead, *Process and Reality, Corrected Edition, ed. David Ray Griffin and Donald W. Sherbourne* (New York: The Free Press, 1978), 343.
26. Ibid.
27. Ibid.
28. Ibid., 345.
29. Reported by A. H. Johnson in his article "Whitehead as Teacher and Philosopher," *Philosophy and Phenomenological Research* 29, (1969), 372.
30. See my *Deep Empiricism: Kant, Whitehead, and the Necessity of Philosophical Theism* (Lanham, MD: Lexington Books, 2007), chaps. 5–6; and "Between Hartshorne and Molina: A Whiteheadian Conception of Divine Foreknowledge," *Process Studies* 39, no. 1 (2010), 129–48. More specifically, I have suggested that there is a trajectory of thought initiated in *Religion in the Making* and carried forward in parts of *Process and Reality* that indicates that Whitehead was (somewhat inconsistently) moving in the direction of a view of the interrelational codeterminateness of the eternal objects as implying the divine apprehension of all possible states of affairs, as such, in their full formal character—not as actual, but as specific (i.e., determinate) possibilities for actualization. And I have argued, further, that it is such a position that Whiteheadians ought to adopt, regardless of whether it was intended by Whitehead, because it provides the strongest basis for the overall view of the nature of reality posited in Whiteheadian-Hartshornean thought generally.
31. As I make clear in both *Deep Empiricism* and "Between Hartshorne and Molina" (and in the preceding note), this last claim and its implications represent my interpretive extrapolation of the logic of several of Whitehead's statements. While I am inclined to believe that the position I am here defending would meet with Whitehead's approval, I am by no means claiming that it is certain that it was his intent to imply all that I am drawing out of my reading of him. Thus I refer to this as a "Whiteheadian" position, not "Whitehead's" position.
32. Whitehead, *Religion in the Making*, 153–54.
33. The one exception to this general rule of usage in Whitehead's thought is his occasional application of the term 'actual' to the primordial pole of the divine nature. Here, too, though, the actuality of the referent is linked to temporality and concreteness since the divine primordial determination is precisely the basis of the emergence of temporality and concreteness out of the eternal abstractness of God's envisagement of possibility.

34. Whitehead's use of the term 'subsistence' (like his use of many other terms) is idiosyncratic and must especially be differentiated from the uses to which some of his contemporaries, such as Alexius Meinong, put it. For Whitehead, 'subsistence' is simply the term for the status of the eternal objects as existent in the divine understanding; it is *not* a third modality alongside of 'existence' and 'actuality' but simply a specific type of existence. (See Whitehead, *Process and Reality*, 46 and, for further discussion, Malone-France, 118–21 and 135.)
35. Whitehead, *Process and Reality*, 32.
36. Whitehead himself used the older terminology of 'panpsychism,' but most current process thinkers agree with David Ray Griffin's replacement of this term with 'panexperientialism' as a way of clarifying that most actual occasions' experiential horizons do not encompass the higher-order forms of experience typically associated with the notion of the 'psyche.' See, especially, Griffin's *Unsnarling the World-Knot* (Berkeley: University of California Press, 1998).
37. Whitehead, *Process and Reality*, 21.
38. Ibid.
39. Alfred North Whitehead, *Science and the Modern World* (New York: The Free Press, 1967), 76.
40. Whitehead, *Process and Reality*, 29, 167.
41. This is, I believe, the correct interpretation of what Whitehead says about the relation between eternal objects and actual occasions in section 2 of chapter 2 and about the 'evocation' of eternal objects by becoming actual occasions in section 3 of chapter 6 of *Process and Reality*, although he uses the terminology of determinacy in those discussions in a way that might, if read superficially, seem contrary to this explanation. In both of those places, Whitehead is speaking about the indeterminacy of eternal objects and possibilities, *not* in the sense of a lack of definite identity conditions but in the sense of their status vis-à-vis the actual course of things prior to the selective actualization of some rather than others of them in the concrescent choice of the relevant actual occasion.
42. See Malone-France, *Deep Empiricism*, 117–18 for a related discussion of Kant's view and my rebuttal of W. V. O. Quine's famous critique of Kant on this point.
43. I am using 'imagination' here in a sense similar to Kant's use of this concept in the second (B) edition versions of the "Transcendental Deduction" and "Transcendental Aesthetic" (see *Critique of Pure Reason, trans. and ed. Paul Guyer and Allen W. Wood* (New York: Cambridge University Press, 1998)—specifically, in his treatment of the notion of the 'transcendental synthesis of the imagination.' For Kant, whereas the 'transcendental synthesis of apperception' is the cognitive procedure by which the *given* manifold of representations (i.e., empirical 'appearances') is made an object of consciousness, the synthesis of imagination is "the faculty of representing in intuition an object that is not itself present" (B 151). Of course, contrarily to my use of the term here, for Kant, the imagination is linked to the deterministic character of the manifold of phenomenal appearances and, therefore, the implicit phenomenal unity of past, present, and future because of its centrality in his deterministic account of the underlying logic of the representation of

temporal successiveness in human subjectivity. (I will say more about the connection between Kant's notion of synthesis and Whitehead's later.)

44. I use the term *precise* here in contradistinction to Hartshorne's conception of possibility as 'vague.' See, Malone-France, *Deep Empiricism*, chaps. 5–6 and "Between Hartshorne and Molina" for further discussion.
45. Luis de Molina, *Liberi Arbitrii cum Gratiæ Donis, Divina Præscientia, Providentia, Prædestinatione et Reprobatione Concordia* (1588; repr., Paris: P. Lethielleux, 1876), hereafter referred to as *Concordia.*
46. Molina, *Concordia*, 368–69 ff.
47. Ibid.
48. See Kant, *Critique of Pure Reason*, B 131–35 and B 406–9. Also, for further discussion of the relation between Kant and Whitehead's views on this point, see Malone-France, *Deep Empiricism*, 46–49.
49. Whitehead, *Process and Reality*, 156.
50. Immanuel Kant, Critique of Pure Reason, trans. and ed. Paul Guyer (Cambridge: Cambridge University Press, 1998).
51. William James, *A Pluralistic Universe* (Lincoln: University of Nebraska Press, 1996), 322.
52. See Malone-France, *Deep Empiricism*, 168–69.
53. Alfred North Whitehead, *Adventures of Ideas* (New York: The MacMillan Company, 1933), 105.
54. Ibid., 88.
55. Ayn Rand, *The Fountainhead* (Indianapolis: Bobbs-Merrill Company, 1943), 259.

CHAPTER 6

1. Alfred North Whitehead, *The Function of Reason* (Princeton: Princeton University Press, 1929), 27.
2. Derek Malone-France, "Process and Deliberation," *Process Studies* 35, no. 1 (2006), 108–33.
3. This term is meant to have a somewhat broader reference than the widely used 'deliberative democratic theory,' which refers more specifically to those elements in the wider movement that have to do particularly with democratic political philosophy and science.
4. See, for example, Seyla Benhabib, *Democracy and Difference* (Princeton: Princeton University Press, 1996); Amy Gutmann and Dennis Thompson, *Democracy and Disagreement* (Cambridge: Harvard University Press, 1996); and James Bohman, *Public Deliberation: Pluralism, Complexity, and Democracy* (Cambridge: MIT Press, 1996).
5. See, for example, Susan Bickford, *The Dissonance of Democracy: Listening, Conflict, and Citizenship* (Ithaca: NY, Cornell University Press, 1996); James S. Fishkin, *Democracy and Deliberation: New Directions for Democratic Reform* (New Haven: Yale University Press, 1991) and *The Voice of the People: Public Opinion and Democracy* (New Haven: Yale University Press, 1995).

6. See, for example, James T. Kloppenberg, *The Virtues of Liberalism* (Oxford: Oxford University Press, 1998).
7. See, for example, Sonja K. Foss and Cindy L. Griffin, "Beyond Persuasion: A Proposal for an Invitational Rhetoric," *Communication Monographs* 62 (1995), 2–18; Gerard A. Hauser, "Vernacular Dialogue and the Rhetoricality of Public Opinion," *Communication Monographs* 65 (1998), 83–107 and "Civil Society and the Principle of the Public Sphere," *Philosophy and Rhetoric* 31 (1998), 19–40.
8. See, for example, Barbara Arnstine, "Developing Students for a Democracy: The LegiSchool Project," *Studies in Philosophy and Education* 19, no.3 (2000), 261–73; Philip J. Burns, "Supporting Deliberative Democracy: Pedagogical Arts of the Contact Zone of the Electronic Public Sphere," *Rhetoric Review* 18 (1999), 128–46; Penny Enslin, Shirley Pendlebury, and Mary Tjiattas, "Deliberative Democracy, Diversity, and the Challenges of Citizenship Education," *Journal of Philosophy of Education* 35, no. 1 (2001), 115–30; and Peggy Ruth Geren, "Public Discourse: Creating the Conditions for Dialogue Concerning the Common Good in a Postmodern Heterogeneous Democracy," *Studies in Philosophy and Education* 20, no. 3 (2001), 191–99.
9. See, for example, George E. Marcus, *The Sentimental Citizen: Emotion in Democratic Politics* (University Park: The Pennsylvania State University Press, 2002).
10. See Jürgen Habermas, *Structural Transformation of the Public Sphere: An Inquiry into the Category of Bourgeois Society* (Cambridge: MIT Press, 1989) and *Between Facts and Norms: Contributions to a Discourse Theory of Law and Democracy* (Cambridge: MIT Press, 1996); and Karl-Otto Apel, *From a Transcendental-Semiotic Point of View* (Manchester: Manchester University Press, 1998) and *Selected Essays, Vols.1 & 2.*, ed. Eduardo Mendieta (Atlantic Highlands, NJ: Humanities Press, 1994–96).
11. See John Rawls, *Political Liberalism* (New York: Columbia University Press, 1993).
12. For a good cross-section of this response, both sympathetic and critical, see Stephen Macedo, ed., *Deliberative Politics: Essays on Democracy and Disagreement* (New York: Oxford University Press, 1999).
13. Bohman belongs in this category. See, also, Joshua Cohen, "Deliberation and Democratic Legitimacy" and Thomas Christiano, "The Significance of Public Deliberation" both in *Deliberative Democracy*, ed. James Bohman (Boston: MIT Press, 1997).
14. Deliberative virtue theories, like contemporary virtue theories in general, owe much to Alasdair MacIntyre's revival of interest in Aristotelian moral theory through his influential works *After Virtue* and *Whose Justice? Which Rationality?* Deliberative virtue theory takes its cue especially from the latter. For a good example of a virtue-based deliberative theory, see Mark Kingwell, *A Civil Tongue: Justice, Dialogue, and the Politics of Pluralism* (University Park: Penn State University Press, 1995).
15. Gutmann and Thompson, I believe, belong in this camp, as does William Galston, who compellingly brings together philosophy and public policy

discussions in his *Liberal Purposes: Goods, Virtues, and Diversity in the Liberal State* (Cambridge: Cambridge University Press, 1998).

16. Bickford's feminist deliberative thought is probably best described in these terms, though it is self-consciously syncretistic. See also, Iris Marion Young, "Communication and the Other: Beyond Deliberative Democracy," in *Democracy and Difference: Contesting the Boundaries of the Political*, ed. Seyla Benhabib (Princeton: Princeton University Press, 1996); and William Connolly, *Identity/Difference: Democratic Negotiations of Political Paradox* (Ithaca: Cornell University Press, 1991).
17. Though the populist bent of deliberative liberalism somewhat ameliorates the strong meritocratic impulse of traditional liberalism, no genuinely liberal model can wholly dispense with intellectual and economic meritocracy.
18. In this context, 'virtue theory' represents a more generic term than either 'communitarianism' or 'republicanism' (in the classical sense), but the historical and philosophical connections between all three terms in American social and political thought are evident, though, as Kloppenberg shows, these connections have often been more complex—and sometimes more conflicted—than has traditionally been supposed.
19. Alasdair McIntyre, *Whose Justice? Which Rationality* (South Bend: Notre Dame University Press, 1989).
20. This is perhaps a somewhat inelegant term, but it is, I think, a well-fitted one. The theorists to whom I am applying this label neither fit neatly into the liberal or the virtue camp (in that they draw on the insights of both fairly equally) nor do they collectively constitute a definite third category that could be accurately characterized without reference to these two more basic conceptual models. (After formulating this category for the purposes of this essay, I came across Kloppenberg's use of the term 'hybrid' in a discussion of the complicated entanglement of 'liberal' and 'republican' ideas in nineteenth-century American political thought and rhetoric [Kloppenberg, *Virtues of Liberalism*, 66, 68]. Though his use of the term is unsystematic and more narrowly focused than mine, I take his account of the historical hybridization of liberal-individualistic and republican social virtue principles as supporting the validity of the term as a label for contemporary versions of the same sort of balancing act between liberal procedural and virtue-dispositional ideas.)
21. There are actually important shades of difference between these two terms, in that 'agonistic' focuses attention on the conflictual nature of deliberative discourse, while 'difference' focuses attention on what is viewed as the primary source of such conflict (namely, the competing and often contradictory presuppositions and claims of diverse identity groups and cultural perspectives). Nevertheless, I use them interchangeably here because these two emphases almost invariably go together.
22. See Karl-Otto Apel, *Understanding and Explanation*, trans. Georgia Warnke (Cambridge: MIT Press, 1988).
23. It is important, here, to note the significance of the qualifying term "hypothetically" in this formulation. Both Apel and Habermas understand the role of the

notion of an indefinite and fully rational community of deliberators in their theories in the same way in which Rawls, in his earlier work, uses the notion of the 'veil of ignorance' and Hobbes, Locke, Rousseau, et al. use the notion of the 'state of nature,' namely, as a conceptual *heuristic device* with normative implications.

24. John Dewey, *Liberalism and Social Action* (New York: G. P. Putnam, 1935), 44.
25. Evidence for this equation can be seen in the parallel between Dewey's formulation of the "problem of democracy" as "the problem of that form of social organization, extending to all the areas and ways of living, in which the powers of individuals shall not be merely released from external constraint but shall be fed, sustained and directed," and his formulation of the "end" of liberalism as "the liberation of individuals so that realization of their capacities may be the law of their life . . . [and] the use of freed intelligence as the method of directing change" (Dewey, *Liberalism and Social Action*, 31, 56).
26. Dewey, *Liberalism and Social Action*, 3.
27. Ibid., 24; emphasis mine.
28. Ibid., 52.
29. Ibid., 46.
30. Ibid., 52–3.
31. Dewey writes that "[s]uch a [society] demands much more of education than general schooling, which without a renewal of the springs of purpose and desire becomes a new mode of mechanization and formalization . . . It demands of science much more than external technical application—which again leads to mechanization of life and results in a new kind of enslavement. It demands that the method of inquiry, of discrimination, of test by verifiable consequences, be naturalized in all the matters . . . that arise for judgment" (*Liberalism and Social Action*, 31).
32. Alan Ryan, *Liberal Anxieties and Liberal Education* (New York: Hill and Wang, 1998), 40.
33. Dewey, *Liberalism and Social Action*, 73.
34. Ibid., 58; emphasis mine.
35. Ibid., 79.
36. Kloppenberg brilliantly details the differences between Weber and Dewey on the question of disenchantment in Chapter 6 of *Virtues*, "Democracy and Disenchantment: From Weber and Dewey to Habermas and Rorty" (82–99).
37. Ibid., 61.
38. For a good sense of how Hartshorne developed the connection between the ontological category of creativity and the theme of human freedom, see "Politics and the Metaphysics of Freedom," in *Creative Experiencing: A Philosophy of Freedom*, ed. Donald W. Viney and Jincheol O (New York: SUNY Press, 2011).
39. Alfred North Whitehead, *Process and Reality, Corrected Edition*, ed. David Ray Griffin and Donald W. Sherbourne (New York: The Free Press, 1978), 133; emphasis mine.
40. Ibid., 47.

41. "Provided that we admit the category of final causation, we can consistently define the primary function of Reason. This function is to constitute, emphasize, and criticize the final causes and strength of aims directed towards them" (Whitehead, *Function*, 26).
42. Benjamin Barber, *Strong Democracy: Participatory Politics for a New Age* (Berkeley: University of California Press, 1984), 175.
43. See Bickford, *Dissonance of Democracy*; Fishkin, *Democracy and Deliberation*; and Fishkin, *Voice of the People*.
44. Bickford, *Dissonance of Democracy*, 2.
45. I have in mind here process thinkers like Jay McDaniel, whose conception of interreligious dialogue, which owes much to Cobb's work, balances genuine commitment to one's own confessional belief system with a humble attitude of openness to the insights of others' perspectives. See Jay McDaniel, *With Roots and Wings: Christianity in an Age of Ecology and Dialogue* (Maryknoll, NY: Orbis Books, 1995).
46. Charles Hartshorne, *Insights and Oversights of Great Thinkers: An Evaluation of Western Philosophy* (Albany, NY: SUNY Press, 1983), 313; emphasis mine.
47. See Gary Dorrien's illuminating biopic article on Meland, "Metaphysics, Imagination, and Creative Process," *American Journal of Theology and Philosophy* 25, no. 3 (2004), 199–224, especially 216.
48. As Franklin Gamwell notes in a related context, "Modern moral and political thought has often focused on the question of human rights: What rights, if any, belong to all human individuals solely because they are human? Within the past two centuries, theoretical address to this question has been marked by a dominant consensus. It holds that a principle or principles of human rights must be independent of any comprehensive telos to which all human activity ought to be directed, that is, a telos defined by reality as such and, in that sense, metaphysical. In contrast, thinkers within the tradition of process thought typically assert that all moral and political principles are dependent on a purpose in the nature of things" (*Democracy on Purpose: Justice and the Reality of God* [Washington, DC: Georgetown University Press, 2001], 322). See, also, Daniel Dombrowski, "Process Thought and the Liberalism-Communitarianism Debate," *Process Studies* 26, no. 1/2 (1997).
49. Whitehead, *Process and Reality*, 21.
50. See, especially Gamwell, *Divine Good* and "Purpose."

INDEX

Abraham, 19, 24, 51–60, 68, 70–71, 73, 82
Abrahamic faith, 19, 49, 54, 68, 70, 124; and "problem" of anxiety, 21; and salvation, 24–25
Abrahamic religions/theologies, 6, 64, 102; and revealed faith, 21, 58, 61; and salvation, 105, 223–24
absolute, the, 106–7; in Kierkegaard's thought, 24
absolute duty, 62–63
abstractness in Whiteheadian metaphysics, 119–34
absurd, the, 35, 94
actual entities in Whiteheadian metaphysics, 116–34, 136–51 passim
actuality, 44; as distinguished from "existence" in process metaphysics 118–19; God's relation to, 108–9; and possibility in the Fall, 23–24, 105–6; in Whiteheadian metaphysics, 114–34
actual occasions in Whiteheadian metaphysics, 120–34, 150–51.
Adam, 22–24
agonistic deliberative democratic theory, 140–54 passim; defined, 142–43
alterity, 67
anarchism, 11, 36
angels in Kierkegaard's thought, 23–24, 27, 106
antiliberalism: and twentieth-century totalitarianism, 13
anxiety, ix–x, 3, 4, 12, 19, 30–33, 36, 41, 49, 93, 97, 99, 101, 105, 109–13; and the Fall in Christian theology, 22–25; in modern Western philosophy and theology, 6–8; as occasion of faith, 96; as problem to be solved, 21, 26–28; and tolerance, 38, 48
Apel, Karl-Otto, 68, 139, 143
Aristotelian physics, 115
Aristotle, 103, 121, 139
Arminius, Jacob, 104
Athens, 54
atomism, 134
Audi, Robert, 85–86
Augustine of Hippo, 103, 126, 157n7
Augustinian theism, 125–29, 132
authenticity, 27, 48
authoritarianism, 58, 74, 108; as latent in Kantian-Rousseauian liberalism, 14
authority, 45, 47, 60, 69, 76, 83, 108–13
autonomy, 15, 31, 52, 61, 64–65, 68–70, 76, 84, 86, 89, 108–13, 143–55 passim; children and, 82; and the Fall, 23–25, 103–7; according to Kant and Rousseau, 12–13

Baader, Franz, 158n14
Barber, Benjamin, 152
Benhabib, Seyla, 140
Berlin, Isaiah, 9–15, 44
Bickford, Susan, 153–54
Board of Education v. Pico, 82
Bohman, James, 140
Bok, Sissela, 72
Brandeis, Louis, 88
Breivik, Anders Behring, 163n30
Brutus, Lucias Junius, 56–57

Buddhism, 161n52
Bultmann, Rudolf, 7, 21, 25
Bush, George W., 58, 73, 75; administration of, 72

Calvin, John, 15, 41, 104, 124
Calvin's contradiction, 41
care, 111
Carnap, Rudolf, 113
Catholicism, 103–4; Molinist controversy in, 124–25; ultraorthodox form of, 15
certainty, 3, 4, 12, 48, 105; glorification of, 108–13; and intolerance, 41; logical vs. epistemological, 17; as opposed to autonomy, 26, 65, 107; and tolerance, 30
Christ, 25
Christian Dominionism, 75
Christianity, 2, 15, 38, 41, 58, 64, 65, 86, 101–2; and the Fall, 22–25; and missionizing, 15; and revelation, 21, 54–55, 60; in Tillich's thought, 90–92
civic virtue, 19, 38
civil society, 142, 145
clash of civilizations thesis, 2
classical conservatism, 143
classical theism, 20, 101–13, 116, 124–34, 136. *See also* Augustinian theism; Thomistic theism
classic liberalism, 3, 9, 10, 30, 41, 77; as opposed to "classical" liberalism, 11; and the recognition of fallibility, 38
Climacus, Johannes, ix, 93–95, 97
Cobb, John Jr., ix, 152, 154
coercion, 14, 17, 25, 31, 36, 37, 65, 84–89, 91, 105, 108–13, 135–37, 151–52
Cold War, 26
colonialism, 15
commerce in Whitehead's thought, 135–36
communication community, 143, 151
communism, 13
concrescence, 120–34, 150
concreteness in Whiteheadian metaphysics, 119–34
Congress (of United States), 72–73
consequent nature of God, 116–34
contingency, 107, 114; and divine foreknowledge, 126–34
cosmic values, 155
creatio ex nihilo, 116
creativity, 111; as related to anxiety in Niebuhr's thought, 27–28; in Whiteheadian metaphysics, 121–34, 155–56
Cromwellians, 8

Danish Lutheranism, 55
Darwin, Charles, 8
Dasein, 159n22
Dawkins, Richard, 40
deliberative democratic theory, 20, 41, 51, 101, 134, 138–54; four main types of, 140–43
democratic deliberation/discourse, 42, 52, 68, 90, 112; and fallibilism, 17, 29; and governmental secrecy, 73; Marcus on role of anxiety in, 30–33
de Molina, Luis, 104, 124–28
demos, 32
Dennett, Daniel, 40
de re modalities, 127
Derrida, Jacques, 54, 58–59, 62, 64, 66–68, 70–71, 74, 82–83, 94, 162n2, 164n38
Descartes, René, 123, 129
despotism, 58, 136; benevolent, 11
determinateness in Whiteheadian metaphysics, 119–34, 170n41
determinism, 114, 122; as antithetical to rationality, 148–51; Augustinian theistic version of, 127; in Kant's ontology, 130–33
Dewey, John: and contemporary deliberative democratic theory, 139, 144–49; and fallibilism, 16–17, 68
disclosure, 58, 64, 69, 84; in Kant's thought, 51

discourse, 70; faith-based negation of, 107; in Kant's thought, 51
discourse theory, 51, 101, 139
disenchantment (Weberian), 122, 148, 161n55
divine anxiety, 105, 107–13
divine foreknowledge, 104–5, 108–11, 114–34
divine omnibenevolence, 108, 133
divine omnicausality, 102, 126, 149
divine omnipotence, 108, 133, 149
divine omniscience, 18, 101–10, 114–34
doubt, 4, 12, 16, 19, 46, 55, 92; absence of, 26, 73; God's experience of, 108; in Hume's *Dialogues*, 35
dread, 110

educating society, 145
efficient causation, 122, 129
Einsteinian physics, 113, 115
Elshtain, Jean Bethke, 87
enduring substances: in classical metaphysics, 120; in Kant's ontology, 131
Enlightenment, the, 7, 9, 12, 29, 30, 48, 157n8; ethical tradition of, 53–54
epistemic anxiety, 3–4, 9, 11, 12, 14, 16, 17, 19, 30–33, 38, 42–48, 65–66, 90, 95–97, 99, 101, 110–13, 137–55 passim; and debate over religion in the public sphere, 86; distinguished from skepticism, 35–36; and humility, 37; as indicator of psychological maturity, 29; Socrates as exemplar, 20, 93–95
epistemic virtue, 4, 29; anxiety as, 26, 37, 41, 111–13; defined, 19
epistemological freedom, 82
Eros, 111
eternal objects in Whiteheadian metaphysics, 118–34, 169n30, 170n41
ethical, the, 53, 62, 94
ethical universalism, 69
evangelical Christianity, 2, 58; role of in Bush administration, 73
evangelium, 25
Eve, 22–24
event ontology, 119
existence: as distinguished from "actuality" in process metaphysics, 118
existentialism, ix, 7, 21, 26, 31, 33, 90–92, 96, 110
ex nihilo nihil fit, 119
experience in Whiteheadian metaphysics, 122–34; preliminary definition, 122
faith, 38–41, 47, 51–63, 66, 68, 83–84, 92, 97, 100–101, 110; and anxiety in Niebuhr's thought, 27–28; and liberalism, 5–6; as paradoxical in Kierkegaard's work, 55, 93–95; in politics, 2; role of in Bush administration, 73, 75; and salvation, 24–25, 105–8; as transformed by epistemic anxiety, 30
Fall, the, 22, 105–6
fallenness, 41; in Christian theology, 22–25
fallibilism, 11, 14, 16, 48, 81, 89, 99–100, 138, 145, 154–56; distinguished from skepticism, 35–36; and liberal-democratic discourse, 20, 137; pragmatic-progressivist form, 16; and reasonableness in public discourse, 66
fallibility, 4, 12–14, 18, 21, 23, 31, 33–34, 36, 45–47, 49, 64, 73, 83, 86, 88, 92–93, 97, 105, 112; and conceptions of the divine, 25; and liberal-democratic citizenship, 29–30; and the logic of liberalism, 38, 137; in modern Western philosophy and theology, 7–8; as transcendental condition of human nature, 28, 68
fascism, 36
fear, 110; as distinguished from anxiety, 31, 109
feelings (ontological) in Whiteheadian metaphysics, 122–34 passim, 151
Feuerbach, Ludwig, 85–86

Fichte, Johann Gottlieb, 13–15
fideism, 40, 42, 101
final causation, 122
finitude, 25, 48, 64, 81, 92–93, 96–97, 157n7; epistemic implications of, 7, 21, 23, 26, 34, 37, 42–43, 49
Fleischacker, Samuel, 158n11
Frankfurter, Felix, 168n17
freedom, 25, 44, 105–6, 110–12; in Kant's thought, 51; problems with political libertarian conception of, 134–36; in Whiteheadian metaphysics, 114–36, 150–52
free knowledge, 125–27, 133.
Friedman, Milton, 11
fundamentalist Christianity, 2, 15, 75, 82

Gamwell, Franklin I., 17–18, 155, 175n48
gay rights, 3, 75, 88–89
general will: according to Rousseau, 13–14
Genesis: on the Fall, 22–24
God, 2, 20, 22, 40, 42, 43, 53, 57–58, 60, 62, 67, 69–71, 88–89, 94, 99, 101, 104; in Bultmann's thought, 25; and the Fall, 24, 106; as "Lord" of history, 103, 108; as moral-political trope, 107–13; Whiteheadian conception of, 108–34
God-world relation, 101, 105, 114–34
government, 11, 14, 32, 72–73, 135–36
Griffin, David Ray, 168n21
Gutmann, Amy, 140–41

Habermas, Jürgen, 80, 139, 143
harm principle, 77, 86
Hartshorne, Charles, 117–18, 149, 154
Haufniensis, Vigilius, ix; on the Fall and salvation, 22–24, 105–6
Hayek, Friedrich, 11
Hegel, G. W. F., 13, 55, 58, 80, 132–33
Hegelian dialectic, 55
Heidegger, Martin, 26, 96, 159n22
Hick, John, 38–39
Hobbes, Thomas, 11, 77, 81, 87
Holocaust, the, 102
Holy, the, 92
human dignity, 13, 16, 47; according to Kant, 9–12
Hume, David, 35–37, 157n8
humility, 8, 19, 29, 42, 46, 112; as grounded in epistemic anxiety, 37
Huntington, Samuel, 2
hybrid liberal-virtue theory, 41; of deliberative democracy, 140–42, 145–48.

Idea, the, 132
ideational, 120
identity politics, 142
imago dei, 101, 108–13
imitatio dei, 101, 108–13
immortality, 94
indeterminateness in Whiteheadian metaphysics, 119–34
innocence: according to Kierkegaard, 23–24, 105–6
Inquisition, the, 15
internal relatedness, 135
Isaac, 19, 24, 52–53, 55–58, 65, 70–71, 73, 82
Islam, 2, 102; alternate version of Moriah story, 164n44; and revelation, 21, 65
Islamist, 65

James, William, 68, 132, 160n46
Jerusalem, 54
Jesus, 43
Judaism, 2, 102; and revelation, 21

Kant, Immanuel, 123; liberalism of, 9–15, 25, 47, 51, 55, 58–59, 68, 80; ontology and phenomenology of, 130–32
kerygma, 25, 90
Kierkegaard, Søren, ix–x, 7, 19, 21, 24, 27, 31, 34, 53–54, 59, 67, 69, 74, 79, 93, 108, 110, 133, 157n6, 158n14, 159n21–n22

Kloppenberg, James, 148, 173n18, 173n20
knight of faith, 34–35, 60, 62–63, 94–95
Kotsko, Adam, 67, 165n7

laissez-faire capitalism, 134
Larmore, Charles, 10–12, 44
leap of faith, 106
Levinas, Emmanuel, 165n6
liberal deliberative democratic theory, 140–56 passim.
liberal democracy, 1–2, 20, 49, 54, 58, 66, 135; and fallibilism, 17, 30, 88
liberal democratic citizenship, 1, 16, 29–30, 124
liberal democratic norms, 6, 30, 41, 44–46, 48, 51–52, 64, 67–68, 89, 99, 134, 155
liberal ethos, 5
liberalism, 14, 42–47, 64, 80, 137, 141, 150; main historical types of, 9–15; Miltonian-Lockean-Millian type, 48; principled vs. pragmatic, 3–4; Rawlsian, 48, 100; and secrecy, 73; and tolerance, 38, 43
liberal-republicanism, 10–12
libertarianism: metaphysical, 126, 129; political, 11, 134–36, 144; social, 88
liberty, 9–15, 48, 52, 144–45; as non-domination, 10–12
Locke, John, 9, 14–15, 38, 79, 81, 83, 87, 129
Luther, Martin, 104, 124

Macedo, Stephen, 1, 3, 162n62
MacIntyre, Alasdair, 141
Madison, James, 77, 160n43, 165n9
Malesic, Jonathan, 58, 63–69, 74, 86, 95, 164n38
Marcus, George, 31–33
Marx, Karl, 13
Marxism, 26, 84
mauvaise foi, 34
May, Rollo, 96
McDaniel, Jay, 175n45
mechanism (ontological), 122, 149
Meinong, Alexius, 170n34
metaphysical telos, 155
Michael (archangel), 24
middle knowledge, 125–29.
Mill, John Stuart, 9, 14–15, 38, 77
Milton, John, 9, 14–15, 38, 81
Molinism, 118, 123–34
monism, 121
monotheism, 41
moral law: according to Kant, 12–13
Moriah, 19, 24, 52, 55, 57, 68, 70–71
movement of faith, 57, 60, 93
Mozert v. Hawkins County Board of Education, 165n8

naturalism in Whiteheadian metaphysics, 122
natural knowledge, 125–27.
natural selection, 39
Nazi Germany, 15
necessity: and self-determination, 23–24, 106; metaphysical, 125–34, 154; propositional, 127–28
negative liberty, 10–15, 77, 83
negotiating society, 146
Neoplatonism, 103
nervousness: as distinguished from anxiety, 31
new atheists, 3, 40
New Testament, 103
Newton, Isaac, 123
Newtonian physics, 115
new traditionalism, 66, 89
Nicene Christianity, 40
Niebuhr, Reinhold, 7, 21, 48, 96; on positive and negative forms of anxiety, 26–28
nihilism, 31
noumenal self, 130–31

Obama, Barack, 3
Ogden, Schubert, 154
Old Testament, 103
ontological anxiety, 96

open theism, 20, 102–14
organic theism, 20, 113–34
orthodoxism, 16; defined, 15; as idolatry, 43, 82; as reaction to anxiety, 28
Other, the, 63–71, 74, 82

pacifism, 36
panentheism, 117.
panexperientialism, 120–34 passim, 151; distinguished from panpsychism, 170n36
pantheism, 109, 129, 133
Patocka, Jan, 64
Paul, 74, 82–83
Peirce, Charles Sanders: and fallibilism, 16
persuasion, 100; in process metaphysics and ethics, 135–36, 151–54
philosophical anthropology, 28
planning society, 145
Plantinga, Alvin, 60
Plato, 129
Platonism as reformed in Whitehead's thought, 114–34
pluralism, 2, 3, 9, 65, 84, 88–89, 155
Popper, Karl: and fallibilism, 16–17
positive liberty, 10–15
possibility, 44; God's relation to, 108–9; and human autonomy, 23–24, 105–6; as "precise," 124–34; role in the Fall, 23–24, 105–6; in Whiteheadian metaphysics, 114–34
pragmatism, 67–68, 149
predestination, 104
preference satisfaction utilitarianism, 85
primary substance, 121
primordial nature of God, 116–34, 169n33
principle of noncontradiction, 18, 36
principle of relativity, 116, 120, 149–50
privacy, 72
problem of evil, 117, 126
process philosophy and theology, 17, 20, 68, 101, 108–34; and deliberative democratic theory, 138–56
Protestantism, 41
Psalms, 108
public/nonpublic/private distinctions, 140, 142; in Kant's thought, 51, 140
public reason/discourse, 66, 76, 137–54; in Kant's thought, 51
public sphere, 72, 137; Marcus on role of anxiety in, 32; Rawlsian conception, 86; religious reasons in, 20, 40, 84–89, 112

qualitative leap, 23
Quine, W. V. O., 170n42

radical responsibility, 58, 61–65, 67, 69, 73, 83, 95, 108
Rand, Ayn, 136
Randian Objectivism, 136
rational egoism, 134
rationality: and emotions in Marcus's thought, 32–33; according to Kant, 12
Rawls, John, 61, 139–40, 161n55
reason, 137; as dependent on final causation, 148; and emotions in Marcus's thought, 32–33; in the Enlightenment, 7; and faith in Kierkegaard's thought, 55; Hume on, 35; Kant on, 12
reasonableness, 46; recognition of fallibility as metacriterion of, 66
relativism, 16
religious exceptionalism, 69
religious exclusivism, 29, 41, 109
religious freedom, 87
Renaissance humanism, 125
representationalism (ontological), 129
republicanism, 11, 58; classical-Madisonian, 147
Rescher, Nicholas, 168n22

resignation, 56–57
respect for persons, 12, 14, 16, 47, 89, 137.
responsibility, 27, 49, 57, 61, 67, 70, 83, 110–13, 126, 150
revelation, 46–47, 75; in Abrahamic religions, 21, 51–72
rhetorical theory, 139
Roark, Howard, 136
Roman Republic, 56
Romanticism, 13
Rorty, Richard, 68
Rousseau, Jean-Jacques: liberalism of, 9–15, 80
Rushdoony, R. J., 75
Russell, Bertrand, 113

salvation, 22–25, 105–7; Paul's advice regarding, 74
Sarah, 73
Sartre, Jean-Paul, 26, 34, 49, 96
Scholasticism, 103, 124
scientific naturalism, 113
scripture, 102–3; and fallibility, 36; Hebrew, 107
secrecy, 58–62, 68, 71–76, 84
self-determination: as emerging through the Fall in Christian theology, 22
selfhood: Kant and Whitehead on, 130–32; social conception of, 135
serially ordered occasional selfhood, 131
Silentio, Johannes de, ix, 19, 54–63, 65–68, 70–71, 73–74, 164n38
sin, 22–24, 110; in Niebuhr's thought, 26–28, 48, 105–6
Singer, Peter, 85
skepticism, 16, 19, 93, 95; Hume on, 35–37
slavery, 36
social conservatism, 3
social contract, 79
societies (ontological) in Whiteheadian metaphysics, 122, 134–35, 150–51.
Socrates, 20, 34–35, 76, 92–95
Socratic anxiety, 35–37, 93, 97
Socratic ignorance, 35, 54, 93–95
Soviet Union, 15
state, the, 142
state of nature, 78
Stein, Gertrude, 168n17
stoicism, 35
Stout, Jeffery, 66, 68, 86, 89
Strauss, David, 8
subjective aim, 120–34 passim, 151
subjective form, 120–34 passim
subject-superject, 120–34 passim, 151
subsistence (ontological), 119, 123; Whitehead's usage distinguished from Meinong's, 170n34
suspension of the ethical, 48
symmetricality of time, 149; according to Kant, 131

tacit consent, 79–80
temporality in Whiteheadian metaphysics, 116–34
temporal modalities, 126–27
temptation: and anxiety, 27, 96
terrorism, 2, 65
Tertullian, 160n48
theological circle, 90–92
Thomas Aquinas, 103, 125–26, 157n7, 160n39
Thomistic theism, 125–27
Thomistic virtue theory, 85
Thompson, Dennis, 140–41
Thomte, Reidar, 27
Tillich, Paul, 7, 21, 26, 90–92, 96
tolerance, 19, 29–30, 38, 43, 48, 52, 66, 100, 112, 143, 155, 162n62
totalitarianism, 13–14, 51
tragic hero, 56–57, 63
transcendental anthropology, 68
transcendental object, 130
transcendental synthesis of apperception, 130–32

Urban, Hugh, 75

virtue, 19, 37, 41–42; anxiety as, 26, 29–33, 47, 111–13; democratic forms of, 29, 140, 142, 145–47, 150; and vice, 28
virtue epistemology, 42, 46
virtue-oriented deliberative democratic theory, 140, 142–43, 145–50 passim.

Wesley, John, 104
Whitehead, Alfred North, 20, 68, 101, 108, 111, 113–37
Wittgenstein, Ludwig, 113
Wolterstorff, Nicholas, 86–87
Wright, Jeremiah, 3

Yeats, W. B., 99

Zagzebski, Linda, 42, 46, 107, 161n51

Printed and bound in Great Britain by
CPI Antony Rowe, Chippenham and Eastbourne